some problems of judgment and feeling

Othello as tragedy: some problems of judgment and feeling

JANE ADAMSON

CAMBRIDGE UNIVERSITY PRESS

CAMBRIDGE

LONDON   NEW YORK   NEW ROCHELLE
MELBOURNE   SYDNEY

Published by the Press Syndicate of the University of Cambridge
The Pitt Building, Trumpington Street, Cambridge CB2 1RP
32 East 57th Street, New York, NY 10022, USA
296 Beaconsfield Parade, Middle Park, Melbourne 3206, Australia

First published 1980

British Library Cataloguing in Publication Data

Adamson, Jane
'Othello' as tragedy.
1. Shakespeare, William, Othello
I. Title
822.3′3   PR2829   79-41437

ISBN 0 521 22368 7 hard covers
ISBN 0 521 29760 5 paperback

Transferred to digital printing 2004

To
Sam Goldberg

Contents

Preface

Like all readers of Shakespeare, I have been greatly stimulated, helped, provoked and incensed by the views of a great many critics. But I especially wish to acknowledge my two largest debts: a long-standing one to the work of L. C. Knights; and an immediate and extensive one to S. L. Goldberg's *An Essay on 'King Lear'* (Cambridge, 1974) – a more radically original book than its modest title may indicate, in its view not just of *Lear* but of Shakespearean tragedy generally, especially in what it suggests about the nature and function of characterization, about the connections between the characters' experience and ours as we engage with the play, and about the argumentative requirements any interpretation has to meet. Neither has written much specifically on *Othello*, but the implications of their work on Shakespeare triggered my own thinking about why this play might in fact be far richer than the comparatively circumscribed one it is usually said to be. On *Othello* itself I owe most to A. C. Bradley and to F. R. Leavis, whose classic but contrary accounts keep pushing one back to the play to work out where each is right, why neither will do, and what they both ignore. On points of detail in the play I have inevitably found myself in agreement with dozens of critics, including many whose over-all sense of it differs from mine, though I have not generally noted such agreements; it seemed on the whole more useful

ix

to restrict the notes mainly to citing views different from mine and to acknowledging conscious debts.

I should perhaps add two further points about the writing of this book. It was originally completed in 1976, very much in its present form, but as part of a larger study of some narratives and plays about lovers whose relationship ends in disaster. I mention this because of my otherwise perhaps rather puzzling concentration on critical writing before that date, and the references I make to poets such as Chaucer and Henryson. It was through thinking about some of their poetry (and, by contrast, Marlowe's) that I first began to realize what makes *Othello* so compelling. The second point concerns the word 'vulnerable', which recurs here quite often. I have used it unabashedly throughout, since some such term is indispensable to my account of the play and I cannot find any accurate alternative. It was once a clear and uncluttered word, and I hope that those for whom in recent years it has been trivialized by self-advertising gestures of 'sensitivity', or tarred with the brush of lonely hearts, will be able to rehabilitate it – at least while thinking about *Othello* as tragedy.

Except where otherwise noted, I have quoted throughout from the following editions: *Othello*, ed. Kenneth Muir, New Penguin Shakespeare (Harmondsworth, 1968); for all other works by Shakespeare, *William Shakespeare, The Complete Works*, ed. Peter Alexander (London and Glasgow, 1968 [1951]).

Introduction

Although *Othello*, unlike *Coriolanus*, is generally considered
one of the great Shakespearean tragedies, it is also quite
widely thought to be the most limited of them. For anyone
like myself who does not share that limiting view of it, the
prime critical task must therefore be to explain why not –
to explain how the play is tragic in the fullest sense of the
word, and why its alleged limitedness is actually the reflection of the reader's own rather cramping moral and
artistic preconceptions.

We can see clearly enough the disabling effect of such
preconceptions in the views of earlier times – Rymer's is
only the most notorious case – yet it is probably no less in
our own. To a quite peculiar extent, the growing mass of
commentary about *Othello* in recent decades seems to have
become stuck in old ruts, old debates and circularities.
Particular aspects of the play have been written about very
finely, of course; nevertheless, we do not seem to be much
closer to any generally shared understanding of it as a
whole. As with no other of Shakespeare's tragedies, criticism
of this one seems to have become arrested or split into two
intransigent camps – not, I think, because of any special
daftness in *Othello's* very various readers, but because of
certain essential features of the play itself. At any rate, the
critical stalemate suggests that as well as reviewing the
common arguments and counter-arguments about it, we

need to re-consider the tragedy in a rather more fundamental way. Hence this book: it is an attempt to turn back to the play again and ask *why* has it proved so hard for critics to reach even a rough general agreement about its basic tenor, about what we make of its hero, and about the kind, depth and scope of the demands it makes on us.

From Albert Gerard's brief and usefully oversimplified summary in 1957 we can perhaps take some bearings on how things have or have not changed in *Othello* criticism since then.[1] Gerard distinguished three main 'schools': a 'traditional' school of 'naturalistic' interpretation; a 'symbolic' school, which tries to 'explain away the difficulties inherent in the traditional psychological interpretation of the Moor by turning the play into a mythic image of the eternal struggle between good and evil'; and another school, according to which 'this tragedy ought to be treated as a purely dramatic phenomenon, created by Shakespeare for the sake of sensation and emotional effect'.

In the twenty years since Gerard wrote, a few changes have taken place. The last-mentioned 'conventionalist' school, for instance, seems to have pretty well faded away (on the subject of *Othello*, at least, though alas not with some of the other plays). Nowadays, it is commonly agreed that *Othello* lends itself best to 'naturalistic' interpretations, and discussions of it in these terms far outnumber the symbolic, allegorical, sociological and other sorts of readings. Even so, it is in this commonest sort of criticism, which addresses itself primarily to questions of character and psychology, that the critical stalemate or impasse has been

---

[1]Albert Gerard, ' "Egregiously an Ass": The Dark Side of the Moor', *Shakespeare Survey*, 10 (1957), pp. 98–106. For a fuller, more challenging discussion of the play's critical history see Helen Gardner, '*Othello*: A Retrospect, 1900–1967', *Shakespeare Survey*, 21 (1968), pp. 1–11, and Robert Hapgood's more recent survey, '*Othello*', in *Shakespeare: Select Bibliographical Guides*, ed. Stanley Wells (London, 1973), pp. 159–70. Gerard's and Gardner's articles are now conveniently available in *Aspects of 'Othello'*, ed. Kenneth Muir and Philip Edwards (Cambridge, 1977).

most acute; and consequently more and more critics in recent years have tried to start (as I shall) by looking once again at the forty-year-old dispute between those who argue for 'noble Othello' and those who denounce 'Othello the egotist'. Generally speaking, the results have not been encouraging. Most attempts to review the dispute seem to end up caught within the very same terms themselves, either modifying and then re-arguing the case for one side or the other, or urging some kind of enlightened compromise. It is hardly surprising that other critics have chosen to side-step the dispute altogether, presumably on the principle of letting sleeping dogs lie; but here too there has been little fundamental change, since the dogs are not really asleep. The issues cannot be resolved by ignoring them. Again and again, therefore, discussion of the play comes back to much the same opposing answers to the same central questions: how are we to see and respond to what Othello is and says and does?

The only way to begin resolving this state of affairs, I believe, is to ask what it is about the play itself that produces it. Clearly, it will not cut much ice simply to announce one's own point of view and illustrate it from the play. Any reading needs more support than that, and what is really needed with *Othello* is an account that includes some thinking about the complicated process by which any view of the play is reached, one that explores the nature and the 'cause' of our own and others' feelings and judgments. In fact, the play's most radical effect is to press us to do just that.

Very broadly, the gist of my argument is that, while all great works of literature enlarge our understanding of how people interpret or make sense of their own experience, *Othello* does so in a unique and challenging way. For it is remarkable how explicitly the play dramatizes and explores the ways and means by which different people 'make sense'

3

of what happens in their lives, including what they merely imagine to be happening. The whole action might be said to germinate from the sort of observation Shakespeare's Cicero makes in *Julius Caesar* (I, iii, 33–5):

> Indeed, it is a strange-disposed time;
> But men may construe things after their own fashion,
> Clean from the purpose of the things themselves.

Throughout *Othello* we watch how every one of the characters construes and misconstrues things, how they all 'fashion' their view of others to fit with their sense of themselves (or vice versa); and increasingly we become aware – as they themselves never do – of how their fears and desires and needs lead to various kinds of emotional confusion and inflexibility, and how this in turn blocks or deforms their sense of what is and what is not. Time and again we see people who, in trying to comprehend what is happening to them (especially when they feel under threat), arrive at some conception or misconception of things, and then, once their mind is 'made up' – to use the common and significantly ambiguous phrase for the process – cannot or will not change it.

Yet if we can allow ourselves to respond fully to what the play puts in front of us, I do not think we can remain so detached and impartial in our own judgments as that kind of description may suggest. Even while we see how the characters ensnare themselves in the traps that feeling lays for judgment and action, we do not always prove much better at avoiding the same sort of traps ourselves. The more deeply we become engaged by the play, the more urgently we too feel pressed to 'make sense' of what is going on; the more readily, therefore, do we ourselves leap to or fall in with some clear-cut, often partial or misguided, but at least decisive, view of things. Like the characters, we too are prone to 'make up' our minds in some inflexible attitude, especially if it is plausibly put to us by others, and (again like the characters) to cling to our judgments through thick and thin, adducing anything and everything as 'confirmations strong' and so tending to overlook, ignore or vehemently deny whatever might disturb our moral certainty. And it is this – the relationship between (on the one side) the characters' treacherous habits of thought and feeling and judgment, and (on the other side) our own in response to them – that is the central focus of my argument. For it seems to me that the power and stature of *Othello* as a tragedy are founded in its power to make us recognize, very painfully, how much we share as human beings with each and every character – even the worst – because of this fundamental link between our needs and our fallibility.

To speak of the play's power to challenge us and bring us to various kinds of awareness implies, of course, that it is a carefully constructed whole, that Shakespeare's imagination pervades and informs the entire dramatic action – creating, construing and organizing *everything* he thereby gives us to construe. To meet it adequately therefore calls for a detailed understanding of the play's construction and of the way its meaning develops. This is why I have tried to make any discussion follow the sequence of that unfolding structure, and why my account of the play is designed (as I hope it will be taken) as a single, continuous whole. However, it will be plain that by 'structure' – unhappily a rather ambiguous word these days – I mean to include all aspects of the play, not just some, and especially not just those which are often described as forming a 'triadic' or 'five-part' pattern. Accounts of the structure of any Shakespearean play in those terms usually oversimplify, focusing attention on the hero to the virtual exclusion of everything else. Othello is at the centre of the play, but he is not the whole of it. I am concerned, not with character-analysis in the usual sense, nor static 'patterns of imagery', but with the developing insights that emerge in the organization of recurring ideas, words, deeds, images, situations.

It will be clear that my whole procedure (like any) has theoretical implications, but I have spelt these out only occasionally. In so far as my account of this particular play does spring from a general view or advocate one, I suppose it could be summarized in two main points: that the meaning of a Shakespearean play lies in nothing less than its total dramatic action, and that the significant 'action' is that which Shakespeare's art produces and activates, or causes to take place, in *our* consciousness as we discern and respond to all the salient details of speech and deed and inter-relationship in which he simultaneously creates, embodies and explores a particular set of lives. The lameness of this abstract formulation really underlines my point, however: the significance and value of the dramatic whole can be realized only in, and as, the specific experience of a mind responding to it as fully and precisely as possible. This is not a new observation, of course, though it is far from being widely accepted or even properly understood. It is certainly not an invitation to mere subjectivism or to any indulgence in one's own private feelings about the kinds of behaviour and situation the play presents, nor is it a symptom of despair about reaching any measure of agreement with others who necessarily see and respond differently. The question for every reader is always what is actually there, in this particular work, to be experienced; and although the question always remains open, it is never, it seems to me, wholly and absolutely open: some interpretations are demonstrably less accurate and adequate than others, and some indeed are demonstrably false.

There are many things about the play that I have not mentioned, of course, since it would be insane even to aim at comprehensiveness, and no doubt also many more I have not seen; but a few of my deliberate omissions perhaps call for brief comment. I have naturally concentrated on the issues I think most important. The old and much-battered question of 'double time' does not strike me as one of them. It may raise some interesting points perhaps, but it seems to me more of a (literally) academic question than one essential to our understanding of the play, tending as it does to lead our attention away from Othello's obsession, towards the kind of details that might obsess an Inspector from Scotland Yard. Another such question, that of Iago's 'motives', is also often treated as one requiring the skills of a detective. On those terms – as if a sleuth could conscientiously sift the evidence, make out a water-tight case for the prosecution, and thereby finally solve the mystery of the play – the question seems to me misconceived and misleading, and I have not discussed it in that form. Rather, for reasons I try to explain, I think Iago's behaviour calls for the same kind of attention we have to give to Desdemona's, for instance, or indeed to everyone else's. A third topic I do not discuss at all is the 'Christian elements' in the play: about these, silence seemed the best reply to those who claim, with great and no doubt sincere insistence, that these 'must' be of 'central importance' in any interpretation.

A better claim might perhaps be made for the importance of Othello's race, on which I have said very little. (On the absurd debate about the exact shade of his skin I say nothing at all.) But here again I think the matter has usually been over-emphasized by twentieth-century critics and producers, or given a quite wrong emphasis by being isolated from other elements in the drama. Othello's Moorishness, far from being a special and separable issue, matters only in so far as it is part of a much larger and deeper one, which does seem to me central: the distinction, which the action constantly leads us to consider and reconsider, between the given, indissoluble facts, and the more open and changeable areas, of people's lives. For the play makes us consider and reconsider not merely what aspects of one's nature and behaviour one can make and change and control, but also the relationships between various ways that things seem 'fated to us': between those that seem fated 'e'en then . . . when we do quicken' (as Othello himself revealingly puts it) – parentage, birth, physical attributes, natural talents and dispositions – and those which our own experiences, choices, actions, commitments, and so on, in all the given circumstances of our lives, gradually accumulate and form into our destiny. Throughout the play, the characters themselves keep confusing all these – as when Othello for example alleges that he is congenitally doomed to be betrayed. Yet their very confusions painfully underline and intensify our own difficulty in maintaining any clear-cut distinction between the 'fated' and the 'free' aspects of the self – especially during the last three acts of the play, when we are made so acutely aware of the baffling complexity of the emotional and moral realities that constitute the characters' experience, and, through them, our own. Are the feelings we cannot help having really 'fated' to us? And in what sense are we free or able to *do* anything about them? All these perennial questions lie at the heart of the play, and it is in terms of these larger issues that Othello's colour (and his temperament and his past) are best considered.

One other matter I have not much emphasized (at least not directly) is *Othello* in the theatre: the question of how it works or might work in performance. In obvious and unforeseen ways it is a magnificent but taxing work for the stage, and my account of it suggests both how and why I think this is so. A Shakespearean critic's job is much less like an actor's than like a producer's or director's, in that he has to concern himself with every role, every speech, every movement, and every relationship between these in the play. On the other hand, the critic's job also differs from the producer's in important ways – not least because the critic can allow for multiple possibilities of interpretation and performance at many points in the drama, whereas the producer has to commit himself to the one single

8

interpretation he thinks best. Thus any critic can learn something – whether positively or negatively – from particular productions; but any critical interpretation worth its salt will also carry with it suggestions, even if they remain implicit, about how the play might best be produced, whether in an actual theatre or in the theatre of the mind.

I

The 'comforts' of praise and blame

> nothing extenuate,
> Nor set down aught in malice.
>
> *(Othello*, v, ii, 338–9)

The crucial test of any view of *Othello* is its last scene, the culmination and climax of the whole drama. We have had to watch the hero vilify and strike his wife; we now have to watch while he kills her for a 'sin' we know she never committed, and then watch while he kills himself as well. At this point, the central critical questions become acute. What does the play eventually bring us to think and feel about Othello? How far, here and all through, are we brought to consider him as the victim, and how far the agent, of his fate? What bearing does our sense of these issues have on our estimate of the nature, scope and quality of the play as a whole? In relation to Shakespeare's other tragedies is *Othello* really a 'comparatively simple', 'rather limited' play, as we have so often been told?

On the first of these questions – what we are to make of Othello's behaviour, especially during the second half of the play – most people seem to have very fixed views. Generally speaking, they tend to take one of two positions about the play: to some, Shakespeare's main impulse is evidently to present the case *for* his hero; to others, it is evidently to present the case against him. On the one side, it is Othello's vulnerability that seems most important. Arguing on much the same lines as Coleridge and Bradley, for example, many critics see Othello's conduct as the natural, and therefore condonable reaction of such a man to extreme pressure; more than anything else, they claim, the play evokes our pity for him as the noble, 'not easily jealous' victim of Iago's hellish cunning. On the other side, it is Othello's culpability that seems most important. Arguing on much the same lines as Leavis, for example, many see Othello as 'noble' in certain limited ways; but more than anything else, they claim, the play judges him (and evokes our judgment of him) as an egotist made brutal by a jealousy that is largely self-generated, a man guilty not only of maltreating and killing his innocent wife, but of not even having the grace, courage or humility to accept his guilt.

Of course, it is understandable that so many readers have tried as honestly and as elegantly as possible to sit on the fence. But (for reasons inherent in the play itself, I believe) such critics inevitably seem to meet the fate of Humpty Dumpty, or to get impaled on the spiky contradictions of the case, or, by evading or failing to recognize those essential contradictions, to ignore precisely those aspects of the play that most challenge, even dislocate, the comforting moral assumptions we usually make about our world.

My point, therefore, in beginning with what everyone knows are the two main views of Othello (and hence *Othello*) is not to adjudicate between them, nor to dismiss both, nor to fence-sit, but to suggest that each answers to something important in the play – which also means that each under-estimates something important as well. For while each has its force as well as its limits, and while they also seem to exhaust the possibilities between them, singly and together they have the curious effect of making the play seem less disturbing and less deeply tragic than I think it is.

The strength of the first view – what we might call the Bradleyan or, better, the 'pro-Othello', view – is fairly obvious; so too is its weakness, at least since Leavis's celebrated (some would say notorious) attack on the sentimentality of Bradley's account of the play. If we can dispense with Leavis's scathing vehemence, we may notice that Bradley does at least insist on the play's power to make us feel *for* Othello in some way. On the other hand, his particular account of those feelings does seem soggy and crude, and is certainly distorted and undermined by his flat refusal, or incapacity, to acknowledge Othello's guilt. After extolling the hero at some length, Bradley arrives at the awkward fact that Othello's record blackens some-what half-way through III, iii. In response to this, however, Bradley calmly remarks, 'but the play is a tragedy, and from this point we may abandon the ungrateful and undramatic task of awarding praise and blame'.[1] It is a neat tactical policy-revision, which has the consoling effect of allowing him to extenuate Othello's abominable behaviour by blaming it all on the villainous Iago, whose skill he covertly praises as well. Like all of Othello's partisans Bradley cannot bring himself to recognize that, psychologically and physically, Othello – and Othello alone – kills Desdemona. As Leavis acidly pointed out, Bradley clings so blindly to the notion that his hero is merely a victim, that his account of the play's final scene actually argues that Othello is now his old noble self again (now that 'chaos has come and gone') and that 'there is almost nothing here to diminish the admiration and love which heighten pity'.[2] Like all such extenuations of Othello – and they are legion – this is open to the crushing objection that it quite overlooks (or reduces to 'almost nothing') our feelings for *Desdemona* at this point. In what sense can the play be called a 'great tragedy' if it urges us simply to admire and pity a man as he disposes of his innocent wife? Indeed, what is true here is true of all such 'noble Othello' views of the play, that they are inadequate precisely to the extent that they over-

[1] A. C. Bradley, *Shakespearean Tragedy* (London, 1957 [1904]), p. 158.
[2] *Ibid* p. 161.

13

look or understate the shocking fact that Othello commits murder.

The problem with the second main view of the play – what we might call the Leavisian or 'anti-Othello' one – is roughly the reverse. Its strength lies in the obvious reasons the play gives us to judge Othello as culpable. Its weakness, however, is that it indulges in judgment and blame of Othello at the cost of any sympathetic feeling for him at all. In this, Leavis's account of the play, which is the classic statement of the anti-Othello view, demonstrates the point most clearly.[1] So determined is Leavis to reject Bradley's sentimentality and to insist that Othello himself, not Iago, is the primary agent of his fate, that he fails even to consider how far Othello, like any human being, is open to pain and suffering. Like all anti-Othello critics, he either ignores such vulnerability or treats it simply as moral weakness based on egotism, to be merely despised. Yet in what sense is the play a tragedy if it leaves us so detached from its hero as scarcely to care when he kills himself – or, rather, scarcely to recognize that he does actually kill himself? Quick as Leavis is to insist that Othello commits murder, he fails to treat seriously the no less crucial fact that Othello then commits suicide.

To understate the reality either of the murder or of the suicide is to ignore or miss one vital reason why the play agitates us as deeply as it does. John Arthos, for example, seems to me wholly mistaken in his view that the killing of Desdemona 'has no such relation to the logic of *Othello*' as does the stabbing of Duncan to the logic of *Macbeth*. Far from being, as Arthos puts it, 'hardly more than the punctuation to the tragedy', Othello's murder of Desdemona and his subsequent suicide are no less central in *Othello* – agonizingly delayed though they are – than

[1] F. R. Leavis, 'Diabolic Intellect and the Noble Hero: or, The Sentimentalist's Othello', *The Common Pursuit* (London, 1952), pp. 136–59 (originally published under a slightly different title in *Scrutiny*, 6 (1937), pp. 259–83).

Macbeth's suicidal murder of his king.[1] The changes Shakespeare made to his 'source' are here even more crucial than usual: in Cinthio's tale, both the Moor and the Ensign together kill Disdemona, and the Moor does not take his own life, but is killed by Disdemona's relatives. Shakespeare's conception is entirely different. As we are made to experience it, the whole thrust of the drama from Act III onwards is Othello's terrible thrust to murder and to suicide simultaneously. It makes us gradually realize how and why his very drive to murder Desdemona is also a drive to kill something deep within himself. It is precisely this double thrust that all Leavisian and Bradleyan accounts of the play equally distort and oversimplify. If there is something morally askew about a view of Othello that sidesteps his murderous atrocity, there is something rather brutal (and morally complacent) about a view of him that sees only moral complacency, egotism and self-consoling fantasy. Indeed, if obloquy and scorn of Othello were the main response the play demanded of us, why would anyone continue to find it interesting at all? The play seems to me compelling just because it neither invites nor allows us to stand in lofty condemnation of the man who, in Act IV, is shown to be so tormented by his feelings that he literally collapses, unable to bear them, and who in Act V stabs himself to death.

As the play presents it, Othello's act of self-destruction is both deliberate and deliberately total. I do not see how we can speak, as Leavis and those who endorse his account of the play tend to, as if this suicide were not really 'real' at

[1]'The Fall of Othello', *Shakespeare Quarterly*, 9 (1958), p. 94. Marvin Rosenberg documents how *Othello* too was threatened in the eighteenth century (especially in France and Germany) by 'those decorous and proper spirits who wanted to improve it with the kind of "poetic justice" that Tate's happy ending had inflicted on *King Lear*': Brabantio (not dead after all) was by some producers allowed to rush in and save Desdemona at the last minute. See *The Masks of Othello* (Berkeley, Los Angeles and London, 1971), pp. 31-3.

all, not an essential part of the main dramatic action. For Leavis, the play's action effectively ends with a mere histrionic *gesture* of suicide, and the gesture is merely the last and most consummate of Othello's self-admiring self-dramatizations. Othello has

> all the advantages of that last speech, where the invitation to identify oneself with him is indeed hardly resistible. Who does not (in some moments) readily see himself as the hero of such a *coup de théâtre*?[1]

But is not the dramatic point and power of Othello's final action (to which this speech leads him) precisely that he is not here 'seeing himself as the hero' at all? He is killing himself. To blur or evade this fact is to evade the crucial question the play explores at length and agonizingly answers: the question of *why* he commits suicide, and, more radically still, why he has to. If Othello's state at the end were merely histrionic and inauthentic, his suicide would represent no more than a sleight of Shakespeare's hand. The play would be a rigged tragedy, with a false because merely arbitrarily appropriate ending. Indeed, since Brabantio is safely dead, and everyone left alive is prepared to fob the blame off onto Iago and to see Othello as merely a 'rash and most unfortunate man', an Othello who actually believed the self-extenuations he utters could have easily wriggled off the hook by telling another of his tall, round and richly varnished 'unvarnished tales'. Alternatively, to think that he kills himself because he is really a noble chap after all is to show either Shakespeare or oneself as morally feeble-minded. Proponents of the case should decide which.

Leavis's reply to Bradley is interesting for another reason as well, however. It snarls itself in, though it does not openly acknowledge, the central dilemma facing anybody trying to come to terms with the play as a tragedy. Leavis contemptuously dismisses what he calls Bradley's 'obtuse-

[1] 'Diabolic Intellect and the Noble Hero', p. 153.

ness to the tragic significance of Shakespeare's play'; yet he is not much clearer himself about what, exactly, that 'tragic significance' might be, even though he discusses what he calls 'Othello's last speech' (it is his second-last, actually) in two separate essays. In the earlier essay, 'Diabolic Intellect and the Noble Hero' (from which I have been quoting), he says that

even, or rather especially, in that magnificent last speech of his Othello does tend to sentimentalize, though to say that and no more would convey a false impression, for the speech conveys something like the full complexity of Othello's simple nature, and in the total effect the simplicity is tragic and grand.

He then goes on to quote and comment on the speech, remarking that its ending is 'a superb *coup de théâtre*';

As, with that double force, a *coup de théâtre*, it is a peculiarly right ending to the tragedy of Othello. The theme of the tragedy is concentrated in it – concentrated in the final speech and action as it could not have been had Othello 'learnt through suffering'. (pp. 151-2)

In his second and later comment on the same speech, however, Leavis declares:

Eliot [in his remarks on Othello's self-dramatizing habit] . . . gives us the cue for saying that the attitude represented by Othello's last speech is radically untragic. This is so obvious as to seem, perhaps, not worth saying: Othello [*sic*], for those who don't join in the traditional sentimentalization of the play, is a very obvious case. The essential point that has to be made is that his valedictory *coup de théâtre* represents a rhetorical inflation, a headily emotional glorification, of an incapacity for tragic experience that marks the ordinary moments of us all.[1]

Is the play a tragedy, or not? Is Othello a tragic hero or isn't he? The contradiction between the two statements points directly to the chief critical problem with the play:

[1]"Tragedy and the "Medium"'" (originally published in *Scrutiny*, 12 (1944), pp. 249–60); quoted here from *The Common Pursuit*, p. 128.

is it possible fully to acknowledge Othello's culpability and his habit of evading it in self-dramatizing rhetoric, and yet at the same time to feel intensely for and with him, without sentimentalizing? To put the issue quite simply, I think we can call the play a tragedy in the fullest sense only if – and only to the extent that – it makes us face squarely the implications of Othello's habitually self-bolstering mode of speech, while simultaneously making us assent to such acute feelings about the ending as, for example, Dr Johnson experienced:

I am glad that I have ended my revisal of this dreadful scene. It is not to be endured.[1]

The tragedy, *Othello*, is centred in but is not confined to the tragedy of Othello. In his famous penultimate speech, Othello enjoins his audience – in words we might well also take as an implicit injunction from Shakespeare to *his* audience as to how we are to respond to the hero and indeed to everyone else in the play –

> Speak of me as I am: nothing extenuate,
> Nor set down aught in malice.   (v, ii, 338–9)

As I have been suggesting, this is exactly what most readers of the play seem to find most difficult – to be sympathetic without extenuating, clear-eyed in judgment without becoming vindictive, meagre-hearted or malign. Yet, as Othello's injunction may suggest, the critical problem is scarcely surprising. Indeed, in one way, it is partly what the play is about. For although the ardour of critical debate usually obscures this fact, the problems of judgment and feeling that *we* experience with the play are very like those we see experienced by everyone within it. It is not by

---

[1]'Notes on Shakespeare's Plays: *Othello*', quoted here from the Yale edition of *The Works of Samuel Johnson*, 8 vols., vol. 8, *Johnson on Shakespeare*, ed. Arthur Sherbo (New Haven and London, 1968), p. 1045. (Except where otherwise noted, all quotations of Johnson are from the Yale edition.)

accident that Othello's long valedictory speech raises the
problem explicitly, nor is this by any means the only time
it is raised in the play. On the contrary, from one end of it
to the other Shakespeare explores the ways and means by
which people's thoughts and feelings – whether about
others or about themselves – can become fatally tangled,
mutually distorting. The very plot is little else than the
causes and consequences of a wide range of feelings,
judgments and misjudgments. Roderigo allows himself to
be grotesquely gulled by Iago because of his feelings for
Desdemona. Desdemona misjudges Othello's state and
therefore persists in urging Cassio's suit. Emilia misjudges
Iago and so gives him the fatal handkerchief. And of course
Othello (like everyone else) grossly misjudges Iago and
therefore comes to misjudge Desdemona. Nor is it at all
surprising that there are so many occasions in the play
where people hotly censure and accuse others, and so many
formal or informal arraignments or trials – in many of
which, we notice, the person accused, whether actually
guilty or (as often) not, tries to exculpate himself, denies
the crime and declares his innocence.

In a play so full of people prepared (often on the most
flimsy or even non–existent evidence) to pronounce extremely hostile or extremely favourable judgments on one
another or on themselves – judgments so often shown to
be governed far less by objective facts than by the subjective
feelings and needs of the judge – we surely need to be
especially wary of supposing that we as audience are
somehow comfortably exempt from the hazardous conditions of judgment and feeling that beset everyone in it. Yet
very few readers pause to reflect on how the play reflects
back on ourselves in this way; criticism of *Othello*, as of the
other tragedies, has always been bedevilled by fault-finding
and inventory-taking of the characters' 'virtues' and
'defects'. But we are surely given no encouragement 'to
play the god with [others'] weak function' (to use Iago's

phrase); on the contrary (as Desdemona's own self-critical comment reminds us), 'we must think men are not gods' and remember that we too are men and women, like those whose lives we watch. To stay aloof, keeping moral scoreboards and meting out praise and blame, is a way of *not* taking stock of the play's own radical inquiry into why people so often come to see the world in terms of what Iago calls 'debitor and creditor' principles (I, i, 31), and into how and why such clear-cut black/white moral accounting systems can go so disastrously awry. As with so many of Shakespeare's plays, *Othello* everywhere reveals how profoundly central to Shakespeare's thinking was the perception that, as Nietzsche observed, it is our needs that interpret the world. And here too what applies in each dramatic character's 'interpretation' of his world equally applies (we come to realize) in our own responses to them.

Really to attend to the play and let it speak to us, without interpreting it away to satisfy our own need of moral simplicities, is to find we need more, morally speaking, than the distribution of clear-cut praise and censure to whomever seems to deserve them. For of course (as in *Measure for Measure*, for instance, or *King Lear*) the complex questions of what is 'just' and of the bases of 'justice' are precisely what are raised with every allegation of guilt and every protestation of innocence in the play.[1] Again and again we are shown the appalling injustices that can go under the name of justice. Iago continually claims that his treatment of Othello is 'just' retribution for Othello's allegedly unfair treatment of him. Othello himself thinks the same of his own proposed treatment of Desdemona: the idea of strangling her in 'the bed she hath contaminated' strikes him as 'Good, good! The justice of it pleases; very good!'

---

[1]Goldberg's *An Essay on 'King Lear'* considers very fully how such questions arise in that play. For a discussion of some aspects of Shakespeare's interest in 'justice' in *Othello* see Winifred Nowottny, 'Justice and Love in *Othello*', *University of Toronto Quarterly*, 21 (1951-2), pp. 330-44.

In the murder scene, he finds that Desdemona's 'balmy breath . . . dost almost persuade/ Justice to break her sword', but we realize only too terribly well that nothing on earth could now persuade 'Justice' to break or even so much as bend 'her sword' here, since 'Justice' is nothing other than a self-reassuring euphemistic rationalization of Othello's fixed sense that he 'must' kill Desdemona. (In fact, it is precisely Desdemona's 'breath', in her speeches when she wakes, that drives 'Justice', alias Othello, to hurry up and kill her.)

As Pascal once said, love or hate alters the aspect of justice. In *Othello*, as elsewhere, Shakespeare realizes further that most other human emotions – desire or fear, for example, or admiration or contempt – can 'alter the aspect of justice' too. Everywhere in the play we see emotions and judgments begetting and misbegetting each other, justice confusing itself with justification (and vice versa), moral censure smothering moral sense, selves forming and malforming themselves by their reflection in others' eyes. The exploration of how and why people seek justice of each other (and of themselves) is both fundamental to the play and very various in its terms. Merely to note some of the more obvious instances is to see how ubiquitous it is.

It begins with the very opening lines, for example, where we can hardly miss how persistently and defiantly Iago tries to justify himself and to insist on his own worth, reasonableness and rectitude: 'If ever I did dream of such a matter,/ Abhor me'; 'Despise me, if . . .'; 'I know my price, I am worth no worse a place'; 'I, of whom his eyes had seen the proof . . .'; 'be judge yourself/ Whether I in any just term am affined/ To love the Moor'; 'such a one do I profess myself . . .'; 'Heaven is my judge . . .'; and so on. Subsequently, we find Othello, and equally Brabantio, Roderigo and Desdemona too, variously insisting on their own worth, rectitude and just deserts: 'my demerits/ May speak, unbonneted'; 'I must be found./ My parts, my title, and my perfect soul/ Shall manifest me rightly . . .'; and so on. The concern with justice and justification is central to the Senate scene; and in Act II the stress on 'merit', 'honour' and 'desert' becomes still more pronounced and direct. For example, there are Cassio's eulogistic judgments of the lovers, which are immediately followed by the rather odd little game of 'praise and blame' played between Iago ('do not put me to't,/ For I am nothing if not critical') and Desdemona:

O heavy ignorance! Thou praisest the worst best. But what praise couldst thou bestow on a deserving woman indeed? One that in the authority of her merit did justly put on the vouch of very malice itself? (II, i, 141–4)

In the following scene, Iago deliberately sullies and undermines Cassio's reputation. ('Do not think, gentlemen, I am drunk', Cassio drunkenly explains.) Othello subsequently takes Iago's malice against Cassio as a generous attempt to extenuate and shield his 'friend': 'I know, Iago,/ Thy honesty and love doth mince this matter,/ Making it light to Cassio.' Cassio is duly blamed and censured, by himself as well as by Othello: 'one unperfectness shows me another, to make me frankly despise myself'. 'Come,' Iago retorts, 'you are too severe a moraller.'

In the later acts of the play this concern with judgment, merit, extenuation and blame flows into wider and deeper channels, mingling with other strong currents of interest. In the fatal third scene of Act III, for example, Desdemona's feelings prompt her to intervene and press Othello to exonerate Cassio: 'For if he be not one that truly loves you,/ That errs in ignorance, and not in cunning,/ I have no judgement in an honest face' – a claim that implicitly raises for us the questions of what allowances can and ought to be made in judging cases of ignorant or unwitting as opposed to 'cunning' error – questions which later obviously bear on and complicate our responses not only to Cassio

but also to Emilia's 'innocent' guilt in stealing the handkerchief for Iago, to Desdemona herself in her persistent suit
('Alas, what ignorant sin have I committed?'), and of
course to Othello's own drastic 'errors'. As we see, subjective feelings can invest mere 'trifles light as air' with the
potency of incontrovertible 'proofs', 'satisfactions'. Human
wishes or fears can turn and sometimes actually need to
turn mere fantasies into supposedly objective 'confirmations
strong'. When Othello's feelings and thoughts about
Desdemona begin to pull wildly in opposite directions he
desperately craves *any* evidence that would stabilize his
sense of her as either fair or foul – 'I think my wife be
honest, and think she is not;/ . . . I'll have some proof . . ./
Would I were satisfied!'; only forty lines later he has
swallowed Iago's allegation so completely that he asserts,
'Now do I see 'tis true.' Again, in Act IV we see Roderigo
likewise demanding 'satisfaction' of Iago, proof that he has
not been gulled, and yet immediately letting himself be
hoodwinked with nothing more solid than Iago's same old
conditional promises: 'your suspicion is not without wit
and judgement. But . . . you shall be satisfied'. There is a
pointed little exchange in v, i, when Iago calls out of the
murky shadows, 'What may you be? Are you of good or
evil?', and Lodovico replies, 'As you shall prove us, praise
us.' The reply neatly states but does nothing to solve the
problem of judgment that every one of the play's characters has to meet as best he can, and which we likewise face
in relation to them. Iago's challenge to Roderigo is also the
play's challenge to us: 'Be judge yourself.' For us truly to
'prove' anyone involves both our power simultaneously to
think and to feel, and the most rigorously honest effort
we can make *not* to let our thoughts and feelings falsify,
corrode or distort each other.

Of course this is to indicate no more about *Othello* than
Shakespeare's broad concern with the workings of human
feeling and judgment – one continuous with that in virtually

everything else he wrote, yet more than usually central and explicit here. His specific insights and thinking are embodied in particulars, and in the gradually evolving structure of responses and judgments and qualifications and revised judgments created – indeed pressed on us and elicited from us – by the dramatic action. Part of the essential substance of the play we have to assess, therefore, is the wide range of the characters' own particular judgments and feelings about themselves and others – and especially about Othello. Significantly, that range includes just such responses to him as those made by critics such as Bradley and Leavis. There are, for example, Brabantio's hot-headed accusations of Othello as a 'foul thief' and a 'devil'; Iago's sneers at him as a 'credulous fool' and a braggart who tells 'fantastical lies'; Emilia's wild vituperations against him at the end: 'O gull! O dolt!/ As ignorant as dirt!' On the other hand, there are Cassio's admiring respect, and Desdemona's love (which leads *her* to extenuate his terrible abuse of her). Meanwhile there are also Othello's own contradictory claims that he is 'honourable', that he is a 'fool, fool, fool!', and (by implication) that he is as despicable as a Turk, a 'circumcisèd dog'. If we are to come to any settled sense of the play's own composite judgment of him (and the same is true in relation to all the other characters in the drama as well) we need to take into account *all* the variously pro- and anti-Othello views (including his own) expressed or implied in the play, and consider their dynamic opposition all through: which means noting not only who says what, but exactly when they do so and why.

This is one reason why the final scene is so crucial, for in the speeches, silences and actions of all the characters in it, the most extreme feelings and judgments for and against the hero collide head-on. Within Othello himself the collision is so dreadful that in the end it is for him quite literally 'not to be endured'. But unlike him – and the distinction here, as always, is an important one – we do 'endure' the play's ending, terrible though we may feel it to be. Just *how* we can endure it without evading the play's impact (and the same is equally true of Desdemona's death) largely depends on how far – if at all – we have been brought to recognize their deaths as both truly terrible and yet truly inevitable within the play's created world, rather than just a Shakespearean whim to make the end pathetic. But our sense of that of course depends on how we have responded to everything else in the play that bears on, conditions or effects the tragedy of love that is the fate of its central figures.

Like some kind of statutory trade-mark on all anti-sentimentalist accounts of *Othello*, T. S. Eliot's remarks about the play's ending have been repeated so often that it is hard now to view them with a fresh eye. This is a pity, because what he said can help us understand why judgments and feelings collide so terribly in the final scene. Many of Eliot's larger claims in his essay – 'Shakespeare and the Stoicism of Seneca' – seem to me both muddled and muddling, and the context (plays by Chapman, Marston and others) in which he discusses *Othello* is in most respects misleading; nevertheless, his comments on Othello's valedictory speech are very suggestive, even if not quite in the sense he meant:

What Othello seems to me to be doing in making this speech is *cheering himself up*. He is endeavouring to escape reality, he has ceased to think about Desdemona, and is thinking about himself . . . [He is] dramatizing himself against his environment. He takes in the spectator, but the human motive is primarily to take in himself.[1]

Eliot's very ability to diagnose Othello's state here is itself the most significant difference between him as

[1] 'Shakespeare and the Stoicism of Seneca' [1927], in *Selected Essays* (London, 1932, enlarged edn, 1934), pp. 130–1.

'spectator' and the 'spectators' left on stage – Lodovico, Cassio and the others. Unlike them (and unlike Bradley) Eliot is not 'taken in' by Othello's rhetoric: he remains sufficiently detached to see that rhetoric as an attempt on Othello's part, not to countenance painful truths, but to shield himself from them.

However, to agree with Eliot (as – *pace* Coghill[1] – I think we must) about the evasive impulse of Othello's speech at this point is not necessarily to agree with Leavis and others that Eliot's perception 'gives us the cue' for an anti-Othello case. It is rather surprising that Eliot's account gives scarcely any sense of the sheer terribleness of the play's ending, and that his remarks about Othello's state sound so coolly analytic. For it was Eliot who in an earlier essay, speaking about poetic impersonality, was moved to add that 'only those who have personality and emotions know what it means to want to escape from these things'.[2] Had he only followed his own hint here Eliot might have seen that, for Othello in the final scene, that 'want' has become a sheer necessity. In so far as his remarks about Othello's valediction prompt us to see this they are illuminating; but in so far as his commentary implicitly gives us a cue merely to censure Othello, it is to that extent misleading. Shakespeare does not reveal Othello's evasiveness to us in order to condemn it as egotism or moral cowardice. The ending makes far deeper demands on our imaginative and moral understanding than that. For at the very same time as we realize that Othello is indeed, as Eliot claimed, trying to cheer himself up, 'endeavouring to escape reality', we realize too the terrible futility of the endeavour. If he succeeds at all, the success is inevitably partial and evanescent. His attempt is to tidy things up, to salvage some dignity from the wreckage of his life; but at the end of the

[1] Nevill Coghill, *Shakespeare's Professional Skills* (Cambridge, 1964), pp xiv–xv.
[2] 'Tradition and the Individual Talent' [1917], in *Selected Essays*, p. 21.

speech, far from having achieved any real self-comfort, he remains so desperate that he kills himself. So we are pushed towards a more basic question, which has been there for us to ponder ever since the third act: why, exactly does Othello so urgently *need* to try to cheer himself up? And the most basic kind of answer the play gives us is (to put it in Eliot's own words in 'Burnt Norton') that

> human kind
> Cannot bear very much reality.
> Time past and time future
> What might have been and what has been
> Point to one end, which is always present.

In short, the last scene makes us face squarely the question of what 'reality' it is that Othello now can bear so little that he kills himself rather than have to face or endure it a moment more. For us, to respond fully to the drama is to treat as 'real' both Othello's rhetoric *and* the act of suicide to which it finally brings him and which it fails to forestall. We have to acknowledge not only that his urgent 'primary motive' is 'to take in himself' but also that he fails. The attempt and the failure are equally crucial and equally significant; and they surely forbid us the simple comforts of extolling his 'nobility' or denouncing his 'escapism' and of assuming that such praise or censure is the upshot of the play's judgment too.

2

'Injuries' and 'remedies': the first two acts

BRABANTIO But words are words; I never yet did hear
That the bruised heart was piecèd through the ear.
(I, iii, 216–17)

IAGO What, are you hurt, Lieutenant?
CASSIO Ay, past all surgery. (II, iii, 251–2)

If we think back from the final scene over Othello's speeches and actions ever since his crisis in Act III, we can see that *all along* his behaviour has been that of a man 'endeavouring to escape reality'. Throughout the whole second half of the play he attempts by every means he can – ranging from aggressive rage to regressive self-pity – to flee from his own scarcely tolerable sense of perdition in the face of what he takes as the fact of Desdemona's betrayal. The one thing he cannot do is submit to the 'facts'. He struggles either to deny them, or to certify and avenge them – tries everything, in short, that might enable him to reject or modify the image of himself as the unloved, impotent and contemptible cuckold that 'reality' seems to force upon him.

But it is not only Othello himself whom we see deploying a whole range of defensive stratagems. Throughout the play we see everyone else doing exactly this as well – consciously or unconsciously adopting various cheering views of their situations, each view designed to avert particular events or to obviate particular realizations. One after another, each of the characters tries as best he can to alleviate the burden of whatever in his experience is (or might prove to be) fearful or inimical to him. The snippets of quasi-'autobiography' they each rehearse to themselves or to others at various points are in this respect importantly revealing – which is why we need to attend very closely to the particular terms in which they make up cheering stories about themselves or project images of themselves, stories and self-images tailored to fit the way they wish or need to see their lives. Iago tries quite obviously and deliberately to evade any unpalatable aspects of reality, acting always to protect his own hide, devising every stratagem with one eye on the main chance and the other on what he coolly calls 'necessity of present life' (I, i, 156). He announces his double policy of opportunism and self-preservation in the opening scene. But we repeatedly see the other characters, drawn into situations whose exigencies they are not just unwilling but in some cases quite unable to face, seizing, for *real* 'necessity of present life' – for psychic self-survival – on whatever might afford some escape or protection. In every case, our attention is drawn to the same basic issue – the one Montano raises very simply and explicitly in the brawl scene in Act II, when he declares he has done nothing to merit or deserve his injury,

> Unless self-charity be sometimes a vice,
> And to defend ourselves it be a sin
> When violence assails us.   (II, iii, 196–8)

Real or imagined violence in some or other psychological or physical form assails every one of the play's main characters, and each of them deploys his instinctive 'self-charity' to try – however unsuccessfully – to defend himself from it.

So various are the different forms and degrees 'self-charity' takes, however, and so complex are their juxtapositions throughout the play, that we are continually being pushed beyond the tidy moral categories of 'virtue' and 'vice' to sum them up. Iago's 'self-charity' earns our severest adverse judgment not just because it issues in such blatant, deliberate self-deception, but also because he so habitually uses the alleged 'necessity' of self-preservation conveniently to occasion, disguise and justify acts of wanton violence to others. His assorted forms of 'self-charity' strike us as vicious indeed. Yet even here we cannot simply categorize them as 'vice' and thus dismiss them from our minds, for the drama makes us recognize that they are peculiar to him not in kind but only in degree and in the untrammelled ease with which he resorts to them. Montano's instinctive act of 'self-charity' in II, iii, for example, is a different matter; but again we cannot simply pigeon-hole it as 'vice' or 'virtue'. As his respectful, apologetic and justly self-exculpatory tone in speaking to Othello implies, he would doubtless have proved himself more foolish rather than more virtuous had he not resisted Cassio's drunken attempt to murder him. And when we see the much more complicated, various (and often self-delusory) 'self-chari-table' efforts of Brabantio, say, or Othello or Emilia or Desdemona, our feelings and judgments become far more profoundly involved, ambivalent and interlocked. Compared with Montano's vigorous, unreflecting self-defence against Cassio's assault, for instance, Desdemona's reactions to Othello's evident intent to kill her seem peculiarly numbed, passive, forgiving, non-retaliatory. But as we ponder what her apparent lack of 'self-charity' means and implies, and how it differs from and also compares with, for example, Othello's (often Iago-like) responses to her, or Emilia's to Iago, we find that such clean-cut ethical categories as 'vicious' or 'virtuous' are even more inadequate to the moral and emotional complexity of what the play gives us to experience here – to feel as well as to judge.

All through *Othello* we can see Shakespeare exploring

something that had also fascinated other great writers before him: Chaucer, for instance, and Henryson, and Wyatt: the fact that (as Dr Johnson once described it) 'almost every man has some art, by which he steals his thoughts away from his present state'.[1] Here, as in his other tragedies, Shakespeare sees too that such 'arts' are sometimes a man's sole means of bearing life or of protecting himself from it: the point at which they break down is often the point at which a man's self shatters. Dismayed as we may be, therefore, by the range and extent of the human capacity for self-bolstering self-delusion that *Othello* everywhere discloses, we are also made to recognize these 'arts' as sometimes a truly necessary (if not always a sufficient) condition of psychological survival.

If we can recognize that our own moral needs require more than the elementary satisfaction of thinking the characters 'stronger' or 'nobler' than they are, or of viewing their infirmities from a safe position of Olympian moralism, I think we can see that *Othello* is largely about the ordinary and extraordinary efforts people make to cheer themselves up, to comfort themselves against what they could otherwise hardly bear. The play searches out the varied grounds on which people really need to console themselves and to escape from real or imagined pain. More than that, it also searches out how and why, in the longer run, most attempts to do so inevitably fail.

In Othello's own case, the crux is obviously the scene (III, iii) in which Iago intimates the possibility of Desdemona's adultery, and Othello with frightful precipitation comes to believe it is an accomplished fact. This scene is so pivotal for the drama as a whole that it is vital for us to grasp not only what happens in it, and how, and why, but also how our responses to it are shaped by the carefully structured scenes that precede it.

[1] *The Idler*, no. 32, in *Works*, vol. 2, pp. 100–1.

Despite its being a commonplace to speak of the 'masterly construction' of *Othello*, nothing very satisfactory ever seems to get said about how, exactly, the play is a single, unified dramatic whole.[1] Although, for example, Leavis declares that it is 'the simplest' of Shakespeare's tragedies, and that 'the theme is limited and sharply defined',[2] he never actually explains what he means by 'the theme', or asks if Shakespeare's concerns in the play are not perhaps more profound and wide-ranging than 'the theme is simple' allows. And – a related point – although Leavis scorns the common error of supposing the play's 'masterly construction' to be in effect synonymous or commensurate with Iago's intrigue, rightly insisting that 'in Shakespeare's tragedy of *Othello* Othello is the chief personage . . . in such a sense that the tragedy may fairly be said to be Othello's character in action', he gives no indication at all that Othello's character is 'central' in the sense that it is only a part – albeit the 'chief' one – of a larger imaginative whole, a part whose dramatic force is to comment on and be commented on in turn by those of all the subordinate characters. To grasp the play's real subject and the substance of its unity we need to grasp why it creates all of these particular people (rather than others) in these particular relationships and situations (rather than others), and what affinities, if any, are revealed between, say, Brabantio's experience and Emilia's or Cassio's, or between Iago's and Desdemona's, or Roderigo's and Bianca's and Othello's.

Like most readers (including Bradley) before him, and like most readers since, Leavis evidently assumes that 'the theme' or main subject of *Othello* is jealousy; and it is this assumption I think we need to question in the first

---

[1]Michael Long has recently tried to remedy this, though by what seem to me severely Procrustean means, in his sociological account of the play, in *The Unnatural Scene* (London, 1976), pp. 37–58.

[2]'Diabolic Intellect and the Noble Hero', p. 136.

place.[1] For one thing, it leaves the relevance of so much in the play – especially in the first two acts – obscure, to say the least. For another, it leads us either (as Bradley does) to accord Iago undue prominence as the chief engineer of jealousy, or to conclude (as Leavis does) that, despite his apparent dramatic solidity, Iago is rather an uneconomical and 'clumsy mechanism'. Moreover, it also seems to lie behind the many claims that the play is peculiarly limited. Of course it is perfectly true that the play is concerned with jealousy: why else, indeed, is Othello's case counter-pointed with so many others – Roderigo, for instance, and Bianca, and (much more fully) Iago? But to trace the structural logic of the drama from the beginning, or to notice the significant ways Shakespeare changed and added to Cinthio's story, is to see 'jealousy' as only one aspect – or, better, one manifestation – of a more basic subject, which holds Shakespeare's imagination everywhere in the play, including the first two acts.

Dr Johnson was nodding – was indeed sound asleep, I think – when he said that,

had the scene opened in Cyprus, and the preceding incidents been occasionally related, there had been little wanting to a drama of the most exact and scrupulous regularity.[2]

This view is still interesting if only because in our own century the dramatic importance of the early scenes has been so little understood. As recently as 1970, another critic of *Othello*, H. A. Mason, in a chapter promisingly entitled 'The Structure of the First Two Acts', said that throughout these acts Shakespeare seems to be floundering

[1] Cf. A. P. Rossiter, *Angel With Horns* (London, 1970 [1961], p. 190: 'I suggest that the whole meaning of *Othello* can be said to hang on how you interpret the half line "of one not easily jealous".' Cf. also D. R. Godfrey, 'Shakespeare and the Green-Eyed Monster', *Neophilologus*, 56 (1972), pp. 207–19.
[2] *Works*, vol. 8, p. 1048.

to discover 'what his general point was to be'.[1] It may be rash to claim better eyesight than so many earlier critics; yet, as I see it, Shakespeare seems to have begun the play in confident possession of his 'general point', and to have outlined it very crisply in the first one hundred lines. It certainly should be no surprise at all that Acts I and II are almost entirely his own invention – not only not derived from Cinthio's tale, but cutting right across the grain of the *novella*. Boldly conceived, they indicate with wonderful succinctness and precision the main concerns of the entire subsequent action, and they clearly prefigure its essential tragic shape.

From the very beginning, I believe, the play focuses on an issue that is formulated quite explicitly by Emilia in her defiant outburst at Othello in the very last scene:

> Thou hast not half that power to do me harm
> As I have to be hurt.   (v, ii, 161–2)

The human 'power to hurt' and the 'power to *be* hurt', and the connection between them: from the start and all through the play Shakespeare is exploring the relationship between culpability (the impulse and capacity to inflict suffering), and vulnerability (the capacity to suffer), until he finally confronts us with the extremest forms of both, in Othello's related acts of murder and of suicide.

The commonest kind of 'hurt' the action turns on is that of being emotionally or physically rejected, maimed or

[1] In Mason, *Shakespeare's Tragedies of Love* (London, 1970), p.88. Ned B. Allen, observing that in Acts III–V Shakespeare follows Cinthio much more closely than in Acts I–II, concludes that *Othello* is made up of two separate parts written 'at different times – in different frames of mind' and then rather carelessly stitched together: 'The Two Parts of *Othello*', *Shakespeare Survey*, 21 (1968), pp. 13–26. This argument is based on the fallacious assumption that the increased adherence to the *Hecatommithi* in Acts III–V reflects a 'change in Shakespeare's attitude to Cinthio'; in fact, in *Othello* (as everywhere else) Shakespeare's genius is brilliantly opportunistic – he takes from his source whatever he likes, ignores what doesn't suit his purposes, and invents whatever else he sees fit.

wiped out: the personal equivalent of being (in Iago's chilling phrase) militarily 'cashiered'.[1] Throughout the play we see the various ways people try to avert this calamity, and the ways they respond to it when it happens (or when they think it has happened). As the action develops, each particular 'cashiering' shows common features with others, while also significantly differing from them; and although we need to examine each particular case in detail, even a quick glance reveals how many there are. The first major case is Brabantio's, when Desdemona bruisingly dismisses his demand for her public acknowledgment that she owes *him* most 'obedience'. An ominously more abrupt and total form of personal devastation is that in II, i – the Turks are suddenly obliterated by the forces of nature in a storm that also threatens, but spares, the Venetians. Soon after, Cassio is 'cashiered', psychologically losing his life in the form of his job, his reputation and, thus, his self-respect. It is before, during and between these events that Iago discloses to us, and begins to effect, his response to having (so he alleges) been maltreated and rejected or cashiered in various ways by various people – plans of destruction eventually realized when Othello comes to believe that he has been cruelly hurt by Desdemona and so proceeds to cashier her.

The first two acts move swiftly from one to the next of these various disasters. Each personal crisis and the sufferer's reaction to it presents itself in terms of 'injuries' on the one hand, attempted 'remedies' or 'comforts' or 'cures' on the other. The many incidents in which people are assailed by 'bodily' or physical violence serve to mirror and sharpen our responses to those – sometimes the same

[1]Clearly, Shakespeare's concern with 'rejection' was always a central one in his work; it appears and re-appears in *Venus and Adonis*, *The Rape of Lucrece*, and of course the Sonnets, as well as in such plays as *A Midsummer Night's Dream*, *Much Ado*, and – in the years leading up to *Othello* – *Twelfth Night* and *Hamlet*.

35

ones – in which the wounds sustained are psychological: a point to which we are alerted quite directly in the brawl-scene in Act II, for instance. When Montano is (as he exaggeratedly puts it) 'hurt to th' death', 'hurt to danger', Othello announces 'for your hurts myself will be your surgeon', a remark followed immediately by Cassio's exaggerated claim that he has been hurt 'past all surgery', and Iago's reply, feigning sympathy, that 'I thought you [meant that you] had received some bodily wound', and his advice about how Cassio might 'mend' the situation and 'recover' his lost dignity.[1]

From the beginning, however, the drama also reveals that attempted 'cures' or 'surgery' are often only further forms of the 'hurts' that prompted them. As early as I, ii, Iago casually mentions 'contrived murder' as an attractively easy panacea, and Roderigo speaks of suicide as a possible remedy or 'amendment' for grief: 'It is silliness to live when to live is a torment; and then we have a prescription to die, when death is our physician' (I, iii, 306–7). This last is a sentiment that, characteristically, Iago scorns:

O villainous! I have looked upon the world for four times seven years, and since I could distinguish betwixt a benefit and an injury, I never found a man that knew how to love himself. Ere I would say I would drown myself for the love of a guinea-hen, I would change my humanity with a baboon.   (I, iii, 308–13)

That way of putting it – 'never found a man that knew how to love himself' – has important bearings on what we later come to see at the heart of Othello's personal case; but the

---

[1]The age-old metaphor of diseases and cures, or injuries and remedies, runs all through Shakespeare's work, of course – though each play (or poem) uses it in a revealingly distinctive way. It is a key one from beginning to end of *Othello*; but it is hardly less so in *Henry IV*, for example, or *Troilus* and (differently again) in *Hamlet*. I think it is worked most searchingly as a metaphor for moral–psychological maladies in the run of plays from *Troilus* and *Measure for Measure* to *Macbeth*, which all focus directly on various questions about whether and how anyone can 'minister to a mind diseased'.

play also takes up and radically questions the notion that one can, without thereby changing one's humanity with a baboon, always so readily 'distinguish betwixt a benefit and an injury'. Time and again it reveals how easily the particular 'remedies' or consolations people seek for their injuries can turn out – by design or by accident – to be injurious, either to others or to the person seeking relief or both. Medicines, whether self-concocted or prescribed by others, are often in effect poisons. Attempts at remedial murder often prove to be suicidal.[1]

'Hurt', grievance and jealous resentment are at the play's centre from the first, both in Roderigo's peevish complaints against Iago and in Iago himself. So, therefore, are defence, remedy, 'self-charity'. After exculpating himself on grounds of genuine ignorance from Roderigo's resentful charge that he knew in advance of Othello's marriage, Iago immediately insists on his own 'cause' against the Moor. To Roderigo, we notice, he puts on a sourly stoical front: 'Why, there's no remedy. 'Tis the curse of service.' Yet of course he hungrily *seeks* a 'remedy' none the less, to cheer himself up. Not being the sort of 'duteous and knee-crooking knave' he scorns, Iago professes himself to belong to the other class – for to his mind there are only two – of fellows who 'have some soul'. 'Service', for him, is merely a disguised way of gaining power. He 'follows' Othello only to exercise his power to hurt, to 'serve my turn upon him' – not out of altruism but pure self-charity, to 'do [himself] homage'. Congratulating himself thus on being the real master in his bond with Othello, Iago naturally refrains from actually applying to his own case the word he so sneeringly applies to that of impotent knee-crooking knaves – 'cashiered'. But we notice at once the alacrity with which this self-styled master seizes on the advantages of having been served ill.

[1] Cf. for example, Part 2 of *Henry IV*, I, i, 137, where even as Northumberland declares 'In poison there is physic', we realize (as he does not) the ironic truth of the reverse.

Even while declaring that he keeps himself invulnerable by the cunning device of not wearing his heart upon his sleeve, he greedily claims and savours the rights of one who has been victimized, 'peck[ed] at'. Enlisting the aid of Roderigo (whom he simultaneously manages to cashier in the simple sense of relieving him of all his cash), like any reasonable fellow Iago discerns and proceeds to adopt the easiest way of inconveniencing the Moor. Far from requiring any special 'intellect' or 'skill' (as has so often been claimed for him), what could be a simpler ploy than arousing the hurt fury of Desdemona's father? No special effort is required to do to Brabantio exactly what Iago likes to think he's had done to himself, and what he later does in turn to Cassio and Othello too – 'poison his delight' and 'throw such chances of vexation on [his joy]/ As it may lose some colour'. It is quite elementary experimental malice.

The sudden 'timorous' and 'dire' disruption of Brabantio's peace is the first violent assault in the play. It initiates a pattern of events that is to be repeated many times, but of course it is only later that we come fully to realize how much Brabantio's case foreshadows Cassio's, for instance, and Othello's and Desdemona's.

We very quickly recognize Brabantio as a more substantial, formidable, and therefore more interesting figure than Roderigo. As Aerol Arnold remarks, Brabantio's 'function as the father of a daughter who elopes is to behave in a way that makes necessary Desdemona's and Othello's public declaration of their love'.[1] But his behaviour is also significant in subtler ways than that suggests, as we begin to realize as soon as he first appears 'at a window' above the murky Venetian street. Roused by Iago's 'scurvy and provoking' taunts, his immediate response is edged with fear: 'What is the reason of this terrible summons?' Out

---

[1]'The Function of Brabantio', *Shakespeare Quarterly*, 8 (1957), p. 51.

of the darkness comes no clear answer, but only a string of frightful, cryptic, jeering hints; and as the taunts grow more brutal – 'Your heart is burst, you have lost half your soul' – and more obscene, Brabantio's reaction turns to angry incredulity: 'What, have you lost your wits?' In a kind of counter-aggression he threatens that his 'spirit' and his 'place' 'have in them power/ To make this bitter' to his insulters. Within minutes the threats backfire. On discovering that Desdemona has indeed made a 'gross revolt' and eloped with Othello, he is shocked:

> It is too true an evil. Gone she is,
> And what's to come of my despisèd time
> Is naught but bitterness . . .
> . . .
>
> Who would be a father?　　　　(i, i, 161–5)

The natural enough impulse of self-pity here strikes us immediately as springing from and feeding a more basic impulse – to seek any and every possible refuge from the dismaying fact that has been thrust on him. Thus he instantly snatches at the idea that perhaps Desdemona has not really abused and abandoned him at all, but that *she* has been abused, unlawfully forced to act against her own volition; and with this to support himself, he reasserts his power to 'command' allies in his 'cause'. Seizing weapons, he rushes off to repay with injury the man who has injured *him*.

In the following scenes, we notice, Brabantio clings with furious tenacity both to his declared right to exact revenge – 'Mine's not an idle cause; the Duke himself,/ Or any of my brothers of the state,/ Cannot but feel this wrong as 'twere their own' – and to his *power* to command punitive justice, a 'power to hurt' that Iago, in a briefing to Othello at the start of this scene, had provocatively rubbed in, when he warned Othello that Brabantio is 'much beloved',

And hath in his effect a voice potential
As double as the Duke's. He will divorce you,
Or put upon you what restraint and grievance
That law, with all his might to enforce it on,
Will give him cable. (I, ii, 13–17)

More significant still, Brabantio's self-comforting hopes lead him to assert, and then to assume, that all the blame for the elopement 'must' be laid on Othello's head:

O thou foul thief! Where hast thou stowed my daughter?
Damned as thou art, thou hast enchanted her:
. . .
Judge me the world, if 'tis not gross in sense
That thou hast practised on her with foul charms,
Abused her delicate youth with drugs or minerals
That weaken motion. I'll have't disputed on. (I, ii, 62–3, 72–5)

Even so, by the time he arrives at the Senate with Othello under virtual arrest, Brabantio has veered once more from retributive fury back to anguish and self-pity at his over-whelming 'particular grief':

BRABANTIO My daughter! O, my daughter!
SENATORS Dead?
BRABANTIO Ay, to me. (I, iii, 59)

This is the first of many subsequent associations of Desdemona with death, and even here it pulls us up with a little jolt. We realize what being emotionally 'cashiered' can mean – that it can be as hard to bear as death would be and perhaps even harder, since it reveals that one has perhaps never been loved in the way one has hoped or expected, or in the way one has given love. Clearly, it is this realization that Brabantio cannot face or support. He insists that Desdemona has been 'abused, stolen from me, and corrupted/ By spells and medicines' (the passive verbs are revealing), flatly asserting that 'For nature [such as hers] so preposterously to err . . ./ Sans witchcraft could not'.

That Brabantio's grounds for his charge of witchcraft are quite irrational is sharply and significantly underlined by the cool political rationality of the discussion just before he arrives at the Senate. This discussion, in which the Duke and Senators soberly weigh on the scales of likelihood all the various guesses and rumours about the Turks' imminent assault on their dominions, is (as always in this play) pertinent to the drama's strong interest in credibility and credulity, and their opposites. 'There is no composition in these news/ That gives them credit', the sceptical Duke declares at the start; but he wisely continues to scrutinize the 'possible' cause for alarm, enlisting an opinion about the Turks' alleged change of target from the First Senator, who explains why

> This cannot be,
> By no assay of reason. 'Tis a pageant
> To keep us in false gaze,   (I, iii, 17–19)

as, in fact, so it proves. By contrast, Brabantio's hot claims that by no assay of reason could Desdemona be thought to have married Othello voluntarily, and that Othello 'must' therefore be guilty of 'witchcraft', are swiftly proved false. But the sheer illogicality of his deductions is precisely the most revealing thing about them – as it will be about Othello's later. Brabantio's accusation of Othello here is based on nothing more solid than his own assertion that its truth is obvious ('gross in sense'), 'probable and palpable to thinking', and on his desperate refusal or incapacity to believe it could be otherwise. In short, he obviously *needs* to deny or to extenuate Desdemona's guilt, and to believe she is merely a victim; and he needs to believe all this for no other 'reason' than the one he fails to admit even to himself – that he cannot bear the possibility that she may have freely chosen to discard or jettison him, preferring someone else, and a 'sooty' 'thing' at that:

> It is a judgement maimed and most imperfect
> That will confess perfection so could err
> Against all rules of nature, and must be driven
> To find out practices of cunning hell
> Why this should be. I therefore vouch again . . .
>
> (I, iii, 99–103)

For Brabantio, it seems a straightforward matter of weighing the 'objective' evidence – Desdemona's 'perfection' (by which he means filial piety and submissiveness) – and coming to the 'rational' conclusion that Othello 'must' be to blame. As his word 'maimed' makes clear to us, however (but not to himself), he is really haunted by the fear, the lurking threat to his own very maimable feelings, that his 'perfect' daughter may be partly responsible for her 'error'. It is an intriguing argument – in both senses of the word: a fascinating case of self-delusion. Interestingly enough, it exhibits precisely the same assumptions on which Bradley based his account of Othello's behaviour in Acts III–V. Unable to face anything that might seem to disprove or qualify the hero's perfect 'nobility', Bradley is 'driven' by his feelings (which assume the guise of judgments) to 'find out practices of cunning hell' to explain away Othello's culpability. Nevertheless, as in Brabantio's case (and Desdemona's own later on), so in Bradley's, I think: the play makes us see how the impulse to extenuate the guilt of others can be a form of comforting self-delusion, but it gives us no warrant to despise the impulse even when it is that. One crucial difference remains, though, between Brabantio's and Bradley's extenuations, in view of which Bradley's emotional needs become severe critical liabilities. Brabantio, being caught within the stringent conditions of 'actual' living – rather than contemplating the fictional experience of others – is soon stripped of his comforting delusion; Bradley, on the other hand, can freely avail himself of every loophole he can find or make that enables him to persist in his. Bradley's 'vouchings' of Othello's nobility meet with no such immediate stern demand for 'proof' as Brabantio's contrary 'vouchings' are met by:

BRABANTIO   I therefore vouch again
That with some mixtures powerful o'er the blood,
Or with some dram conjured to this effect,
He wrought upon her.
DUKE   To vouch this is no proof,
Without more wider and more overt test
Than these thin habits and poor likelihoods
Of modern seeming do prefer against him.
(I, iii, 103–9)

At this point, of course, Othello does what he so signally fails to do at a similar crisis later in the play when Desdemona is alleged to be guilty: he promptly calls on her testimony to 'witness' his innocence. But even before this 'more overt test' is made, the Duke (who is not notably disinterested) advises Brabantio to abandon the suit, to make a virtue of necessity: 'Good Brabantio, take up this mangled matter at the best'. Brabantio refuses, and consequently it is *he* who ends up 'mangled'. For (just as Othello later does in a grotesquely opposite way in Act IV) Brabantio clings desperately to the view he needs to take, in the face of all evidence to the contrary:

Come hither, gentle mistress;
Do you perceive in all this company
Where most you owe obedience?   (I, iii, 176–8)

The question certainly puts Desdemona on the spot. Although neither she nor Othello shows any sign of wanting to hurt her father, his attitudes and actions unfortunately make injury unavoidable: simply by plain-speaking, by being gracious to her husband as well as to him, she wounds Brabantio. She uses the word 'challenge', but her speech

43

none the less seems gentle; its defiant edge is softened by a conciliatory tone and an urgency that implicitly appeals for his agreement. But the opening sentences of her answer, as she looks directly into his face, trying at once to reassure and acknowledge him as properly 'my father', are not enough to satisfy his huge demand. So her word 'hitherto', toughening the drift of her speech, inevitably ushers in the turn to 'but' – 'But here's my husband'. Courteously, but with a now distancing formality and firmness (and in terms that for us anticipate Cordelia's in a similarly public speech about 'bonds' and 'duty' to *her* father in the first scene of *King Lear*), she denies Brabantio the acknowledgment of undivided love and allegiance he wants:[1]

> My noble father,
> I do perceive here a divided duty:
> To you I am bound for life and education;
> My life and education both do learn me
> How to respect you. You are lord of all my duty,
> I am hitherto your daughter. But here's my husband;
> And so much duty as my mother showed
> To you, preferring you before her father,
> So much I challenge, that I may profess
> Due to the Moor, my lord.   (I, iii, 178–87)

'I am hitherto your daughter. *But . . .*': we are to be reminded of this cashiering 'but' several times later in the play. Here, with a small shock, we realize what the word so sharply thrusts at Brabantio's heart: that no matter what security a 'bond' may have had 'hitherto', this does not automatically guarantee its continuance in the present and the future.[2] To the extent that 'bonds' of loving are freely

---

[1] In doing so, we may notice, she uses the same terminology as Iago did in the opening scene.
[2] Cf. for example Ulysses' 'time' speech in *Troilus and Cressida* (III, iii, 145ff.). As in *Troilus* and the history plays, the precariousness of office, of fame and reputation, as well as of relationships, is strongly felt throughout *Othello*.

chosen, *not* just duties, they are always open to annulment by such a 'but'. Love worth the name inevitably entails that risk. And in this particular instance, Brabantio is utterly crushed.

This last, surely, is the most potent dramatic point here. Certainly, Brabantio's assumptions and attitudes as a father have struck us as neither admirable nor humane ('How got she out? O treason of the blood!'), and his response to his catastrophe – the vengeful claim that if he had any other children 'thy escape would teach me tyranny/ To hang clogs on them' – is shockingly ugly and brutal. All of this suggests, though the play does not enforce the point, that Desdemona and Othello may have had good reason to act surreptitiously as they did. But on this issue – unlike the later issues of Othello's treatment of Cassio in Act II, for instance, or of Desdemona – Shakespeare saw fit neither to invite nor to pursue in the play questions of whether Desdemona treats her father 'justly' or 'unjustly', or (to put it the other way) of whether or not Brabantio 'deserves' all he gets. Such questions are bypassed and rendered unanswerable here by Shakespeare's concentration on something else, viz. Brabantio's power to be hurt in despite of all his crusty protestations of his own power to injure others and to 'command' weaponed supporters in his 'cause'. If, up to this point, we have shared something of Iago's sneering and Othello's cool contempt for the old man's blustering violence, and something of the Duke's impatience, we have also during the Senate scene come to feel something *for* him too. We may dislike the dog yet feel some pity for the underdog in him, and it is that sympathy which now, I believe, comes to the fore – sympathy for this old man who is not a dear old man. One reason it does so (as in a different way with the mortified Malvolio, for example) is that everyone around him seems so ready to brush his grief aside. Most producers of the play, hurrying on to what they see as its 'main business', also gloss over it, swiftly drawing our attention elsewhere. But to attend to him, to let his shock arrest us for one sharp moment, *is* to attend to the play's main business; for what is made clear to us if we do is that, simply by loving Desdemona, even in his own peculiar tyrannous, possessive way, Brabantio's heart exposes itself to such a severe injury, and in the end no attempted self-delusions can serve to protect him from it. That he indeed loves his daughter and loses his 'heart' in losing her comes out clearly in his speech following her denial; for the first time, Brabantio's voice is very small, very subdued:

> God bu'y! I have done.
> Please it your grace, on to the state affairs.
> I had rather to adopt a child than get it.
> Come hither, Moor:
> I here do give thee that with all my heart
> Which, but thou hast already, with all my heart
> I would keep from thee. For your sake, jewel [Desdemona],
> I am glad at soul I have no other child. (I, iii, 187–94)

The blunt simplicity and audible pain of his comment to Othello differ quite markedly from, say, Lear's brusqueness to France at the comparable moment in that play (I, i, 262ff.); the gentle directness of his phrase 'For your sake, jewel . . .', spoken amidst his distress, is in tone far more like Lear's prefatory words to Cordelia – 'And now our joy . . .' – than like Lear's hysterically self-lacerating outbursts against Cordelia that follow her denial of him. Even here, when Desdemona has refused to say what he wanted to hear, Brabantio cannot help acknowledging what Lear with such desperate vehemence struggles to deny: that although he cannot possess and keep her, his daughter is still his 'jewel', that 'I have no other child', and that 'all my heart' goes with her, however he might strive to withhold it. The quietness of his speech is its power, its control the clearest sign of his stress. The courteous entreaties to the Duke – 'Please it your grace, on to the state affairs'; 'I have done, my lord'; and (later), 'I humbly beseech you, proceed to th'affairs of state' – are those of a man who is humbled, humiliated and really hurt. And because Shakespeare troubled to give us this lucid glimpse inside the old man's 'particular grief' before it tips into tyrannical aggression again, we retain and later recollect this sharp impression of a private wound which had rudely sought redress and got public exposure. Shock, pain, and complete isolation: these are what he experiences on being discarded thus.

Hence, the Duke's proffered cheer-up, to the effect that there's no use crying over spilt milk, seems, under these circumstances, rather stupid or callous or at any rate unheeding (as is his later, tactless, suggestion that Desdemona return to her father's house for the duration of the war in Cyprus):

> When remedies are past the griefs are ended
> By seeing the worst which late on hopes depended.
> To mourn a mischief that is past and gone
> Is the next way to draw new mischief on.
> What cannot be preserved when fortune takes,
> Patience her injury a mockery makes.
> The robbed that smiles steals something from the thief;
> He robs himself that spends a bootless grief.
>
> (I, iii, 200–7)

The Duke pronounces these and other such maxims as though they were self-evident facts. (Some obvious comparisons that spring to mind are Rosaline's ironic 'for "past cure is still past care" ' in the final scene of *Love's Labour's Lost*; the numerous exhortations to be 'patient' in *King Lear*, especially Edgar's, which likewise strike us as easy enough to utter but not easy at all to live; Paulina's assertion in *The Winter's Tale* (III, ii, 218–19) that 'what's gone and what's past help/ Should be past grief', wherein 'should' indicates that in actual fact human grief might prove more refractory; or again, Lady Macbeth's pro-

nouncement of two still more dramatically ironic 'shoulds'
(*Macbeth*, III, ii, 8–12): 'Why do you keep alone,/ . . . Using
those thoughts which should indeed have died/ With them
they think on? Things without all remedy/ Should be
without regard.') Clearly, the preoccupations of *Othello*
develop from those of *Hamlet*, for example, and point ahead
to these later plays. The Duke's claim that to mourn a
'mischief' – a stronger word than our use of it, being
synonymous here with calamity – is to court further injury
grossly ignores the human reality of Brabantio's 'mischief'
and his 'o'erbearing sorrow'. Brabantio's sardonic rejoinder
marks the vast gap between his personal *experience* of grief
and the Duke's mere abstract notion of it. The jangling
couplets, mimicking the Duke's, alert us to the choric
function and effect of Brabantio's lines; but their powerful
dramatic effect derives from the authority of the very real
personal anguish out of which Brabantio speaks:

> So let the Turk of Cyprus us beguile,
> We lose it not so long as we can smile;
> He bears the sentence well that nothing bears
> But the free comfort which from thence he hears;
> But he bears both the sentence and the sorrow
> That to pay grief must of poor patience borrow.
> These sentences, to sugar or to gall
> Being strong on both sides, are equivocal.
> But words are words; I never yet did hear
> That the bruised heart was piecèd through the ear.
> I humbly beseech you proceed to th' affairs of state.[1]
>
> (I, iii, 208–18)

For a 'bruised heart' what might be a source of comfort
causes pain, since (as Iago later mock-sympathetically puts

---

[1]Again, this speech is strongly reminiscent of others in other plays: Adriana's
to Luciana (about 'a wretched soul, bruis'd with adversity') in *The Comedy
of Errors*, II, i, 33–41, for example; Benedick's remark in *Much Ado*, III, ii,
25–6, that 'every one can master a grief but he that has it'; and, more
especially, Leonato's replies to Antonio in *Much Ado*, V, i, 1–41.

it to Roderigo) 'what wound did ever heal but by degrees?'
For Brabantio, real grief makes all palliatives 'equivocal'.
Emotional benefits – even the consolations of philosophy –
must inevitably be paid for, must exact their own cost.
Psychological 'medicines' always contain some poisonous
element, and therefore work 'to sugar or to gall'.

After Brabantio, the next major casualty is that of the
Turkish fleet. To miss the significance of this event – even
though it is only reported – is to miss how closely Act II is
related to Act I. H. A. Mason, for example, argues that
Shakespeare reaches the end of the first act 'without
finding a *donnée*', and that in Act II,

> though there are one or two small new developments, there is
> as yet no sense that Shakespeare has fully opened his mind or
> imposed on the play any unifying powers to create anything
> that we could dignify by the name of a general point or *donnée*.
> Indeed, we might well believe that Shakespeare was playing the
> first Act over again *because* he had not yet seen what his
> general point was to be.[1]

This seems to me to miss not only the dramatic import
of Act I, which does considerably more than give us Shakespeare's 'general point', but to overlook the way Act II
continues and develops that import.

Act I ends ominously when Othello 'assigns' Desdemona to Iago's 'conveyance': 'Honest Iago,/ My Desdemona must I leave to thee'; and when the lovers have
retired to spend 'but an hour' together before their parting,
Iago persuades Roderigo to persist in his suit for Desdemona
and then soliloquizes darkly on how best to wreak simul-
taneous vengeance on Othello and Cassio. The rather lurid
violence of his language may prompt us to hope that his
villainy will prove to be what he had sneeringly claimed of

---

[1]*Shakespeare's Tragedies of Love*, pp. 86, 88.

Cassio's soldiership – 'mere prattle without practice'. He gloatingly plots how

> To get his place and to plume up my will
> In double knavery. How? How? Let's see.
> . . .
> I have't. It is engendered. Hell and night
> Must bring this monstrous birth to the world's light.
>   [*Exit*]
>   (I, iii, 387–8, 397–8)

Couched in such apparently melodramatic terms as these, his threat (like Brabantio's famous warning to Othello – 'Look to her, Moor . . .') may well seem, as we hear it, absurd in its vagueness. Yet we can hardly feel very comfortable even so. The particular kinds of emotion (and the intensity of emotions) that this first act of the play has dramatized already seem too intractable to herald a comic sequel.[1] And any hopes we may yet have for a painless dénouement are promptly drowned in Act II. The opening of Act II gives a dreadful physical reality to Iago's mental violence. The 'monstrous birth' of inner 'hell and night' he threatens to induce is immediately echoed by – indeed linked and even identified with – the 'monstrous mane' wrought up by the 'desperate', 'foul and violent' tempest of nature that shakes the battlements of Cyprus and puts at risk the lives both of the Venetian forces and of the invading Turks.

---

[1]Cf. Mason, *ibid.* p. 73: 'Anyone seeing *Othello* for the first time who was called away after the first act would have to admit that he might have been witnessing the opening of a comedy'; and (p. 88) 'another impression strengthened . . . is that so far [by the end of Act II] the play is still a comedy'. This last seems to me a large overstatement. The comic elements are much more ambiguous, and by the end of Act I, still more of Act II, we are surely very aware of what many critics have commented on: Shakespeare's tendency in *Othello* 'to parody or twist to a tragic issue the forms usually associated with comedy', as Emrys Jones puts it in *Scenic Form in Shakespeare* (Oxford, 1971), p. 138. Jones suggests some interesting links between *Othello* and the earlier comedies; his remarks about Shakespeare's self-borrowings from *The Merry Wives* are especially suggestive (pp. 124–7).

MONTANO If that the Turkish fleet
Be not ensheltered and embayed, they are drowned:
It is impossible they bear it out.   (II, i, 17–19)

Othello himself and the rest of his fleet do manage successful 'defence against the elements'; as Cassio puts it, the
General's 'bark is stoutly timbered', and 'therefore my hopes
not surfeited to death,/ Stand in bold cure'.

Juxtaposed as it is, though, with the emotional tumults of
Act I and with Iago's dark threats, the storm obviously
prefigures the dangerous psychic tumults still to come.
(Seeing the play on stage, one can hardly fail to take the
point immediately, but as usual with Shakespeare – as in
Lear and *Macbeth*, for example – the symbolic function of
the storm is clearly and thoroughly underscored in the
verbal text itself.) As it happens, Othello's boat happily
'hold[s] the mortise'; but we are not left wholly confident
that he will therefore prove sufficiently well-fortified to
survive Iago's threatened 'molestation' in which the
elements will be inner ones. The fate of the Turks here
forbids, or at least severely qualifies, any such assurance.
Like Brabantio, they had tried in 'warlike brace' to assert
their power; but like him again, not being 'ensheltered',
they met sudden catastrophe, becoming the victims not
merely of 'grievous wrack and sufferance' but of 'mere
perdition', total annihilation. To us, the warning is clear.
The lovers happily escape this 'disastrous chance'. But the
Turks' fate reminds us that storms do indeed unleash
possibilities of real destruction, possibilities of the sort
fleetingly mentioned in Act I and which we can now no
longer regard as merely romantic exaggerations or melodramatic fantasies – for instance, those suggested in
Othello's eloquent phrases about his past life being full of
'most disastrous chances', 'moving accidents by flood and
field', 'hair-breadth 'scapes i'th' imminent deadly breach',
and so on; or Desdemona's strange reference to 'My

downright violence and storm of fortunes'; or Iago's scornful hammering iterations to Roderigo about the absurd possibilities of 'drowning', as well as his mutterings about hell and night.

These possibilities are not only given a fuller and more threatening force in the storm-scene. The delicately ironic placing of Cassio's panegyric on Desdemona also makes us feel their threat edging nearer the lovers:

> Tempests themselves, high seas, and howling winds,
> The guttered rocks and congregated sands,
> Traitors ensteep'd to clog the guiltless keel,
> As having sense of beauty, do omit
> Their mortal natures, letting go safely by
> The divine Desdemona.[1]   (II, i, 68–73)

Cassio's claims here are genuinely heartfelt, but we can hardly miss the element of hyperbolic fantasy in them, an element that underlines the dangerous – because tranquillizing – sentimentality of such a view of nature's forces. Desdemona may indeed be worthy of high praise, but she is clearly not 'divine' – she is human and destructible; and the terrible power of storms and rocks is their power to wreck *any* hapless wayfarer. Despite Cassio's enthusiastic anthropomorphism – or rather because of it – we are made all the more aware that nature is neither hostile nor clement, but totally indiscriminate; its powers own no reverence for moral worth and no benevolent 'sense of beauty' that might cause them to 'omit their mortal natures'.

Significantly, we are also made aware that the same

[1]Although Muir gives 'enscarped' (for the Quarto's 'enscerped') at line 70, I have substituted the more commonly preferred (Folio) reading, 'ensteep'd', which links with the imagery of later speeches – 'Steeped me in poverty to the very lips'; 'Wash me in steep-down gulfs of liquid fire' – that are related so ironically to the hopes and joys expressed in the storm scene. At line 72 the usual (Folio) reading, 'mortal natures', is dramatically much more pointed than the Quarto's 'c·nmon natures' (which M. R. Ridley accepts in the Arden edition).

applies to Iago and his projected tempest and guttered rocks. Cassio's naïve but endearing veneration is immediately followed by Iago's rebarbative cynicism in his (only half-frivolous) banter with Desdemona. He dismisses all distinctions between 'fairness' and 'foulness' in women in a way that makes clear his lack of any discriminating 'sense of beauty' or reverence for moral worth, which might lead him mercifully to 'omit' the mortal nature of his designs. If, like Othello's, Desdemona's escape from destruction in the storm is plainly fortuitous and not a result of 'merit', so neither her 'beauty' nor the fact that she is 'guiltless' will avail to 'let her go safely by' Iago's treachery. Certainly, this is Iago's own view. As he puts it in one of his self-admiring speeches in IV, i, which tellingly echoes Cassio's own word here, 'guiltless':

Work on,
My medicine, work! Thus credulous fools are caught,
And many worthy and chaste dames even thus,
All guiltless, meet reproach.[1]   (IV, i, 44–7)

The terrible irony of Cassio's speech about Desdemona's safety is of course not fully brought home until the final scene – where, in fact, her own closing speech unwittingly echoes his word: 'A guiltless death I die.' Yet even as Cassio speaks it we are much less aware of safety than of potential peril, '*mortal nature*'. Essentially, what we glimpse in the storm-scene and in the obliteration of the Turks is what we had glimpsed in Brabantio's case: the ominous fact that some 'dangers' are quite literally a matter of life and death, since some 'hurts' are so 'flood-gate and o'er-bearing' as to be irremediable, without any comfort or cure.

*

[1]This may well remind us of Laertes' famous remark (*Hamlet*, I, iii, 38): 'Virtue itself scapes not calumnious strokes', or Hamlet's 'be thou as chaste as ice, as pure as snow, thou shalt not escape calumny' (III, i, 136–7).

The scene in which the next major 'cashiering' occurs, Cassio's (II, iii), at once furthers and complicates the dramatic action in a number of ways. Before the scene begins we know very little of Cassio's nature except that he is devoted to Othello and admires Desdemona. At moments in the storm-scene, and again later in the play – in the eavesdropping scene, for instance – Shakespeare seems rather uncertain and even rather slapdash in his creation of Cassio. (For example, Cassio's reply when Iago declares Othello is married, 'To who?', sorts very oddly with the fact – so we learn elsewhere – that he knew of and helped the courtship; perhaps this is cunning disingenuousness on Cassio's part, though I think the contradiction more likely results from absent-mindedness on Shakespeare's.) But the scene of Cassio's cashiering is confidently and finely dramatized, affording us a sharp, particular and coherent sense of the kind of man he is. And it raises, explicitly or implicitly, a number of important moral issues, each of which helps to form our responses to Othello's crisis soon after.

Among these issues the one usually singled out as especially important is whether Cassio 'deserves' his dismissal or whether Othello's treatment of him here is 'unjust'. In fact, this seems to me the least problematical, since it is not only raised explicitly in the scene itself but answered in plain and quite specific terms. Right at the start of the scene, Othello in a tactful and companionly way cautions Cassio to 'look you to the guard', and to remain in a state of 'discretion'. Presumably he is aware (as Cassio himself and Iago are) of Cassio's tendency to be 'rash and sudden in choler' when under the influence of drink.[1] Both the warning itself and Cassio's undertaking that 'with my personal eye/ Will I look to't' actually serve to underscore

[1]However, we are given every reason to suppose that Iago grossly exaggerates when, in reply to Montano's query as to whether Cassio was often drunk, he says ' 'Tis evermore the prologue to his sleep' (II, iii, 124).

our sense of his culpability when, very shortly afterwards, he manages to get uncontrollably drunk and obstreperous.

Notwithstanding the disapproval of loftier-minded readers, it seems to me hardly surprising that Othello is furious when he has to leave his marriage-bed in order to deal with a brawl started by the very man he had asked 'not to outsport discretion'. Cassio being too drunk and distressed and Montano too badly hurt to explain it, Othello naturally calls for Iago's account, and of course receives what we know (though no one in the scene does) is a distorted explanation. And before we rush on to diagnose a 'lack of self-control' in Othello here we do well to notice one important fact about his dismissal of Cassio: everyone in the scene regards the cashiering as just. What Shakespeare stresses is the simultaneity of Othello's anger and his strict self-discipline. One of the main dramatic points of Othello's famous speech about how blood begins to rule his safer guides, 'collying' judgment and assaying to lead the way, is precisely that it shows Othello's own acute awareness of the dangers of letting any private feelings influence professional judgments:

> Give me to know
> How this foul rout began, who set it on;
> And he that is approved in this offence,
> Though he had twinned with me, both at a birth,
> Shall lose me. (II, iii, 203–7)

Coming so soon after Othello had warmly addressed Cassio as 'good Michael' at the start of the scene, the conditional 'though he had twinned with me' sharply attests both Othello's real fondness of Cassio, and his determination not to let his personal affection and sense of disappointment overrule his judgment as a soldier, which dictates that the culprit must be sacked, not excused.[1]

---

[1]Clearly, it is the same ethic as prompted the 'skillet' speech (I, iii, 258ff.) as well.

This speech clearly parallels the Duke's avowal to Brabantio in the previous 'trial' scene:

> Whoe'er he be that in this foul proceeding
> Hath thus beguiled your daughter of herself
> And you of her, the bloody book of law
> You shall yourself read in the bitter letter
> After your own sense, yea, though our proper son
> Stood in your action.   (I, iii, 65–70)

Whereas the Duke's promise of disinterested justice was (as Iago had predicted) effectively revoked as soon as the culprit turned out to be someone with whom 'the state cannot with safety' dispense, Othello's promise of impartiality is promptly honoured – at obvious pain to himself as well as Cassio. Both the differences and the similarities between the two incidents are suggestive, not least because in both of them (as elsewhere throughout the play) Shakespeare pointedly accentuates the almost inevitable problems that come with *any* combination of public with private concerns, as well as the inevitable unhappiness caused to somebody in any situation where public and private interests must be sternly kept apart. In this respect the incident in II, iii, amplifies our understanding of Othello's earlier unease about how matrimony and generalship will combine; and his vehement stress here on the need to remain absolutely impartial naturally also prepares our perspective on subsequent events, especially Othello's disquiet when Desdemona insists that he *should* let private allegiances dominate public ones. And this important function of the cashiering scene no doubt explains why Shakespeare gives explicit extra emphasis here to the need and significance of professional impartiality, in Montano's warning to Iago:

> If partially affined or leagued in office,
> Thou dost deliver more or less than truth,
> Thou art no soldier.   (II, iii, 212–14)

If we ourselves can remain impartial witnesses of the scene
we see that, judged by the standards of everyone involved,
the dismissal of Cassio represents nothing short of the
'wholesome wisdom' that Emilia subsequently declares
Othello has termed it.[1] Even Cassio himself regards his
drunkenness as a gross dereliction of duty, and though he
longs to be pardoned, at no point does he challenge the
justice of Othello's act. He blames himself – as in this
speech to Iago:

> I will rather sue to be despised than to deceive so good a
> commander with so slight, so drunken, and so indiscreet an
> officer. Drunk! And speak parrot! And squabble! Swagger!
> Swear! And discourse fustian with one's own shadow!
>
> (II, iii, 270–4)

If, then, the incident suggests anything about Othello's
capacity for anger, the suggestion is not that he lacks self-
control. It is subtler than that, and we realize it only
retrospectively. In the event itself our attention is mainly
directed not to questioning the fairness of Cassio's dismissal but to the terms in which Othello effects it, terms
which make clear the painful personal cost to Othello
(accentuated by his sense of the professional necessity) of
having to dismiss him:

> Cassio, I love thee,
> But nevermore be officer of mine.
>   [*Enter Desdemona, attended*]
> Look, if my gentle love be not raised up.
> I'll make thee an example.   (II, iii, 242–5)

[1] After the dismissal – not when it takes place – Desdemona (who is nowhere
exactly *au fait* with military proprieties) does try to persuade Othello that
he acted less than justly; but by this stage she avowedly has an axe to grind,
and we suspect she rather wishes than believes her allegation to be true:
> In faith, he's penitent:
> And yet his trespass in our common reason –
> Save that, they say, the wars must make example
> Out of their best – is not almost a fault
> T'incur a private check. When shall he come?   (III, iii, 63–7)

'I love thee,/ But nevermore . . .': it recalls the similar cashiering 'but' that Desdemona had earlier pronounced to her father. And if we notice here the (of course unwitting) ambiguity of 'I'll make thee an example', it may well make us realize that Othello could conceivably, one day, utter just such a 'but' to another and dearer 'love', his 'gentle love', Desdemona. In fact, there are a number of small but disquieting hints and forebodings of that possibility all through Act II.

Cassio's case serves to warn us not to treat such hints too lightly. For there were also a number of little signs, prior to the brawl, that led us to anticipate some such rupture of the bond between him and Othello as this scene puts before us. The public 'displanting' of Brabantio, for example, was still very fresh in our minds when Iago, in Act I, first announced his intention to throw vexation on Cassio's joy (as on Brabantio's) by usurping his 'place'. In the storm-scene, the strangely iterated remarks about Cassio's physical separation from Othello might also have seemed ominous: 'They [Othello and Cassio] were parted/ With foul and violent tempest'; 'I have lost him on a dangerous sea'; 'O, but I fear! How lost you company?'; 'The great contention of the sea and skies/ Parted our fellowship.'

As Cassio's rupture with Othello is foreshadowed in this way, so in turn it provides a number of disquieting fore-shadowings of Othello's future. There is something doubly sinister in Iago, just before the fight, speaking to Montano about Cassio in exactly the same sort of terms as Montano has just used of Othello, as 'a soldier, fit to stand by Caesar/ And give direction'.[1] For Iago then goes on to point out Cassio's 'ingraft infirmity' of drunkenness:

[1] This echo of Montano's praise of Othello,
> Pray heaven he be [safe]
> For I have served him, and the man commands
> Like a full soldier,   (II, i, 34–6)

naturally jolts us into remembering Iago's earlier aspersions on Cassio's soldiership, in the first scene.

> . . . and do but see his vice:
> 'Tis to his virtue a just equinox,
> The one as long as th'other. 'Tis pity of him.
> I fear the trust Othello puts in him,
> On some odd time of his infirmity,
> Will shake this island. (II, iii, 118–23)

Of course, far from fearing or pitying that result, Iago deliberately seeks it, capitalizing to the full on Cassio's 'infirmity'; it is we who now 'fear the trust' Cassio puts in *Iago* and who already begin to fear the trust Othello likewise puts in him. Much later, we are to be reminded of Iago's fake expressions of solicitude for Cassio here, when – with exactly the same ulterior motive – he utters exactly the same sentiments to Lodovico apropos of Othello himself, in the scene in which Othello in *his* 'infirmity' strikes Desdemona: 'He's that he is: I may not breathe my censure/ What he might be' –

> Alas, alas!
> It is not honesty in me to speak
> What I have seen and known. You shall observe him,
> And his own courses will denote him so,
> That I may save my speech. Do but go after,
> And mark how he continues. (IV, i, 278–83)

There is another disturbing suggestion of the future possibility of discord between the lovers in Othello's description of the brawl as a 'monstrous', 'private and domestic quarrel', a suggestion which – given that the fight has violently disrupted the lovers' first, joyfully awaited hours of privacy together since their marriage – is reinforced by another in Iago's account of the 'barbarous brawl', when he says he does not know who began it:

> Friends all but now, even now,
> In quarter and in terms like bride and groom
> Devesting them for bed: and then but now –
> As if some planet had unwitted men –

59

> Swords out, and tilting one at others' breasts
> In opposition bloody. I cannot speak
> Any beginning to this peevish odds.　　(II, iii, 173–9)

Nor can we miss the suggestive way Iago brought the 'peevish odds' about. Beginning with an experimental 'parley to provocation', he had tried insinuations about Desdemona's sexual disposition – 'Methinks [her eye] sounds a parley to provocation' – alleging (more directly than he at first dares do to Othello in the next act) Desdemona's sexual gaminess, her open 'alarum to love'. When Cassio failed to respond to this bait he tried another – on a side where Cassio frankly declared himself vulnerable: 'I have very poor and unhappy brains for drinking . . . I am unfortunate in the infirmity and dare not task my weakness with any more.' (Just so, Othello, before Iago's onslaught, will declare where *he* is most vulnerable: 'Perdition catch my soul but I do love thee.') Against men as open as this, Iago hardly needs diabolical skill. It took very few and small waves of assault against Cassio's fortifications to bring him to acknowledge his sense of friendship, duty and courtesy by drinking the General's health: 'I'll do't, but it dislikes me.'[1] Like Brabantio's before him ('t'incur a general mock') and Othello's later ('Dost thou mock me?'; 'to make me/ A fixed figure for the time of scorn'), Cassio's fury was exacerbated by a sense of being mocked, denigrated, laughed at: as Iago put it so suavely, a sense of 'indignity/ Which patience could not pass'. Like Brabantio's too, Cassio's aggression recoiled on himself: in trying to cure the initial 'hurt' he only inflicted a worse one on himself, a public and final dismissal.

In all of this, the most striking and significant aspects of Cassio's case, I think, are, firstly, his surprising inability to withstand Iago's pretty mild persuasions, and, secondly,

---

[1] Compare Iago's phrases in badinage with Desdemona: 'Fled from her wish, and yet said "Now I may" ' (II, i, 148).

the sheer speed and completeness with which he capitulates and becomes drunk. Both these features are to have their counterpart in Othello's case, of course, and not only do they raise moral questions at the very centre of our understanding of the play, but the fact that they do marks the crucial difference between Shakespeare's tragedy and a morally simplistic, Cinthio-like tale of villainy perpetrated on innocence.

One such question is whether 'capitulation' is in fact the right word for Cassio – the question, that is, of how far we have to judge Cassio as having fallen or as having been pushed. As I have suggested, the play itself questions how far, by military standards, Cassio must be held responsible for his drunken behaviour, and it finds him, as he finds himself, wholly to blame. We notice, too, that in lamenting his conduct, he uses active rather than passive verbs to describe it: 'O God, that men should put an enemy in their mouths to steal away their brains! That we should . . . transform ourselves into beasts!' He is mortified by what he is and has done: 'I am a drunkard!' (This capacity for quick, spontaneous self-condemnation and remorse – not common in this play – further endears Cassio to us and strengthens our respect for him, for it goes with his capacity to recognize and praise true merit in other people such as Othello and Desdemona. Both these traits mark his nature as the reverse of Iago's.) But we also notice that his regret and self-disgust clearly spring from his sense that his misconduct was not just professionally criminal but also morally reprehensible – that he has dismally failed in his duty to Othello as a friend. And it is here that the play demands of us a more subtle and difficult moral response. For while we realize the extent to which Cassio is indeed culpable, the agent of his own folly, we are equally conscious of the extent to which *Iago* is culpable and Cassio really the unlucky 'fly' (as Iago gloatingly puts it), ensnared in the spider's 'web'. We have to recognize both facts: that Cassio's dismissal would not have happened thus without Iago's malign opportunism in provoking the brawl, and yet that it would not have happened thus without his own act of accepting drink – an act made in full knowledge of his own 'weakness'. But the inadequacy both of mere blame and mere exculpation does not only complicate our appraisal of Cassio's behaviour. Even here we recognize its wider implications – most centrally and specifically, in our sense of Othello's possible fate, which we already suspect is being obscurely brought to 'monstrous birth'.

Viewing this possibility from the perspective afforded by Cassio's cashiering we may remember that in Act I, when the green-eyed monster Iago first projected his plan to diet his revenge simultaneously on Cassio and Othello, he had confidently declared that the Moor 'will as tenderly be led by th'nose/ As asses are'; and just prior to the brawl-scene he had again regaled himself with the prospect of making Othello 'thank me, love me, and reward me/ For making him egregiously an ass' (II, i, 299–300). Yet the brawl-scene itself, in presenting us with the spectacle of *Cassio's* being so tenderly led by the nose, also sharply puts us in mind of the other side of the old adage: it's easy enough to lead an ass to water, but not even an Iago could persuade a wholly recalcitrant ass to drink. Just as Roderigo's gullibility arises from his own hot hopes rather than from any skill of Iago's, Cassio's confessedly 'poor and unhappy brains for drinking' make him easy to exploit. He needs very little coercion. Half-voluntarily, half against his own will, he drinks the very poison he professes not to want, and it steals away his brains. The latter phrase is his own, and it reminds us how, in Act I, Othello had been wrongly accused of 'abusing' Desdemona 'with drugs or minerals/ That weaken motion'. And just as in that case Desdemona was, on her own admission, 'half the wooer', readily acquiescing in Othello's 'indirect . . . courses', so too with Cassio, who swallows drugs that (temporarily) 'subdue' his judgment – indeed disastrously 'poison [his] affections'.[1]

We can scarcely fail to be apprehensive, therefore, when Iago, at the end of this scene (II, iii), describes the poison he intends to use on Othello – 'I'll pour this pestilence into his ear:/ That she repeals him for her body's lust'.[2] Moreover, well before Iago actually begins to do so, we have been prompted to question the susceptibility in Othello that will be the necessary and perhaps (as with Cassio) the virtually sufficient condition of Iago's success. For this, surely, is the most troubling moral question Cassio's case raises in our minds: is not 'poisoning' effective only when men are susceptible to it? Even before Othello's crisis, we are brought to suspect that if he too falls when he is pushed, it will be because – like Roderigo and Cassio and Desdemona, all in their different ways – he is an active, a *collaborative* victim. Inevitably, we begin to be uneasily on the lookout for any signs of infirmity in Othello's emotional or moral fortifications.

Before going on to consider the scene of Othello's collapse, however, we need to ponder Iago's nature, and the light (as well as the blight) it casts on other lives in the play.

---

[1]Brabantio's phrases (I, iii, 111–12).
[2]Obviously, the treatment in *Othello* of this metaphor of moral poisoning is developed from Shakespeare's extensive usage and exploration of it in *Hamlet*.

3

'Pluming up the will':
Iago's place in the play

> let me see now;
> To get his place and to plume up my will
> In double knavery. How? How? Let's see.
>
> (I, iii, 386–8)

So many critics over the years have made so much sense (not
to mention nonsense) of Iago that one naturally hesitates
to dig over the plot again.[1] Yet much of the debate about
his 'character' and about his 'symbolic' status has tended
less to clarify than to obscure his place in the dramatic
design, and it still seems worth insisting on what by now
ought to be a commonplace – that Iago's intrigue and what
prompts him to undertake and persist in it, are imagined
and judged in the same terms as apply to everyone else in
the play. His speeches and actions continually illuminate
and are themselves illuminated by those of all the other
characters. As Bradley rightly pointed out, Iago is not
arbitrarily introduced into the play to represent inexpli-
cable evil or Evil. Certainly, his behaviour cannot be
accounted for by any or all of his own declared motives for
it, nor did Shakespeare see fit to explain how Iago *came to
be* as he is; but – and it is a 'but' whose force we cannot
afford to ignore – the way Iago thinks and speaks is dramatically conceived and dramatically 'placed' in relation to
everything else in *Othello*. At times knowingly and at times

[1]Marvin Rosenberg, 'In Defense of Iago', *Shakespeare Quarterly*, 6 (1955),
pp. 145–58, offers a convenient summary of some of the main views.

unwittingly, Iago reveals – or rather Shakespeare gives him speeches that reveal to *us* – aspects of his nature that strike us as significantly (and often dismayingly) akin to those of his 'victims', especially Othello, even while in other more obvious respects he is shown to differ from them.

Iago's dramatic function in the play is certainly complex. Clearly he is an interesting and significant figure in himself – though not, I would argue, one that warrants the kind of exclusive attention he has often been given.[1] For he does not merely act in and upon the world the play dramatizes: he is himself a defining aspect of it. More specifically – though this point too has not commonly been recognized, still less understood – Iago serves as a crucial *limit case* in the play, a man whose life and being vividly demonstrate, in extreme form, certain habits of feeling, certain ways of viewing and responding to the world, that the drama gradually makes us recognize as to some extent character-istic of everyone in it (and of us watching it), each in his own particular (and definitive) form and degree. In short, no less than Desdemona, or Emilia, or Roderigo, Iago embodies an essential part of Shakespeare's integrated thinking in *Othello*: his life, his mode of being and of responding to his world, demonstrate one basic human premise, as it were, in the play's unfolding logic.

To put the point another way, I think that Bradley and others have not only exaggerated Iago's importance, but have thereby distorted it as well. Iago needs to be de-mythologized. But in trying to do just that, Leavis and other anti-Bradleyan critics have again, as it seems to me, pushed too hard, and so distorted the facts in an opposite way. Iago

---

[1]Cf. for example W. H. Auden's assertion that 'any consideration of the Tragedy of Othello must be primarily occupied, not with its official hero, but with its villain'; *The Dyer's Hand* (London, 1962 [1948]), p. 246. Perhaps the most ambitious example is Stanley Edgar Hyman's *Iago: Some Approaches to the Illusion of His Motivation* (New York, 1970). This is offered as 'a display of pluralistic literary criticism' (p. 3), but the result seems only 'perplexed in the extreme'.

is too distinctive a dramatic figure, too forcefully real, to be reducible to a mere theatrical device – the conventional Villain – or to a (luridly coloured) 'mechanism' necessary to the plot. This is not to say that he does not fulfil any technical function. Obviously he does – but only because he is dramatically realized *as* a dramatic character inhabiting the same world as the others.

For example (as has often been remarked), he is the main means by which Shakespeare affords us – one might almost say inflicts on us – an unrelievedly ironic perspective on the action as it takes place before us. His soliloquies obviously affect how we view him, but they also condition how we see, and how we cannot see, everyone else. The way Shakespeare presents him robs *us*, totally and forever, of any chance to remain innocent of the snares we see others in the play innocently falling into. Hence, even in the early scenes we can never share the relatively simple clarity of Desdemona's view of the world, say, or Emilia's, or Othello's own, not only because our view of a drama is always larger than that of any of the characters in it, but because in this case Iago makes us sharply aware, right from the start, that there is a particular *kind* of moral fact in the dramatic world, which the other main characters are somehow too innocent, too unsuspicious, or too unperceptive – too 'honest' – to reckon on. 'Innocence' may be comfortable, but it is a comfort we are never allowed. But neither, of course, are we allowed the comfort of being able to do anything about the malignity we witness. Iago's disclosures leave us, as mere onlookers, with no option but to remain silent with him as if in forced complicity, excruciatingly bound to him by the knowledge we cannot share with those who (if we only could speak) might avert the disasters which will otherwise befall them.

This is surely one reason why *Othello* is so continuously painful. Having to watch, we are in no way free to act on the crucial information Iago reveals to us, even though it urgently excites our natural wish to tell what we know and so forestall calamity. This kind of helplessness is a necessary function of all play-watching, of course; indeed, some people would argue that part of our interest in drama is always an unacknowledged wish to witness 'disaster' whilst being free of responsibility for causing or failing to avert it. But although the sustained dramatic irony of *Othello* is by no means peculiar to it among Shakespeare's plays – *Cymbeline* and *Twelfth Night*, for example, are only two among many other cases – it is arguable that only in some of the late plays, and not in the other great tragedies immediately following *Othello*, did Shakespeare again rely so much on this pervasively ironic mode of presentation which *Othello* shares with the earlier comedies. Certainly, in no other Shakespearean tragedy, and perhaps in no other Shakespearean play, is our foreknowledge of what the protagonists are ignorant of so deeply and so *unrelievedly* burdensome. More importantly, this prolonged anxiety – this lurching between the extremes (as Bradley put it) of 'sickening hope and dreadful expectation'[1] – which we experience because of what we know but cannot forestall or 'amend' is comparable with and so brings us more fully to understand the unrelieved tension Othello himself experiences because of what (so he thinks) he 'knows' yet cannot change, ignore or bear.

It is Iago whose speeches force that burden of 'knowing' upon us. Nevertheless, like the main protagonists, we know even more – in particular, various moral and emotional realities – that Iago himself is ignorant of. He is like anybody else in that the terms as well as the spirit in which he views the world delimit what he sees and fails to see in it. As Marlowe put it in *Hero and Leander* (Sestiad 1, 174),

---

[1] *Shakespearean Tragedy*, p. 143; see also his rather Johnsonian remark on p. 146: 'Nowhere else in Shakespeare do we hold our breath in such anxiety, and for such a long time as in the later Acts of *Othello*.' In observations like these Bradley seems to me much truer to our actual dramatic experience than the coolly analytic distance most anti-Othello critics suggest we can and should maintain.

'What we behold is censur'd by our eyes' – an insight that, for Shakespeare, became a basic assumption and working-principle of his art (as it was to become a basic assumption of writers like Blake and Lawrence after him). What a man sees or does not see reflects what he values; what he values reflects what he is; and no less than in Shakespeare's other tragedies (perhaps most especially in *Antony and Cleopatra*), this is both the basis on which all the characters in *Othello* are dramatically realized, and also partly what the tragedy is about.

All through the play, the presence of Iago brings this home to us with particular force. In the first two acts we may notice for example how often particular characters recognize in others, or project onto others, qualities which in fact they themselves possess, though often without their being conscious that this is so. When Iago appears, we can hardly miss the point. When he declares that Emilia is like all women – 'saints in your injuries, devils being offended' (II, i, 110), these phrases immediately strike us as far more suggestive of Iago's own self-righteous vindictiveness than of Emilia. When in the same scene Desdemona asks Iago, 'what praise couldst thou bestow on a deserving woman indeed?', the very terms of her question reveal her own qualities. The terms of Iago's reply reveal his scorn for fairness even more vividly: 'She that was ever fair . . . was a wight, if ever such wight were . . . to suckle fools and chronicle small beer'. In the same scene again, the qualities Othello recognizes and praises in the master of his ship are precisely those – for example, the 'authority of merit' – he values in himself: 'He is a good one, and his worthiness/ Does challenge much respect.' But we cannot fail to notice the point when, at the end of the scene, Iago speaks to Roderigo of Cassio:

a knave very voluble; no further conscionable than in putting on the mere form of civil and humane seeming for the better compassing of his salt and most hidden loose affection . . . a slipper and subtle knave, a finder out of occasions; that has an eye can stamp and counterfeit advantages, though true advantage never present itself; a devilish knave . . . a pestilent complete knave. (II, i, 231–40)

Clearly, all these judgments of other people reveal as much (or more) about the judge as about the judged; and I think it was to underline the significance of this that Shakespeare included in the scene I have been quoting from (II, i) the otherwise rather odd game of praise and censure played by Iago and Desdemona – an incident that has no parallel at all in Cinthio.

The point of it is usually overlooked, perhaps because the game seems so clumsily imposed on the story. Certainly, Desdemona's excuse for amusing herself at this time ('I am not merry, but I do beguile/ The thing I am by seeming otherwise') is pretty weak, whichever way we look at it: it obliges us to take at face value the sort of 'I am not what I am' explanation that on Iago's lips would be most suspect, and so it distracts us into wondering (even while we sense it is beside the point to do so) why, if she isn't merry, she should feel obliged to pretend she is, and further, why she proves so *able* here to 'give out such a seeming'. In trying to account for her part in the game it hardly seems adequate to speak (as Coleridge did, for example) about her courtesy and consideration for others' feelings here: after all, these would seem a pretty thin reason for (even dissembled) frivolity in a newly wed wife whose husband may be drowning while she thus chatters on to cheer up his friends. Besides, her 'counterfeit' merriness doesn't exactly strike one as an effortful disguise of anxiety. Perhaps a more convincing line of argument would link this quay-side discussion with Othello's later speech where he denies that Desdemona's gregariousness (the fact that she 'loves company,/ Is free of speech') is a cue for jealousy, and thus take the game as illustrating her easy sociableness; her aside ('I am not merry . . .') could then be regarded as a

sign of her slight shame or embarrassment in catching herself at being so playful – and even a bit coarse-grained –
when she ought to be reserved or worried. The trouble with
that explanation however, is that it leaves us with a
Desdemona whose taste for superficial chat is evidently
stronger than her love (why is she *not* worried?) and who is
able to fool or 'beguile' herself simply by declaring 'I am
not merry' when obviously she *is*.

But Shakespeare challenges, he doesn't need protection
from, our critical scrutiny; and surely the truth of the
matter here is simple enough: finding himself unable, or
unwilling, to invent any very convincing motivation for
Desdemona's behaviour at this point, he perfunctorily put in
her aside as at least a plausible explanation of it. Indeed,
though he never troubled to improve it, the dialogue hints
perhaps at his own faintly sheepish but amused sense that
the game-scene is all rather laboured and clumsily managed.
Iago's remarks about *his* difficulty in inventing witty
repartee are dramatically apt to his character and thus
repellent in the casual brutality of his images (so out of
place in the chit-chat situation); but in a more relaxed and
good-humoured sense they could also apply to the self-
conscious dramatist himself at this point:

> invention
> Comes from my pate as birdlime does from frieze –
> It plucks out brains and all. But my muse labours,
> And thus she is delivered.   (II, i, 124–7)

In any case, there seems little need to fuss over the laboured
and clumsy delivery of the game: the important thing is
that Shakespeare felt he needed such a dialogue between
Desdemona (not anyone else) and Iago, and the main
question to concentrate on is, why?

The answer lies in its general import and effect. While
the game makes us realize how self-revealing are particular
people's views of others, it also shows us, in an apparently

frivolous context, the collision of two radically different moral outlooks. Desdemona's, which – like Cassio's – generously inclines to see and affirm 'true merit' in others (as was so beautifully attested by her language in the previous scene, for instance, when she spoke of how 'I saw Othello's visage in his mind/ And to his honours and his valiant parts/ Did I my soul and fortunes consecrate'), here collides with Iago's fundamentally different outlook or disposition – that of a natural defiler and desecrator, for whom the notion of 'consecrating' oneself to anyone else is romantic claptrap ('A fig!'), and who thus always 'profanely' denies any merit besides his own. 'Profane' here is Desdemona's word for Iago's attitude (II, i, 160), and in using it, however light-heartedly, she implicitly appeals to the moral standards she herself lives by, which are once again emphasized by Iago's characteristic perversion of the same language of moral sanctity. Her word may remind us of Iago's own perverse use of it in an earlier soliloquy:

> For I mine own gained knowledge should profane
> If I would time expend with such a snipe
> But for my sport and profit.   (I, iii, 378–80)

Of course the clash between Desdemona's and Iago's moral styles in this quay-side scene is minor, polite, ostensibly joking and cast in hypothetical terms ('O, fie upon thee, slanderer!', Desdemona blithely cries). Only later, amid Iago's more gross slanders and Othello's wild delusion that she must be foul, do we grasp just how revealing, indeed how paradigmatic, this strange little game actually was. Even at the time, however, we feel quite sharply that Iago's habits of mind are no laughing matter. We notice, for example, that Emilia is well aware of his unwillingness to recognize any real worth in others. She seems to speak from bitter experience in remarking to Iago, 'You shall not write my praise.' She implies (and hence makes us aware) that his judgment of her would be merely a sour product of his own sour disposition. And we begin to grasp the darker implications of this fact about Iago when we also notice – or rather deduce – Emilia's pragmatic assumption that it would therefore be utterly futile to challenge him or to try to persuade him to see things her way. Though provoked, she refuses to take an active part in the game. She withdraws and lapses into silence. But we also notice that unlike Emilia and despite her comments, Desdemona entirely missest he point about Iago (just as she later fails to see it abour Othello). She naïvely presses him with the question, 'What wouldst thou write of me, if thou shouldst praise me?'; and despite his wry warning – 'do not put me to't,/ For I am nothing if not critical' – she childishly persists: 'Come on, assay . . .'; 'Come, how wouldst thou praise me?'

Flippant as they are, Iago's comments in this scene make very plain to us that, for a mind as warped as his, terms like 'fair' and 'foul' do not answer to anything objectively real. They are merely labels he applies or withholds as it happens to suit him. Indeed, he treats them as interchangeable. In slick little couplets he applies them in handy-dandy fashion, inverting them in accordance with his own personal whim, his own 'pride and purposes'. Of course, he is teasing Desdemona here, but the fact that his teasing takes this form betrays a good deal about him. (We can't readily imagine Desdemona or Cassio, for instance, trotting out these cynical generalizations.) There is always a virulent sting in the tail of Iago's 'praise'. He is nevertheless not the kind of man who would ever raise even to himself a philosophic question like that Troilus asks, in II, ii, of *Troilus and Cressida*, for instance: 'What's aught but as 'tis valued?' Iago's cast of mind is much rougher than that, much more meanly pragmatic, much less self-reflexively intelligent. He simply assumes that everything depends on his own valuation of it, and sees himself as the sole accurate judge in a world that is wholly manipulable. His personal 'vouchings' are his 'proof' that merit comprises nothing more than a ridiculous fitness 'to suckle fools'. In short, the main thing about Iago that emerges from the quay-side game confirms what we had glimpsed in the opening scenes of Act I: for all his air of coolly detached objectivity, Iago's judgments are not shaped by objective realities at all, but by subjective feelings as hot as any that Brabantio or Othello exhibit in their blackest moments of panic or rage. And, like Emilia, we begin to see that such a man could never be persuaded that the world is other than he 'judges' it to be. That is what Desdemona fails to grasp during the course of the game, and what makes rather frighteningly ominous her innocent inability to realize it. Iago's mind is not one to produce what she calls 'old fond paradoxes', simply 'to make fools laugh i'th' alehouse'.

As I see it, Shakespeare's main interest in Iago from beginning to end of the play centres on the various forms of *imperviousness* Iago cultivates in himself. The action continually makes us scrutinize the nature and source of these attempts to make a shell around himself, the degree to which they work or fail, and the relationship between this impulse in him and his destructiveness.

The first two acts strongly reveal the sort of moral stupidity that is Iago's way of remaining *morally* impervious to life. All his early speeches show what the quay-side-scene confirms: that his 'thoughts' are composed of 'certainties' which swing with his current feelings and which he hugs to himself too tightly for them to be ever assailed by conscious doubts. It never occurs to him to wonder whether they might not be open to question. And it is this terrible blind fixity of Iago's moral outlook which makes him often seem to us – to borrow some phrases from Ted Hughes's poem, 'Thrushes' – 'more coiled steel than living': he acts always with 'bullet and automatic/ Purpose' to size up everyone (or size them down), with a sudden devouring 'efficiency which/ Strikes too streamlined for any doubt to pluck at it/ Or obstruction deflect'.

His very first speech evinces clearly enough his mental habit of rigidly categorizing people into two kinds – those foolish enough to get used and abused, and those (like himself) clever enough to do the using and abusing themselves. For him, people are starkly polarized into victims and victimizers. Yet he himself, as we notice right from the start of the play, exploits the practical advantages of both. When it suits him to do so, he likes to claim that others have criminally stabbed him in the vitals. At the same time, he likes to think of himself as having absolute governance over himself and his world. He understands human relationships solely in predatory terms. His assumption that life consists either in hurting others or getting hurt oneself is reflected in his every speech and action – his most characteristic verbs (and actions) being those such as 'gyve', 'ensnare', 'enfetter', 'enmesh' and the like. If we refrain from sharing his fascination with his own cleverness and really observe him, we notice that his sense of his cunning and his manipulative skills is grossly inflated. Increasingly clearly, we realize that his power as a hunter and 'poisoner' derives, not from any splendid intellect, but far more from the particular constitutions of his chosen victims. This is true not only in his relations with Othello, but equally with Roderigo and with Cassio, with Brabantio, even (in a rather different way) with Emilia and Desdemona. In each case Iago is more a catalyst that precipitates destruction than a devil that causes it: without his victims' infirmities – including their propensity to trust him – he is in fact utterly impotent.

Iago's self-conceit, impervious to reality, rests on his alacrity in seizing not just on the practical but also the emotional – especially the self-aggrandizing – advantages of *both* views of his relations with his world: he congratu-

74

lates himself on what he considers his potent ingenuity in
snaring others, whom at the same time he swaggeringly
despises for being so easily snared. He sees it as his special
prerogative to victimize whomever he pleases – usually by
inducing people to injure one another for his own 'peculiar
end'. Equally, he coolly assumes that for him – though of
course not for others – it is fair rather than foul play to
trap people in their own infirmities, to poison them with
the distilled essence of what they are at their weakest or
worst. He views everyone (except himself) as he views
Cassio, of whom he declares that his (Cassio's) 'vice' is 'to
his virtue the just equinox'. To Iago's mind, in short,
personal qualities are mutually cancelling, good and bad
merely 'the just equinox' of each other; and since, like
'fair' and 'foul', 'vice' and 'virtue' are (for him) interchangeable, he finds it just as easy to make others' 'virtues'
instruments to plague them as he does to capitalize on
their 'vices', 'playing the god' with their 'weak function'.
Virtually anything serves as fodder for his consuming
appetite to negate (for the appetite is to feed and affirm
the only 'self' he can acknowledge); and this is his deliberate
policy with everyone on whom he preys – not least, Desdemona:

> For 'tis most easy
> Th'inclining Desdemona to subdue
> In any honest suit. She's framed as fruitful
> As the free elements . . .
> . . .
> And by how much she strives to do [Cassio] good,
> She shall undo her credit with the Moor.
> So will I turn her virtue into pitch,
> And out of her own goodness make the net
> That shall enmesh them all.   (II, iii, 329–32, 348–52)

Desdemona's earlier reference to such 'merit' as would
'justly put on the vouch of very malice itself' emerges – in

75

the light of Iago's soliloquies – as an attractive but dangerously sentimental illusion, comparable with Cassio's remarks about the storm's readiness to '[let] go safely by the divine Desdemona'. Clearly, nothing would ever 'put on the vouch' of Iago's malice. His soliloquies blast any budding hopes or illusions *we* may have that moral virtue makes a moral universe.

Iago's, then, is an essentially simple mind, for whom life is correspondingly simple. He reduces everything to his own terms, his own labels, his own certainties. Nothing in life as he sees it can't be pigeon-holed. And this outlook – this apparent imperviousness to any moral stress or perplexity – naturally attracts not only men like the callow, vacillating Roderigo, who is a fool any knave could handle, but men like Cassio and Othello too. The kind of 'honesty' Iago cultivates is that of the simple soldier-man – a 'realistic', or rather cynical, blunt man-of-the-world, unimpressed by fine emotions and super-subtle manners, a 'man's man', who cuts through to the nub of a matter, and preserves a firm self-sufficiency.[1] (At least, so it appears.) Nor is this sort of 'honesty' merely a façade, as Iago's very last words in the play demonstrate so clearly: 'Demand me nothing; what you know, you know:/ From this time forth I never will speak word.' This exhibits the real potency of his moral outlook: the pragmatic, simplistic, reductive habit of mind that makes his attitudes and schemes so plausible and so attractive to men caught in complex emotions and situations. What they do not reckon on, of course, is Iago's positive need – in Lawrence's phrase – to 'do the dirty' on life; in as much as they are drawn to or sucked in by his defiling view of things, however, they nevertheless share it themselves.

In some ways the simplicity (or the sheer crudeness) of Iago's mind, his complacency, his assumption that the

[1]A pertinent study of the play's critique of the 'male ego-ideal' is John Fraser, '*Othello* and Honour', *The Critical Review*, 8 (1965), pp. 59–70.

world is at his disposal, are very like Lady Macbeth's.[1] The similarities remind us that in *Macbeth* (as well as in *Lear*) Shakespeare is still pondering the strong allurement, and the crippling cost, of various kinds of moral and emotional insusceptibility. Like Lady Macbeth's, Iago's superficial 'wittiness' turns out to be mere knowingness: for instance, his knowing speech about love as a 'mere permission of the will' is comparable with Lady Macbeth's characteristic tone, as for instance in her speech (I, v, 58ff.) about reading the 'book' of Macbeth's face. Lawrence's remark about her in his poem 'When I Read Shakespeare' – 'such suburban ambition' – applies just as well to Iago too. Like her, he makes murder or injury to others sound quite rational, even conventional: both of them speak, not of 'murder', but of sensible self-advancement. No wonder then that Iago finds it as easy as Lady Macbeth does to put others in a state of moral stupefaction, and for much the same reason: moral simplicity is always seductive to those whose lives are complicated and anguished. For Iago, as for Lady Macbeth, nothing is easier than coping with emotions and moral complexities (they even suppose they cope with their own), since they assume it needs only a mere act of will to eradicate feelings and (as Iago puts it) 'turn virtue into pitch'.

Thus Iago assumes and argues that anybody with a proper sense of his own 'pride' and 'place' can readily tell the difference between an advantage and a handicap, and can readily 'stamp and counterfeit advantages, though true advantage never present itself' (II, i, 236–7). To meet frustration, hurts and disappointments, a man need only – as he says to Roderigo – 'know how to love himself':

If thou wilt needs damn thyself, do it a more delicate way than drowning. Make all the money thou canst. If sanctimony and a

[1] On this point, and for a number of other insights about *Macbeth*, I am gratefully indebted to an unpublished study of that play by Jillian Redner (Melbourne).

77

frail vow betwixt an erring barbarian and a super-subtle Venetian be not too hard for my wits and all the tribe of hell, thou shalt enjoy her – therefore make money. A pox of drowning thyself! It is clean out of the way. Seek thou rather to be hanged in compassing thy joy than to be drowned and go without her.

(I, iii, 348–55)

For Iago, people – other people, that is – are such knaves that one can easily toy with them for 'sport and profit', as he does with Roderigo here. He has the same attitude to everyone, and exploits them each in exactly the same way. Despite his own (and Bradley's) vast admiration for his cunning, his 'wit' is in fact remarkably stereotyped and inflexible. One after another, he scoffs at people for not showing due self-regard and proper forwardness in discerning and battening onto whatever works for their 'good'. To exactly the extent that he intends to abuse each, he advertises his own disinterested generosity and usefulness in indicating and promoting his 'friend's' best self-interest. The admonitory speech to Roderigo just quoted, for instance, is recognizably a parallel and extended version of an earlier speech to Brabantio, advising him likewise to look sharp and distinguish between benefits and injuries:

Zounds, sir, you are one of those that will not serve God if the devil bid you. Because we come to do you service, and you think we are ruffians, you'll have your daughter covered with a Barbary horse; you'll have your nephews neigh to you, you'll have coursers for cousins, and jennets for germans.

(I, i, 109–14)

In another situation, and in a different tone, this might strike us as a comically creative fantasy. But here, as always in Iago's accent, relish is so hotly mated with scorn and revulsion that the product is obscene as well as grotesque. To put this speech and others like it beside, say, those of Falstaff in *Henry IV* (especially Part 1) is to see at once that for all the apparent vitality and earthiness of his speech at times, Iago's methods of converting others' benefits to injuries are far less various and far less inventive, as well as more malignant. His stature as a 'wit' and an adroit manipulator of circumstance is barely ankle-high beside Falstaff's capacity to 'turn diseases to commodity': indeed that very Falstaffian word 'commodity' is itself far more comic, droll and genial than any of Iago's terms or euphemisms for self-profit – terms in fact much closer to the less imaginative Hal's, whose method of gaining 'respectability' consists, not in turning 'diseases to commodity', but rather (as Warwick predicts) in 'turning past evils to advantages'.[1] But Iago's talent as 'ingener' (to use Cassio's word) is cruder still – and practically as minimal as that of another sterile malcontent, Thersites in *Troilus and Cressida*. Like his, Iago's *tone* varies hardly at all throughout the play (compare Emilia's), and his 'invention' likewise twists everything into the same contorted shape, and by the same means.

The paucity of his 'inventiveness' plainly reflects the spiritual bankruptcy that prompts it. He merely repeats with Cassio, for example, what he does to Brabantio and Roderigo, being predictably the first to offer (hypocritical) sympathy for the 'hurt' he has in fact engineered, the first to draw attention to his generosity in offering help, and in advising Cassio to change the facts of his situation by changing his attitude to it: after all, he says, 'you have lost no reputation unless you repute yourself a loser'. And he goes on to point out, in what *we* realize are appallingly ambiguous terms, the easiest steps by which Cassio might 'remedy' his pain and 'mend it for your own good':

Our General's wife is now the General . . . This broken joint between you and her husband, entreat her to splinter; and my fortunes against any lay worth naming, this crack of your love shall grow stronger than it was before.   (II, iii, 306, 312–17)

[1]Falstaff's characteristic phrase comes at the close of Part 2, I, ii; Warwick's narrowly pragmatic one (symptomatic of the play's imaginative contraction during Part 2) comes in IV, iv, 78.

And once again we find him at the end of the scene coaxing
Roderigo out of his misery (at having been hurt in the
brawl) by urging him likewise to look on his injury as a
benefit consisting of an injury to Cassio:

> How poor are they that have not patience!
> What wound did ever heal but by degrees?
> Thou know'st we work by wit, and not by witchcraft,
> And wit depends on dilatory time.
> Does't not go well? Cassio hath beaten thee,
> And thou by that small hurt hath cashiered Cassio.
>
> (II, iii, 359–64)

It is perfectly simple for Iago thus to play off against one
another the self-despising Cassio and the naïvely optimistic
Roderigo, cajoling each to undertake the course of remedial
action that, unbeknown to themselves, must necessarily
cost them most dear. And we already begin to suspect that
his advice and procedure with Othello in the following acts
will be exactly the same.

It is part of Iago's dramatic function to illuminate the
behaviour and attitudes of other characters in the play by
comparison as well as by contrast. He is, for example, by
no means the only one who self-interestedly exploits or
abuses others, and who cannot or will not acknowledge as
real anything that clashes with his own wishes or needs.
Roderigo and Brabantio are obvious cases in point. Each
heatedly tries to deny or refuses to acknowledge that
Desdemona might really be in love (and stay in love) with
Othello. They do so, we see, because each of them wants or
needs not to believe it. Not only does Iago of course deny
this too, but even Othello himself in Act III – because of
his peculiar needs – also comes to assert that it 'cannot be'.
Nor is Iago the only one prepared to tread on people's
necks or manipulate or exploit them to get what he wants.
All through the Venetian world, social and political aims

as well as personal ones are often implicitly thought to justify – even, indeed, to necessitate – some form of what we might call 'practised imperviousness' to others' feelings. Iago's comments in I, i about the power and mastery to be got from 'service', for instance, are immediately echoed by Othello himself in the next scene, when he calmly declares that 'My services, which I have done the signory,/ Shall out-tongue [Brabantio's] complaints.'

In the following scene, the political version of the same sort of attitude is revealed in the behaviour of the Duke and Senators. Brabantio had asserted that 'if such actions [as Othello's] may have passage free,/ Bondslaves and pagans shall our statesmen be' – by which he seems to mean that the lower classes will marry into the aristocracy and thereby assume power in matters of state. But to us his words suggest something else as well, something confirmed when Othello's actions do have passage free – not because they are proved guiltless but because his past and more especially his future services can so readily 'out-tongue' and 'non-suit' Brabantio's challenge.[1] Venice's statesmen are to that extent already surreptitious 'bondslaves' to their political ends.

The details make their point with a nice irony. When the aggrieved Brabantio bursts into the Senate chamber, we notice that, despite the First Senator's clear announcement, 'Here comes Brabantio and the valiant Moor' (in that order), the Duke is so engrossed in thinking about the Turks' attack and Othello's consequent usefulness to the state that he greets Othello first and Brabantio second, and then justifies this rudeness with a placatory white lie:

DUKE Valiant Othello, we must straight employ you . . . [*To Brabantio*] I did not see you: welcome, gentle signor.

With more pressing matters to deal with than Brabantio's

---

[1] Cf. Iago's phrases in I, i, 12ff.: 'But he [Othello] . . ./ Evades [my supporters] with a bombast circumstance . . ./ Non-suits my mediators'.

domestic disaster, the Duke first of all swiftly assures Brabantio that 'whoe'er' has done 'this foul proceeding' will be duly punished; and he then, when the invaluable General is alleged to be the criminal, sweeps this promise quietly under the mat. Although he now quite properly (if somewhat tardily) insists that Brabantio's allegations must undergo a wider and more objective test, the Duke proves quite prepared to accept Othello's 'vouchings' as proof – even before Desdemona arrives to confirm them. Othello has only to announce his version of the courtship, a version which for all its eloquence merely gainsays Brabantio's, and the Duke at once urges Brabantio to back down. We cannot help noticing the double shuffles, I think; and even if they seem reasonable enough in the circumstances (given that we know how irrational Brabantio's tale about 'witchcraft' is), we also cannot help noticing how peremptory the Duke is. Indeed, throughout the scene, the ducal imperatives reveal both his lack of interest in anything not in accord with his own concerns, and his habit of ignoring or overriding everything that conflicts with his will: 'we must straight employ you'; 'take up this mangled matter at the best'; 'you must therefore be content to slubber the gloss of your new fortunes'; 'you must hence tonight'.

Of course, the Duke's concerns are those of the state, not merely private ones; and since his public responsibilities are so evident, neither we nor anyone in the play judges it wrong in him to treat the current international crisis as more important that a domestic complaint. But the very fact that we mentally make these qualifications is interesting. (In fact we tend to speak as though the Duke's public office not only explained his attitude but automatically absolved him from any personal responsibility for the cost his imperatives exact from those he overrides.) For it suggests that we – like the characters in the play – quite happily assume that a strong element of heartlessness (or, as we might say less bluntly, a high degree of human imperviousness) is a necessary and therefore self-justifying condition of political wisdom and success. One effect of the Senate scene is simply to make us aware of the ease with which, when it suits us, we too assume that personal morality and political morality are somehow separate and distinct. And that, in turn, reminds us that in *Othello* Shakespeare is interested in the close relationships between the two, even though this interest is clearly less central here than in those plays more explicitly concerned with politics.

One effect of the whole business about the Turks, I am suggesting, is to make us realize that Iago is not the only person in the play who unthinkingly assumes that his own ends are paramount and self-justifying, and acts accordinly. It would be comforting to be able to hive him off into a special category labelled 'villainous' and treat him as a wholly unique phenomenon in the drama. But the Turkish affair makes it very plain that the same Venetian world that is later (like us) to censure Iago's personal opportunism as the fell morality of a 'Spartan dog' allows free and approved passage to *political* opportunism of a comparably ruthless kind. Shakespeare's wish to suggest this irony is presumably one of the main reasons he includes such details as he does about the Venetians' attitude to the Turks, and (by implication) the Turks' attitude to Venice: both sides take it for granted that, in this sort of struggle for power, self-interest is the sole consideration. Thus everyone (including us) tacitly accepts that as head of state the Duke *has* to think in terms of the same political calculus the First Senator imputes to the Turks. Yet, watching the drama, we also realize what those taking part in it cannot. Even though it is necessary (if the Venetians are to survive the Turks' aggression), their cool reckoning of profit and loss is not essentially very different from the computations of personal self-interest Iago practises and preaches and which we so detest in him:

83

When we consider
Th'importancy of Cyprus to the Turk,
And let ourselves again but understand
That as it more concerns the Turk than Rhodes,
So may he with more facile question bear it,
For that it stands not in such warlike brace,
But altogether lacks th'abilities
That Rhodes is dressed in. If we make thought of this,
We must not think the Turk is so unskilful
To leave that latest which concerns him first,
Neglecting an attempt of ease and gain
To wake and wage a danger profitless.   (I, iii, 19–30)

Of course it is because the Venetians are themselves so adept at such calculations that they are not taken in by the Turks' deceptive tactics. They see at once that the Rhodes expedition is a mere front, 'a pageant/ To keep us in false gaze' – a phrase admirably suitable for Iago's characteristic tactics. So too are the messenger's phrases when he reports that the Turks now 'restem/ Their backward course, bearing with frank appearance/ Their purposes towards Cyprus'.[1]

However, in suggesting that Shakespeare makes us aware of such affinities as these I do not at all mean to imply that Iago finds 'just' external corroboration in the Turks' or Venetians' political behaviour for the kind of power-game he likes to play in the realm of personal relationships. The drama makes us see very clearly that there is *not* that sort of corroboration in Iago's world. Hence the significance of the fact that Iago likes to suppose there is. On the whole, the world of *Othello* is a trusting one – as Desdemona's, Cassio's and Roderigo's behaviour, for example, keeps reminding us; and even in the political sphere there is a

---

[1] Iago's 'frank appearances' disguise his 'purposes' as heavily as do his 'backward courses' – see for example III, iii, 191ff., when he begins his grossest deception by declaring, 'now I shall have reason/ To show the love and duty I bear to you/ With franker spirit'.

considerable degree of dignity, courtesy and trust amongst the Venetians. And since it is thus not a Marlovian, cynical, stab-in-the-back world that we are shown in *Othello*, we are not inclined to say of Iago (as we might of, say, Barabas, in *The Jew of Malta*) that he's a 'nasty chap, yes, but in a world such as this, how else could one survive?' That is not my point, therefore. Rather, it is that such similarities as we do observe between Iago's personal style and others' actions whether in the public or the private sphere give us cause to think more deeply about the ways in which certain moral assumptions, if given 'passage free', can easily harden into Iago-like extreme destructiveness. Iago's vicious egotism is not corroborated, but neither is he a total freak in the play's dramatic world – and it is this that we begin to realize when we notice, for example, that in the political sphere of Acts I and II nobody hesitates to hope for others' disasters, or to treat them when they occur as their own merited gains. Cassio, for example, 'speak[s] of comfort touching the Turkish loss', and, later on, 'Othello's pleasure' is that every man should 'put himself into triumph' upon certain 'beneficial news' 'importing the mere perdition of the Turkish fleet' (II, ii, 1–6).

It is just this kind of equation of others' injuries or perdition with merited benefits for oneself that the play dramatizes in one way or another not only in Iago but in Roderigo, Brabantio and, later on, Othello as well. Every one of the main characters at some point in some way disregards or uses or abuses others' lives or feelings; and we ourselves become partisan in just this way as well, of course. Which of us does not icily discountenance Iago's wounded feelings for example? Which of us is not prepared mentally to cashier or eradicate him to get what we want? Our willingness to consider him as a beastly 'thing' in our road (to use Brabantio's word for Othello) is not made less dangerous or more admirable by the fact that it is on others' behalf that we 'want' his removal. He is the thorn in the

85

side of our own feelings and these are what make us yearn to 'remedy' the situation by lashing out at him. Indeed – for reasons I shall come to later – part of Iago's dramatic function is precisely to arouse our intolerant loathing, and to make us realize how extreme our own intolerance can be. (Whatever grains of truth there may be in a remark like Johnson's, 'I like a good hater', such an attitude to Iago is possible only if we remain far more detached than the play's action and poetry really allow or enable us to be.)[1] We would love to make him pay in kind for the damage he does to others' lives; we too, in other words, are not above equating another's ill with our own good; and it is the dangerous implications of just this tendency that the play makes so painfully visible, especially in its last three acts. The upshot of Shakespeare's exploration of it, however, as we realize during Desdemona and Emilia's highly pertinent discussion of these issues in the willow scene in Act IV, is not simply to make us condemn it. The play presses us not towards any new, bright-eyed programme of moral reform or re-armament, but towards a fuller understanding of how and why people respond to unhappiness, whether others' or their own. We are brought gradually to recognize (in the characters and in ourselves as we watch them live their lives) the unacknowledged fears and desires and needs that impel people to see the world in this way: the psychological states whose twists and turns reveal or disguise themselves in this sort of moral outlook.

Iago's is the extreme case; and in him as in all the other characters those twists and turns are revealed most clearly in his most energetic efforts to disguise them – in the

[1]For a very different view of our relationship with Iago, see for example E. A. J. Honigmann's discussion of *Othello* in his *Shakespeare's Seven Tragedies: The Dramatist's Manipulation of Response* (London and New York, 1976). (Honigmann's opening chapters set out some of the same general issues I am also concerned with, though his discussions of particular plays do not seem to develop his opening suggestions as far as they deserve.)

various ways in which he seeks to justify himself, to cheer
himself up and protect or fortify himself against real or
imagined threats. In fact, Iago busies himself with self-
justification more continuously, obsessively, than any other
person in the play. He is always dictating to others how
they are to think of him. Of course, most of these self-
images are designed to deceive others; but the 'frank'
revelations of his nature and aims in his soliloquies are
different only in being designed (and managing) to deceive
himself. Actually, it is the very urge to justify himself,
which is there right from the beginning (and which he
never seems to notice), that is most significant. Even in the
first scene of Act I, for instance, before we really know he
is exploiting Roderigo, his 'honest' self-revelations strike
us as remarkably over-insistent – almost as though he were
trying to convince himself as well as Roderigo of the
truth and justice of his claims. Thus from the very moment
he first appears, with his swaggering air of being an 'all-
in-all sufficient' man, we are pressed to query the real nature
and extent of his self-sufficiency. From the beginning, we
cannot help suspecting a large dose of self-consoling fiction
in the bits and pieces of autobiography he so eagerly and
superfluously recites to Roderigo. His protestations are
indignantly self-righteous, repeatedly appealing to external
guarantees, external testimony and sanctions: 'be judge
yourself'; 'by the faith of man'; 'I, of whom his eyes had
seen the proof'; 'Heaven is my judge'. This last comes in
an extraordinary speech in which, by way of asserting and
congratulating himself on his own total autonomy, Iago
calls on (of all things) 'Heaven' to judge, attest, underwrite
and sanction his falseness to others and his truth to
himself:

> In following him, I follow but myself.
> Heaven is my judge, not I for love and duty,
> But seeming so for my peculiar end:
> For when my outward action doth demonstrate

The native act and figure of my heart
In complement extern, 'tis not long after,
But I will wear my heart upon my sleeve
For daws to peck at – I am not what I am.[1]

                                    (I, i, 59–66)

This is a highly revealing speech in many respects, and
one that makes it clear that Shakespeare knew exactly
what he was about right from the very beginning. With
consummate precision and control he here alerts us both
to the particular propriety and significance of this speech
as *Iago's*, and also, more widely, to his own essential subject
and dramatic procedure for the whole play. The play's
'outward action', comprising what all its people do and say,
dramatically 'demonstrates' to us, 'in complement extern',
the 'native act and figure' of Shakespeare's vital concerns
as he imagines and projects this particular total dramatic
action. And likewise – despite Iago's point about conceal-
ment and hypocrisy in real life – each individual dramatic
character's 'outward actions' (including his silences and
failures to act) are the means by which his inner being is
revealed to us. Iago's act here, for example, in making this
very speech, demonstrates to us what he is – more clearly
than it does either to Roderigo or even to himself. The
speech itself, and more especially his impulse or need to
make it, all too clearly reveal to us 'in complement extern'
the native act and figure of the heart whose power to be
hurt it is so busily trying to deny. Despite his claims that
his power to wound others cleverly manages to prevent
them from injuring him, Iago's images, his tone, his characteristic, watchful sense of all life as predatory, betray a
man who feels deeply threatened by others but is totally
unable to acknowledge his fear, and who therefore has to
reassure himself by scorning 'daws' and cheering himself

---

[1]Muir follows Rowe's second (1714) edition in giving 'compliment' at line
64; but because it catches the more far-reaching meaning of the pun, I
have substituted the spelling of the Folios and Quartos, 'complement'.

up with his cleverness in outwitting their power to 'peck at' him.

Charles Lamb once praised a particular actor's performance as Iago because, as he put it, Iago's speeches were rightly delivered in a triumphant tone natural to his general consciousness of power. Many others too have followed Iago's own lead in supposing he gloats because he is so powerful. Yet once we notice how intensely Iago loathes and fears any form of subordination to others (the play's careful emphasis on military rank is not just ornamental),[1] and notice how much he loathes and fears any *in*subordination from others (for instance, Emilia at the end), we are hardly struck by a 'consciousness of power' in him. What appears is rather the reverse – a scorching need to dominate whatever might dominate him.

In this respect, Iago's fleeting, late-in-the-day acknowledgment of Cassio's fineness is as rare as it is revealing:

> He hath a daily beauty in his life
> That makes me ugly.[2]   (v, i, 19–20)

It betrays the vestiges in him of a lurking 'sense of beauty' which he everywhere suppresses by transforming it into a 'certainty' that 'fair' really means 'foul' and 'foul' (himself) is 'fair'. As Sen Gupta remarks, Iago's 'allergy to the daily beauty' of others' lives clearly springs from something much more radical than (as Bradley claimed) a mere 'itching for superiority'.[3] The 'itching' is simply part of a remedial endeavour. All through, Iago is eaten up by the suspicion that others are more worthy of respect than he and so make him 'ugly' – a suspicion which Othello comes frightfully to duplicate, and which in Iago is so corrosive that he usually cannot admit it at all. But he is a clear enough

---

[1] See John Robert Moore, 'Othello, Iago and Cassio as Soldiers', *Philological Quarterly*, 31 (1952), pp. 189–94.
[2] There are some interesting comments on this in William Empson's essay on *Othello*: see *The Structure of Complex Words* (London, 1951), p. 234.
[3] S. C. Sen Gupta, *Aspects of Shakespearian Tragedy* (Calcutta, 1972), p. 17.

example of the general truth of Bacon's dictum about riches: 'they despise them that despair of them'. As with Edmund in *King Lear*, for instance, the very extremity of Iago's compensatory devices reveals to us the raw nerve in him they attempt to cauterize.

Thus, surely, we should interpret his sour contempt for those who 'dote' on 'obsequious bondage', and his mocking pretence of obsequious bondage to Othello and Cassio (whom he gloatingly terms 'Lieutenant' only when he himself has practically robbed him of the job). Hence, too, we should interpret as a mark of impotence rather than power his habit of always taking the benefit and giving others the injury of any doubt, his incessant need to besmirch, belittle and take down, his need to cut the world back to manipulable size and shape so as to immunize himself to every possible threat it might contain. Not surprisingly his own scorn for 'this counter-caster' (Cassio) is what first alerts us to the fact that he himself is the most obsessive scoreboard-keeper or counter-caster in the play. His scheming 'debitor and creditor' economy, his itchy-fingered calculations of how, at least cost to himself, he might turn others' profits to losses and his own losses to gains, are precisely what show him as irrecoverably self-impoverished. The man who so busily promotes disease in others' lives, so busily preaches the moral hygiene of self-interest, so busily hawks about poisonous medicines for others' woes, is powerless to cure his own ills. His only balm is to spread his sickness, to watch others suffer what he cannot admit he suffers himself.

Like others in the play (and probably like most of us who watch it too), Iago's most 'heart'-felt acts are not those in which he edits the version of himself he wants others to read, but those in which he edits the version of himself he needs for his own consciousness. He is extraordinary only in the vast liberties he takes as an editor. As Shakespeare dramatizes Iago's self-justifications and self-explanations, he exposes to our gaze, very clearly indeed, the inner realities they are designed to dissolve, deny or hide. In his speech to Roderigo about 'daws' for instance (I, i, 59–66), we realize the obvious sense in which Iago's claims are valid: we see that, for the unwitting Roderigo, Iago is indeed not what he seems to be. But I think we also begin to realize what is further confirmed every time Iago opens his mouth: that the false 'forms and visages' he puts on to mask from others what he takes to be his real self also serve in a different but equally successful way to mask his real self from what he himself takes it to be.

The major thing that Iago cannot admit into his picture of himself is his own capacity to be hurt – his capacity, that is, for feeling. His will is always prompted by the need to guard against or neutralize wounded feelings (especially self-disgust), precisely as he urges the same remedy on others. In a much-quoted speech to Roderigo in I, iii, he explains his contempt for people who allow themselves to be overwhelmed by emotions. When Roderigo confesses that 'it is my shame to be so fond [of Desdemona], but it is not in my virtue to amend it', Iago's retort comes pat. Brusquely sweeping aside the emotional reality of 'fond', he treats it as merely a synonym for 'foolish', and sweeping aside the moral implications of 'virtue', he converts the issue into a simple matter of manly strength and power. As always, he overrides others' feelings and doubts by jeering at them – 'O villainous!'; 'Blessed fig's end!':

Virtue? A fig! 'Tis in ourselves that we are thus, or thus. Our bodies are our gardens, to the which our wills are gardeners. So that if we will plant nettles or sow lettuce, set hyssop and weed up thyme, supply it with one gender of herbs or distract it with many, either to have it sterile with idleness or manured with industry, why the power and corrigible authority of this lies in our wills.[1]   (I, iii, 316–23)

[1] For reasons which I hope will be plain from my argument about the play's examination of 'will-power', it does not seem to me in the least worth while

This is a speech crucial both to our sense of Iago and our understanding of his place in the total action. Of course, he has an ulterior motive here – to stampede Roderigo into complying with his (Iago's) will, by persuading him that he can and ought to exercise his own. But his speech also expresses an attitude he really believes in and likes to think he acts upon. Just as he likes to think the external world is entirely malleable, disposable according to his personal predilections, so he refuses (or is unable) to acknowledge anything in his inner experience that might prove intractable to his will. This is why his admonition to Roderigo comes so easily and with such slick plausibility. Every turn of phrase is revealing. The oppositions slide out neatly, one after another – human lives are seen as passive 'gardens' to be acted upon by 'gardeners' who can simply arrange, as they see fit, to have the garden 'sterile with idleness' or 'manured with industry', and who have the 'power and corrigible authority' to 'plant' or 'weed up' whatever they please, whether this be 'nettles' or 'lettuce'. We can hardly miss how well, in some respects at least, his terms here accord with his own relations with other people, whom he always likes to treat as objects to be cultivated or rooted up ('displanted') at will. But his claim that *inner* experience can be pruned, weeded and fertilized by the will is another matter – one which the whole play is quite centrally directed to exploring.

What Iago asserts to Roderigo is just what he everywhere needs and is pleased to suppose applies to himself – that

to enter into the interminable debate about the relationship of this speech to Christian doctrine, as conducted by, for example, Bernard Spivack, *Shakespeare and The Allegory of Evil* (New York, 1958), pp. 423–4; J. V. Cunningham, *Tradition and Poetic Structure: Essays in Literary History and Criticism* (Denver, 1960), pp. 150–3; Roland Mushat Frye, *Shakespeare and Christian Doctrine* (Princeton, 1963), pp. 159–60; Daniel Stempel, 'The Silence of Iago', *Publications of the Modern Language Association of America*, 84 (1969), pp. 252–63; Ruth Levitsky, 'All-in-All Sufficiency in *Othello*', *Shakespeare Studies*, 6 (1970), pp. 209–21. The real significance of this speech surely lies in its *dramatic* context and implications.

any man has the right, and (more to the point) the power, to control his inner life so that, because he can simply choose what to feel, he *does not have to suffer anything*. No wonder that this argument cheers Roderigo up. It would cheer anyone up – if (as Iago assumes) it were really as easy as that. The consolations of Iago's philosophy are as obvious as they are large, and it takes in not only Roderigo and (in a more fundamental way) Iago himself, but also many of the play's critics. For it is relatively easy to exonerate Othello of guilt by taking this speech of Iago's at face value, and regarding Iago's will as an irresistible power. After all, did he not succeed in his schemes? This is precisely Iago's view of it. He elevates his will to the status of an irresistible cosmic power: events 'in the womb of time' – that is, the events he wishes to occur – 'will be delivered'; nature 'must bring this monstrous birth to the world's light'. To Roderigo he peddles the same kind of story about Desdemona's will. She too, he says, having planted love must inevitably wish to weed it up; everyone has 'reason to cool our raging motions', and love is nothing but a 'scion' of our 'unbitted lusts'. When the love-sick Roderigo demurs, 'It cannot be', Iago echoes and contradicts him, repeating that love is merely 'a permission of the will':

It cannot be that Desdemona should long continue her love to the Moor . . . She must change for youth: when she is sated with his body she will find the error of her choice.

(I, iii, 338–9, 345–7)

He comes back to the same point later on:

Now for want of these required conveniences [sympathy in years, manners, beauties], her delicate tenderness will find itself abused, begin to heave the gorge, disrelish and abhor the Moor. Very nature will instruct her in it and compel her to some second choice. Now, sir, this granted – as it is a most pregnant and unforced position . . .

(II, i, 224–8)

93

Whether or not Iago believes this of Desdemona is dramatically far less important here than his characteristic logic. He assumes that to lack any 'required conveniences' is to find oneself 'abused'; nature's instructions inevitably become compulsions which 'must' be obeyed; desire is equated with necessity: a 'want' automatically 'compels'. Anyone – in particular, himself – can justly have, do, become, or feel whatever he fancies.

Yet what deludes Iago and others in the play ought not to delude us quite so readily. A moment's thought should make it obvious that Iago's actual behaviour everywhere gives the lie to his claims about his power and right to master the world. If, as he likes to think, he can simply determine what to feel and what not to feel, how does the thought of anything come to 'gnaw [his] inwards/ Like a poisonous mineral'? Why is his life so full of nettles instead of lettuces? Why does he not simply root up his envy and plant satisfaction in its place? If his will is indeed so omnipotent as he claims, why does he need to plot and plan so elaborately to plume it up? The more we watch him in action the more his much-vaunted powers of 'will' seem as mythical as his much-vaunted powers of 'wit'. Indeed, it is precisely because his 'wit' and 'will' are so impotent that he needs so energetically to plume them up. He is not nearly so much the master of himself and others as a man enslaved by the need to think himself that. His self-bolstering and self-fortifying postures, his assertions of limitless personal power, betray an emotional susceptibility he masks from his own consciousness by the iron screen of cynical 'realism'. In short, his conviction of power is revealed to us at a last-ditch defensive stratagem: his whole mind's endeavour is rigidly and permanently geared to prevent him from having to see his own vulnerability.

The play's concern with the human need for insurance against and remedies for hurt or rejection is obviously not confined to Iago alone.[1] It is significant in a number of ways, for instance, that Iago's first major statement about the will's power to rule the heart is placed where it is, as early as I, iii. It is in this same scene – the dramatic juxtaposition is highly revealing – that the Duke pontificates to Brabantio in a way remarkably similar to (if more pompous than) the way Iago then explains to Roderigo that his grief and distress are an unnecessary waste of time and energy. Roderigo lacks the gumption to point out, as Brabantio does to the Duke, how almost totally impracticable this philosophy is. Nevertheless, Brabantio's reply to the Duke is fresh in our minds as Iago speaks, and Iago's insistence that the will has sovereignty over feelings is thereby immediately set in dynamic opposition to Brabantio's reply to the same idea. Brabantio at least can see and insist that no bruised or broken heart was ever mended by the power of mere exhortatory words, that human feelings are *not* subject to the dictates of the will and have to be suffered in order to be alleviated, and that the only effective way to 'pay grief' is to borrow patience and bear one's pain until it heals – or (as we later learn has been the case with Brabantio) until it kills.

This same opposition is sustained throughout the play: between, on the one hand, assertions like Iago's that one can just *choose* not to suffer, and on the other hand the actual experience of people like Brabantio when they find themselves abruptly discarded or shut out. In Act II, for example, when Iago argues to Cassio what he had earlier argued to Roderigo, Cassio is sufficiently honest with himself to see and say at once what he is later to realize more painfully still: that one cannot just decide not to feel emotions – self-contempt, for instance – and that it involves more than a simple act of will to change one's nature: 'I will ask him for my place again; he shall tell me I am a

[1]A fascinating study could be made of how words such as 'sure', 'assured', 'satisfied', 'secure', 'safe', operate throughout the play.

drunkard. Had I as many mouths as Hydra, such an answer would stop them all.'

Paradoxically, therefore, a crucial part of Iago's dramatic significance in the play is to underline both the need and the cost of *having* to feel rejection, bewilderment, grief and even shame and guilt. Eventually, as we see in the last three acts, it is within Othello himself that the two ways of responding to this fact (that one *has* to feel) collide most terribly: on the one hand, Iago's method of denying one's deepest feelings and trying to substitute other, more tolerable ones in their place, and, on the other hand, the kind of response Desdemona is brought to make: recognizing (as Marlowe's famous couplet so succinctly puts it) that 'It lies not in our power [to choose whether] to love or hate', that one cannot just plant and root up feelings in oneself, for 'will in us is over-rul'd by fate' – by those parts of one's nature that lie beyond the will's reach. In the end, it emerges, one is fated to be the self one is: for all the possibilities of growth and change, one has to live within the limits and potentialities of one's own individual being. And since this includes far more than the conscious will, the will cannot really preserve the self intact – except, of course by, killing it.

Iago's significance, I am suggesting, centres on his un-remitting efforts to deny or suppress the feelings that consume him, and to transform them into other feelings that might at once allow and justify a course of retributive action, instead of his having impotently to suffer fear, loss and self-disgust and negation. As we see it, Iago deals with what he is afraid of partly by denying that he fears anything at all, and partly by turning himself into it, becoming the monster who fills him with monstrous dread: he represents the very destructiveness and malignancy he so perpetually, so anxiously, expects from others. Watching him, we are faced with the fact that, like storms, people are indeed capable of wrecking others' lives. Thus, another part of his dramatic function is, in being so persistently present and active in the play's world, to prohibit *us* from dismissing as merely absurd or mad such suspicions, such fearful wariness, as Iago's own or Othello's. His very existence formidably demonstrates that life can indeed be fraught with dangers even more terrible than those one feared, dangers which are real precisely because they can lurk in the quarter where one least suspects them – in one's own self, for instance, or in the person of one's trusted 'friend'. Fears of being destroyed can turn out to have been totally justified – yet the very harbouring of them can destroy the self they were meant to preserve.

Iago's lust for imperviousness perverts his whole life and being, and, paradoxically, it is this that both sets the limit on our capacity to care for him as a fellow human being, yet forces us to acknowledge him as such. The need to protect and preserve oneself, to make oneself psychologically less vulnerable to the injuries life can inflict, is one we recognize in various forms in everyone else and in ourselves, and recognize as naturally and definitively human. But the problem with Iago – which aggravates our need totally to deny our kinship with him – is the extent to which, on the face of it at least, he actually succeeds in making himself morally and emotionally impervious to life. As John Bayley puts it, 'Iago maintains to the end the dreadful integrity of his own ignorance.'[1]

The extremity of Iago's self-preservative arts and the degree to which they succeed are what most clearly mark him off as a limit case in the play: his permanent and absolute *impatience* of life, his insistence on the supremacy of his will, his incapacity ever to be driven to admit (even to himself) the indomitable actuality of anything in his self or his world. He makes himself incapable of any form of conscious self-recrimination, self-doubt or guilt – utterly

[1] *The Characters of Love* (London, 1960), p. 146.

incapable, that is, of really risking anything of himself. But his entire life is consumed in the perpetual obsession with keeping up all his life-assurance policies. To make himself able to lose nothing, he inevitably (and unawares) makes himself capable only of negative and self-negating gains. When at the end Othello insists that Iago is an honest man 'who hates the slime that sticks on filthy deeds', even though we fully recognize the absurdity of the claim we cannot think that, on the contrary, Iago 'loves' slime. He enjoys sliming and begriming, gets a deep, cheap thrill of fascinated revulsion as he vicariously savours others' (imagined) bestiality – as we discover very early on from the excited insistent rhythms of 'Even now, now, very now, an old black ram/ Is tupping your white ewe'. Yet for all that, what we have seen in him is not only that (as Albany puts it in *King Lear*) 'filths savour but themselves', but further that even Iago's 'savouring' is very short-lived – dull and finally unsatisfying to him. Hence the double irony of his taunts at Othello in Act IV, for instance – 'Satisfied? . . . How satisfied? . . . Where's satisfaction?' Even after he has got Othello to request and authorize Cassio's assassination, for example, he cannot rest content for a moment but can keep his relish simmering only by keeping on tormenting Othello about the handkerchief. And even in v, i, when he finds himself at the crisis-point he has engineered for others – 'it makes us or mars us', 'it makes me or foredoes me quite' – the 'peril' of the situation turns out to have no real piquancy for him at all. In fact, there is nothing in him to 'make' or 'foredo', nothing he will allow to be open to benefit or injury. This becomes unmistakable in the very last scene, when he is finally cornered. He refuses to yield an inch: 'Demand me nothing' – for what *could* he yield? Othello speaks more truly than he knows when he declares 'If that thou be'st a devil, I cannot kill thee.' He cannot, nor could anyone else, kill Iago's heart, not because Iago is a 'devil' but because he – alone of the

98

central figures – is incapable of committing himself to another, and is therefore not open to serious, even fatal injury at anyone else's hand.

In this respect his is a peculiarly significant case, because throughout the play Shakespeare is exploring the capacity of the human heart to break or be broken, and of men to die of grief or, in Emilia's words, 'Kill [themselves] for grief' (and of course for guilt too). Whereas no one other than himself can ever seriously hurt Iago, Cassio finds that the loss of his honour and Othello's love 'e'en kills me'. Even Roderigo is almost fatally wounded because in his own inimitable fashion he loves Desdemona.[1] The last scene presents many deaths, each of which symbolically reinforces the play's stress on the necessary link between loving and vulnerability: Brabantio, Emilia, Desdemona, Othello – they are all killed, emotionally and physically, solely because they were willing to love.

Iago's absolute unlovingness, absolute unforgivingness – his commitment to the supreme safety of *non*-commitment – underline the fact that we come to care about the other characters in the play in direct proportion as they do dare risk themselves, do dare to care about others. For him no one is ever in any real sense '*you*' (though of course he uses that word), but always an object – 'she' or 'him'; and his cool competence in dealing with 'problems' is obviously continuous with his cool brutality in dealing with people. But, to compare him again with two not dissimilar characters in other plays, whereas Lady Macbeth's defences

---

[1]Roderigo is usually said by critics to be 'killed' at the end, but Shakespeare is careful to qualify Lodovico's phrase 'the slain Roderigo' (v, ii, 306) with Cassio's 'and even but now he spake/ After long seeming dead – Iago hurt him,/ Iago set him on' (v, ii, 323–5). His severe yet *un*mortal injury symbolically confirms our sense of Roderigo's genuine yet relatively shallow and accidental love for Desdemona. Despite his assertions in I, iii, he doesn't (unlike Othello) have to call on death as his only 'physician'. Less radical 'surgery' will do.

eventually collapse, and Goneril is prepared to die because in her own way she loves Edmund – facts which convince us that neither woman has entirely (in Iago's phrase) changed her 'humanity with a baboon' – Iago, who never loses his conviction that his will can protect him from any and every human susceptibility, seems so far gone that it is hard indeed for us to acknowledge his membership of our own species, our own human 'tribe'.

That very difficulty is highly significant. For Shakespeare's presentation of Iago challenges us to dare *not* to shield ourselves from what the drama shows: that Iago's inhumaneness is itself the clearest sign of his humanity. It cannot be safely fenced off into a category labelled 'devilish', 'unhuman'. Despite its best (or its worst) efforts, Iago's will cannot enclose itself totally and permanently in protective armour-plating. Its rapacious need to try to do so betrays the hidden existence of a somewhere-vulnerable self that needs protection, just as the insatiable need to justify his destructiveness makes us see him as destructible – capable, not of being destroyed by another, but of destroying himself in his very craving to make that impossible.

What I am trying to get at here is Iago's dramatic effect on *us*, what his life brings us to see. Bradley remarked of Iago's 'egotism' and 'want of humanity' that Iago 'tries to make them absolute and cannot succeed'. But, as I have tried to suggest about all the other characters, our response to Iago is significantly modified by the considerable degree of success as well as the ultimate (and by him unacknowledged) failure of his self-preservative stratagems. What we find most loathsome is not his unscrupulousness *per se* but his success in continuing to delude himself that it is justified. Somehow, we feel, it would be deeply satisfying to us to make him face the immitigable horror of his own vileness. What hurts us most (and so makes us yearn for the 'comfort' of being rid of him) is just this fact that he retains the comfort of self-delusion.

If we pause to reflect on the emotional logic of that response, we soon realize – with whatever degree of dismay – that Iago's dangerous, gnawing resentment of others' 'benefits' and 'comforts' is exactly mirrored in our potent resentment at *his*. He is so vigilant in protecting himself that it is impossible for us to feel any 'inwardness' with him in the usual sense of that term, since he alienates our sympathies as successfully as he alienates himself from any possible sympathies in his own being. But that very sense of total alienation from him is precisely what makes us bound to him for ever. Our 'inwardness' with him, we might say, is mediated by – indeed, it consists in – our violent antipathy to him. Our hatred and fear of him is commensurate with and duplicates his hatred and fear of life. The multiple 'cause' we so quickly find to 'do justice' on him, the scorching need for retributive action that burns in us and, because frustrated, grows more acute as we watch, corresponds and is equivalent to the same arts of self-preservation, the very destructiveness we abhor in him. It is a chilling thought. But in a play that presses us so hard to realize the implications of all our habits of feeling it is one we can evade only if, Iago-like, we successfully delude ourselves.

Like his towards the world, our inhumaneness towards him is a symptom of our humanity, though a part we normally like to deny the existence of in ourselves. Just as his aggressiveness and his real or imagined vulnerability go hand in hand, so do ours. Yet for us to recognize this is not to find any ready way to sever the connection. And this too is an important truth the play pushes us to see: that our natural impulse to shun or lessen our emotional vulnerability to such a person as Iago is not in itself necessarily culpable, but our every attempt to translate it into action (for example, by wishing for some dire fate to befall him) is bound to be destructive, bound to resemble the behaviour we judge criminal in him.

It is perhaps useful to add here two further obvious but important points. The first is that the old adage, 'tout comprendre c'est tout pardonner' does not – and I believe cannot – apply to our response to Iago. For one thing, we do not really comprehend 'all', and for another it is probably true that the more we understand him the *less* we are inclined to forgive. We blame him because he will not or cannot love or forgive others, but to recognize in ourselves a corresponding refusal or incapacity to love or forgive him does not dissolve or diminish it – or even make us believe we ought to try to muster more charity.

The second point is a related one. If it is a sentimental falsification to suppose that the play makes mercy and love flow warm and tender in all our veins, it is no less sentimental to suppose that the resemblance to Iago's behaviour that we find in our own response to him is tantamount to identification with him. Whilst our reaction to him is in significant ways like his own to others, our response to others is in equally significant ways unlike anything Iago is capable of. Although I have stressed his dramatic function in objectifying our own potential destructiveness, a linked and certainly no less crucial part of his function in the play is to underscore how much we *do* care about those whose joy he plots to annihilate.

Most critics would of course agree that Iago is quite crucial in the dramatic design. What I have been trying to suggest, however, is that this is true in a sense rather different from those usually meant. The basic contradictions in Iago as Shakespeare conceived him are the essence both of his dramatic 'character' and therefore of his dramatic importance – so essential, in fact, that it is perhaps useful to summarize them before turning to consider Othello, who has so much in common with his 'friend' and yet who differs so vitally from him.

From beginning to end of the play, Iago represents, in

an extreme form, the urge to shield oneself from hurt and injury by the exercise of sheer will (on others and on oneself) and the effect of doing so: a ruthless *maiming* of life both inside and outside the self. Iago's contempt for others is significant because it is so clearly the other side of an unacknowledgeable self-contempt – a sense of injury and resentment aroused by feeling disregarded and therefore denigrated by others, but masking itself from conscious recognition by a conscious 'philosophy' of cynicism and a readiness to find 'causes' for injuring everyone else. Indeed, some of his phrases to Roderigo concerning will-power are also strikingly apt to the manifold motives or 'causes' he offers himself for his own behaviour: according to his whim or 'necessity' of the moment, he 'sets' or 'weeds up' any suitable rationale that springs to mind, his policy being simply to 'supply [his mind] with one, or distract it with many'. No one cultivates his motive-garden more assiduously than Iago does. Nor does it take us long to see that (to use the Duke's words in Act I) 'there is no composition' (consistency) in Iago's claims about himself 'that gives them credit'.

The inconsistencies are strongly emphasized. To act as he does, Iago needs to think of himself as a persecuted and wounded victim, even while pluming up his will by asserting and seeking to prove that he is too tough and clever to be woundable. On the one hand, identifying himself with what he claims is his autonomous will, he sees himself as free, omnipotent and thus invulnerable because moved only by self-chosen emotions; on the other hand, he identifies himself as the scandalously victimized object of *other* people's malignant wills, thus justifying his chosen methods for remedying the 'injuries' allegedly done to him. This sense of himself as both victim and agent allows him a wonderfully flexible sense of his own freedom. It enables him not to recognize how much he is bound by emotions and fears he cannot choose either to have or to discard;

at the same time, it enables him to absolve himself of any sense of culpability by supposing that everyone behaves (or ought to) in the same way:

> And what's he then that says I play the villain,
> When this advice is free I give, and honest,
> Probal to thinking . . .
> . . .
> How am I then a villain
> To counsel Cassio to this parallel course
> Directly to his good? Divinity of hell!
> (II, iii, 326–8, 338–40)

In Iago, the need of sheer will-power, and the contradictions it betrays, are more deep-seated and thus more extreme than in any of the other characters; but in varying forms and degrees all the others exhibit these as well. Roderigo, Brabantio and Cassio all veer on occasion between a sense of being unfairly victimized and a sense of being a free agent rationally justified in injuring others. In the last three acts of the play, as we shall see, even Emilia and Desdemona (each in her own fashion) veer between assertions of their autonomy and a sense of being helplessly negated by others. Similarly, but most terribly of all, Othello careers wildly from one sense of himself to another, or tries to entertain both simultaneously in a frantic effort to avert total self-disintegration. Yet in each case the drama is concerned with more than the mere fact of such habitual contradictions in people. It probes the underlying causes why they think of themselves in these ways, and further, the reasons why people often, in times of real or imagined crisis, *must* do so in order to survive at all. Again and again *Othello* shows how, in the face of potential or actual threats from others or from one's own feelings, the only comfort or consolation an individual can sometimes find, and which he instinctively clutches at or even invents, is some or any relatively clear-cut sense of himself and of his place in the world. When external conditions in one's life prove (or seem to prove) intolerably refractory, a fluctuating – or, better, an ever-adaptable – sense of *oneself* is often the only means of 'coping', though (as Shakespeare makes crystal clear in this as in virtually every play he wrote) to 'cope' with a problem is always costly and not at all necessarily the same as 'solving' it. In Iago's case, the gymnastic leaps from one sense of himself to another are revealed as gratuitous, glibly opportunistic, usually a simple function of 'required convenience'. But at the other extreme from Iago we find Desdemona also striving to find some steady foothold, some steady sense of herself, amid the changing current of her life, and struggling the more desperately to retain it as her experience grows more and more turbulent. For her and for Othello alike, the maintenance of any clear, true and yet still bearable, still livable, sense of themselves and of each other not only becomes more difficult as the action develops, but becomes in the end a tragic impossibility, grounded in their love itself.

As it progresses, the play explores and brings home to us the ways in which each of the lovers' attempted defences against shock and grief differ from, resemble or combine the defensive stratagems employed instinctively by each of the other characters. Of these, the most revealing cases are perhaps Cassio's, where the stratagems are the most frankly self-acknowledged, and Iago's, where they are the most fixed, far-gone and indissoluble. Iago is the only one of all the main characters who cannot be crushed by grief; the defences of each of the others become eroded and broken at last by the engulfing tide of their experience. This seems to me another reason why the play is so deeply disturbing. In showing us how *all* its people seek at times to evade, deflect or master their insurgent feelings, and in showing us how and why they all (except Iago) ultimately fail, it shakes the ground beneath our own habitual props and shelters. It makes us realize both the naturalness of the human need for self-consolation, and the delusions involved in such necessary efforts to cheer ourselves up. Iago's case reveals to us the essential human hollowness of one who can never recognize what every other character is eventually, at vast emotional cost, forced and able to see: that one's freedom begins only in realizing how far one is necessarily bound by the feelings that grow in and around commitments one can neither ignore nor change; that the 'will' is therefore subject to the core in human beings that makes them susceptible to pain as well as being capable of inflicting pain on others – that it cannot be autonomous any more than it can make one impregnable. More clearly than any other character, Iago exhibits why human life ultimately cannot, for all its need to, insulate and defend itself in mere will, or find any citadel worth defending that is stronger than its own power to hurt and to be hurt.

4

Personal and professional identity: Othello in the first two acts

OTHELLO   [She] bade me, if I had a friend that loved her,
I should but teach him how to tell my story,
And that would woo her.   (I, iii, 163–5)

MONTANO   I have served him, and the man commands
Like a full soldier.   (II, i, 35–6)

From the start, I have suggested, *Othello* is concerned with the nature, the making, and the rupturing of 'bonds', and the kinds of freedom and constraint different people find within the 'bonds' they enter into. In this sense, it is continuous with Shakespeare's earlier comedies, especially *The Merchant of Venice* and *Twelfth Night*. But in *Othello* the personal costs and gains, the constraints and liberations people discover in their commitments are explored more subtly than in the earlier plays, and it looks forward to the same concerns (taken up in a new way) in *Measure for Measure* and *King Lear*. Almost at once, for example, Iago's claims in the opening scene about 'bondage' and 'duty' and whether or not he is 'affined/ To love the Moor', are dramatically set against, for instance, Desdemona's speeches in the Senate about 'duty' and obligation to her father, and her commitment to Othello. Throughout the play Iago exploits Roderigo by reassuring him he is 'knit to thy deserving with cables of perdurable toughness', and Roderigo, ever gullible, accepts his obsequious bondage with Iago, little realizing that the friendship he thinks so helpful is no more than a trap. Brabantio claims Desdemona's filial bond to him by claiming she must have been 'bound' in 'chains of magic' by Othello. Or, to take another, more central case, in an early speech to Iago, Othello talks about 'circumscription and confine', the necessary personal cost of loving Desdemona – a recognition soon dramatically set against his overbrimming happiness, his sense of freedom and benefit, in II, i: 'O my sweet,/ I prattle out of fashion and I dote/ In mine own comforts'; 'Come, my dear love,/ The purchase made, the fruits are to ensue:/ That profit's yet to come 'tween me and you.' All through the play the human bonds are claimed, established, broken, disrupted. Each party to such a bond sees it – what it consists in, and what it entails – in his own way, and this may coincide with the other's sense of it or may widely diverge from it. Not surprisingly, therefore, the play is concerned to explore how and why human 'affection' so often tends to alter when it alteration finds.

The connection and the opposition between 'bound' and 'free' are continually invoked, but most of all, as we might expect, in that central scene (III, iii) where the vital bond of mutual love between Desdemona and Othello is jarred and then so fractured that nothing can 'repair' or 'mend' the 'unkind breach' between them. Here, significantly, the word 'bound' and its derivatives and synonyms recur again and again, underlining the terrible ironies the scene is structured to expose. Despite its length the scene drives forward, emotionally speaking, with an almost sickening speed and a tense, tightly wrought logic – a logic wrought by Shakespeare as dramatist, that is, not by Iago as villain. Iago is here quite finally exposed for what he is, but he also gradually recedes to the fringe of our attention. It is now Othello himself, and what is happening within him, and why, and what it means, that increasingly rivet our attention as we watch.

So full and complex is this scene, so densely and profoundly imagined, that it really defies critical summary even while its dramatic and theatrical power drives us to try to give some account of it as best we can. Even as we witness it, we come to realize it is a single, carefully unified whole; and perceiving its unity we come more fully to grasp its significance in the play as a whole.

Part of its significance lies in its dramatic framing – a point that critics and producers seem invariably to overlook. It is flanked on either side by two *tableaux* – one at the start and one at the close – in each of which a 'bond' is formally acknowledged. Moreover, both vows of allegiance are linked by verbal echoes and inversions so that they stand in fundamental contrast with each other and epitomize the momentous change effected by what happens in between. In the first, as III, iii opens, we see Desdemona speaking out of confident faith in her relationship with Othello, and warmly assuring her friend Cassio that she will do 'all my abilities on thy behalf' to heal and restore the broken bond between him and Othello. Cassio's gratitude is heartfelt:

> Bounteous madam,
> Whatever shall become of Michael Cassio,
> He's never anything but your true servant.
>
> (III, iii, 7–9)

Fully aware of Cassio's unhappiness and trying thus to comfort and cheer him up, Desdemona keeps repeating her assurance.[1] 'Do not doubt, Cassio', she says, 'Assure thee,/

---

[1] It is through her multiple reassurances that Shakespeare alerts us to the dramatic irony of this colloquy. *Our* confidence that her 'abilities' will achieve what she presses Cassio to believe can hardly fail to be called in question when, in the space of 26 lines, she over-protestingly enjoins him, 'Be thou assured . . . do not doubt . . . be you well assured . . . do not doubt that . . . I give thee warrant . . . . Assure thee. . . . Therefore be merry.' It is also a strong signal that the rest of this scene will focus on the human need for assurance, confidence, secure certainty.

If I do vow a friendship, I'll perform it/ To the last article.'

The central scene finally ends with the second vow of allegiance: Iago's undertaking to 'give up/ The execution of his wit, hands, heart,/ To wronged Othello's service', to destroy and avenge the allegedly adulterous bond between Desdemona and Cassio – in short, to perform his friendship to the last article and to be Othello's true servant:

> Let him [Othello] command,
> And to obey shall be in me remorse,
> What bloody business ever. (III, iii, 464–6)

Othello, in terms that unwittingly reflect Cassio's, duly expresses his gratitude: 'I greet thy love,/ Not with vain thanks, but with acceptance bounteous.'

Unlike Othello himself, we of course are acutely aware of Iago's secret purpose here. For us, his behaviour is merely a repeat-performance – decked out in more sumptuous emotional robes – of his earlier hypocritical protestations to Cassio(II, iii) and Roderigo: 'I have professed me thy friend . . .; I could never better stead thee than now . . . Thou art sure of me . . . Let us be conjunctive in our revenge against him' (I, iii, 333ff.). As we see it, therefore, Iago's 'noble' bond with Othello here immediately strikes us as a shocking travesty of the genuine friendship between Desdemona and Cassio it is pledged to avenge. Where their bond is committed to restore, this is committed to destroy – and is itself the means by which Iago initiates the destruction of Othello. The easy brutality with which he agrees to murder Cassio – 'my friend is dead' – not only clinches our knowledge of what the word 'friend' means in his mouth. We know all too well that in Iago's hopes 'my friend is dead' implicitly applies to his 'friend' Othello too, and is a real possibility just because the latter so readily acquiesces in this depraved abuse of human language and feeling.[1]

[1] The same applies to Iago's words to Montano in II, iii, 138–9: 'I love Cassio well, and would do much to cure him of this evil.'

Even more appalling, however, is Iago's next appeal
– an appeal for restraint which is really a covert incite-
ment to further action: 'But let her live.' By now we
sense what Othello's response will be: 'Damn her, lewd
minx!' Where Desdemona's generous heart had led her to
reassure Cassio that 'thy solicitor shall rather die/ Than
give thy cause away', her words re-echo here in our minds,
twisted now from hyperbolic hypothesis to a dreadful
likelihood, as Othello goes off to seek 'some swift means
of death/ For the fair devil'.

The bond Iago and Othello swear not only debases the
attributes of real friendship and its language; it does the
same with military relationships too, illicitly using the
language of real martial honour: 'service', 'command',
'obey', 'Now art thou my Lieutenant'. More than that,
their vow is a hideous travesty of marriage: a grotesque
marriage of perverted minds. As they ceremoniously kneel
to make their mutual pledge, their strange exalted language
(with its pious resort to the third person) grossly exploits
the rhetoric of matrimonial bonds:

OTHELLO   Now, by yond marble heaven,
          In the due reverence of a sacred vow
          I here engage my words.
                                [*He kneels*]

IAGO   Do not rise yet.
                                [*He kneels*]
          Witness you ever-burning lights above,
          You elements, that clip us round about,
          Witness that here Iago doth give up
          The execution of his . . . heart,
          To . . . Othello's service.
                              [*They rise*]
          . . .

OTHELLO   I greet thy love,
          . . . with acceptance bounteous;
          . . .

IAGO   I am your own for ever.   (III, iii, 457ff.)

It is no accident that Othello's words here echo not only Cassio's earlier in the scene, but those he himself had spoken in the Senate, in Act I (supporting Desdemona's request of the Duke that she might accompany him to Cyprus):

> Vouch with me, heaven, I therefore beg it not
> To please the palate of my appetite
> . . .
> But to be free and bounteous to her mind.
>
> (I, iii, 258–62)

The pledge between Iago and Othello, in short, is revealed as an abominable parody of the very marriage whose destruction it commits itself to, sets in train and ensures.

Othello and Iago's vow is not in itself a sudden new development in the play, however. It is the culmination, the formal registration as it were, of a bond that has been drawn tighter and tighter during the course of this scene. Between the opening vow of Desdemona and Cassio and this pledge at the scene's end, the action has channelled itself irrevocably towards a fatal end. However strongly our hopes continue to pull against the tide of events, we realize by the end of this scene that for the lovers themselves there can probably be no going back. Although neither of them yet knows it, the compulsive course of Othello's feelings has swept them both far out of their depth and beyond help. To explain *why* this is so, however, we need to understand exactly what has happened during this crucial scene.

At a first glance, what has happened may seem to be the subversion of one relationship by another: Iago seduces Othello away from Desdemona, and usurps her place in his heart – 'displants' her, as well as usurping Cassio's 'place'.[1] Or, to put it slightly differently, it may seem that Othello, realizing his wife's supposed falsity, promptly

---

[1] This is Stephen Rogers's view, for instance: '*Othello*: Comedy in Reverse', *Shakespeare Quarterly*, 24 (1973), p. 216.

transfers his allegiance from her to Iago, just as in Act V
Emilia, on discovering her husband's real treachery,
transfers all *her* allegiance to Desdemona. No doubt there
will always be critics and producers who find a covert or
overt homosexuality at the centre of *Othello*, and many
who, even if they do not stress that particular aspect of it,
hold that Iago's and Othello's alliance is the most important
thing in the play, and that III, iii should thus be staged so
as to emphasize the blossoming emotional intimacy between
the two men – reinforcing it with much physical contact
between them here: comradely thumps on the back,
embraces, cheek-by-cheek or eyeball-to-eyeball dialogue,
and so forth. (Producers seem especially fond of showing
Othello literally under the thumbs and fingers of Iago as
masseur.) I think any such interpretation vastly oversimpli-
fies and distorts what happens. To give Iago such a central
importance in the scene is seriously to misplace the main
dramatic stress. For that surely falls, not on Othello's
developing relationship with Iago, but rather on the dynamics of Othello's inner state, his shifting sense of his bond
with *Desdemona*, and his turbulent, shifting sense of himself
that conditions and accompanies it. For all their elaborate
rhetoric, the two men do not enter into any intimate
mutual relationship with each other. They are bound together only by Iago's insinuations about Desdemona, and
it is the supposed facts about *her* that Othello's attention
and emotions concentrate on – just as it is his attention
and emotions that absorb our interest (and indeed Iago's
interest as well). Iago of course thinks he is supremely
important in producing those emotions in Othello; nevertheless, as we are made to see it, Othello's being is subdued
not by Iago's power, but by Desdemona's, and his own
power to be hurt by her. Thus the reasons why the scene
develops in the frightful way it does are to be found not in
Iago's nature, but in Othello's, in what is at stake for him
in his marriage. To understand exactly what happens in

this scene, therefore, we have to consider it in its full
dramatic context – in the light of what the first half of the
play has revealed of the lovers and of the meaning each
takes or finds in their bond. Desdemona's sense of it is
obviously linked with Othello's, though differing from it
too; but for the moment we may leave discussion of her
aside, and consider Othello as we see him in these early
acts.

A pointedly significant omission in the first two scenes of
Act I is any mention of Othello by name. He is referred to
only in such coarsely disparaging terms as 'an old black
ram', 'a Barbary horse', a 'lascivious Moor', 'an extravagant
and wheeling stranger', a 'foul thief', a 'thing', an 'abuser
of the world', and so on, or simply as 'the Moor' (usually
with a pejorative stress), or as 'the General'. When he
actually appears, we notice at once the force with which
his own speeches implicitly rebut such terms. He sets them
aside in a perfectly calm, collected manner that sharply
contrasts with the heated, aggressive tones and behaviour
of everyone else so far. He exhibits a cool confidence that
at once claims and confirms a very different nature from
that attributed to him by his assailants. But not until the
Senate-scene (I, iii) is he at last directly addressed and
referred to by his proper name: 'Valiant Othello, we must
straight employ you.'

The tone and manner of the Duke's address are extremely
revealing. This very first time Othello's name is used it is
spontaneously yoked with the epithet 'valiant'. No sooner
is he given his name than his usefulness for 'employ' is
assumed, and a claim upon it immediately made. In fact,
all through this scene, Othello is identified with his job.
The respect accorded him is inextricably bound up with his
usefulness to the state. Even Iago, we notice, who has every
wish to denigrate and deny the Moor's talents, has had to
admit sourly in the opening scene that Othello's military

expertise is such as to make him indispensable: 'the state
. . . cannot with safety cast him'; 'Another of his fathom
they have none/ To lead their business.' Nobody in the
play disputes Othello's excellence as a soldier. The worst
that even Iago can find to say is that Othello brags and
exaggerates his skills – a claim we can hardly treat as a
disinterested judgment coming from that source (especially
when we realize that the point about bragging applies to
Iago himself). Furthermore, as soon as Othello first speaks
(II, i, 6ff.) there is no doubt that he himself 'knows his
price' and rests assured that he is (as Iago would say)
'worth no worse a place' than that of much-respected
General.[1] Quite unperturbed by the news of Brabantio's
imminent challenge, he coolly observes that 'My services,
which I have done the signory,/ Shall out-tongue his
complaints.' The circumlocution ('my services, which I
have done') only seems further to attest his confidence.
When actually confronted by Brabantio's 'officers', all
brandishing weapons, he merely remarks – with crushing
because unruffled dignity – that,

> Were it my cue to fight, I should have known it
> Without a prompter. (I, ii, 83–4)

When he speaks of 'my services', or says that 'my parts,
my title and my perfect soul/ Shall manifest me rightly',
it is plain that he too identifies his inner self with the
honour and valour that can be outwardly 'found' and
'approved'.

The basis of Othello's *personal* self-assurance in these
scenes, then, is what Robert Heilman calls 'positional
assurance'.[2] He relies on the knowledge of being (like the
pilot of his boat in the storm) of 'very expert and approved

---

[1] Reuben Brower, *Hero and Saint* (Oxford, 1971), pp. 1–28, makes some
acute comments on Othello's language in these early scenes and what
happens to it.
[2] *Magic in the Web* (Lexington, Kentucky, 1956), p. 180.

allowance' as a military man. Once we notice the point it is obvious, of course, yet the play stresses it too persistently for us to suppose it is unimportant. Montano's remark in II, i, 35–6 – 'I have served him, and the man commands/ Like a full soldier' – only confirms what is shown to us in its personal aspect in Act I. Off the battlefield, as he is said to do on it, he calmly exhibits his power to 'lead' and 'command' others. His tone is everywhere that of a man who simply expects to have his orders obeyed, no matter what the circumstances:

> Keep up your bright swords, for the dew will rust them.
> Good signor, you shall more command with years
> Than with your weapons.   (I, ii, 59–61)

This last – at least, the first line of it – is one of the most frequently quoted of Othello's speeches, and it does, very crisply, display his characteristic qualities through the first two acts.[1] His quietly masterful dignity here is what clinches his point about Brabantio's lack of it. Furthermore, all through these early scenes, his commanding eloquence is *itself* the incontrovertible mark of his military and personal authority. That is, his sovereign soldiership is given reality for us not only by hearsay evidence – his own and others' accounts of it – but in his potent verbal assumption and demonstration of it. His habitual mode of speech expresses socially his earned warrant to think of himself (and, equally, to be thought of) as professionally 'all-in-all sufficient', one whose manifest 'parts' and 'solid virtue' the 'shot of accident nor dart of chance/ Could neither graze nor pierce' (as Lodovico later puts it). He is dramatically realized, in short, as a man whose worth and courage in military service have won him the right to be personally respected, deferred to and obeyed.

If Othello's language in Acts I and II convinces us of

[1] See Matthew N. Proser's interesting account in *The Heroic Image in Five Shakespearean Tragedies* (Princeton, 1965), pp. 92–170.

his worth, it is hardly strange that it has already convinced Desdemona. The unsurprising naturalness of her being won over by his eloquence is explicitly underlined for us by the Duke's comment: 'I think this tale would win my daughter too' (I, iii, 170). What we notice in the Senate-scene, indeed, is that despite Othello's disclaimers of rhetorical skill, he himself is sharply aware, more so than anyone else, of his power to sway the Senate and to sway Desdemona's heart by his capacity richly to 'speak' his past – recreate it in words. No one else is more expert in, nor more perpetually conscious of, the power of language. 'Rude am I in my speech/ And little blessed with the soft phrase of peace', he declares in soft, eloquent phrases, 'And little of this great world can I speak/ More than pertains to feats of broil and battle'. Yet what follows can be described only as a most successful 'feat' of 'speaking', even though it is ostensibly no more than a straightforward description of the feat of speaking by which he won Desdemona's love. We already recognize as characteristic of him the fact that no sooner does he claim, 'little shall I grace my cause/ In speaking for myself', than he proceeds to grace it by volunteering to do just that: 'I will a round unvarnished tale deliver/ Of my whole course of love'. Before he delivers it, moreover, he refers several more times to the importance of spoken testimony. He asks that Desdemona be sent for to 'speak of me before her father./ If you do find me foul in her report/ . . . let your sentence/ Even fall upon my life', and 'till she come . . ./ . . . justly to your grave ears I'll present/ How I did thrive in this fair lady's love,/ And she in mine'. When it comes, the 'tale' (as we expect from its elaborate prologue) is not only varnished, but highly polished in every phrase and cadence.

As we hear this speech (I, iii, 127–69), we can hardly now fail to notice Othello's own persistent stress on the power and importance of speech: 'Her father . . ./ Still questioned

me the story of my life'; 'I ran it through, even . . ./ To
th'very moment that he bade me tell it:/ Wherein I spake
of . . .'; 'my travels' history'; 'It was my hint to speak';
'Desdemona [would] . . . with a greedy ear/ Devour up my
discourse'; 'I would all my pilgrimage dilate'; 'I did speak';
'My story being done . . .', and so on. The emphasis grows
still more marked when he describes the upshot of his
story-telling:

> My story being done,
> She gave me for my pains a world of sighs:
> She swore, in faith 'twas strange, 'twas passing strange,
> 'Twas pitiful, 'twas wondrous pitiful;
> She wished she had not heard it, yet she wished
> That heaven had made her such a man. She thanked me,
> And bade me, if I had a friend that loved her,
> I should but teach him how to tell my story,
> And that would woo her. Upon this hint I spake:
> She loved me for the dangers I had passed,
> And I loved her, that she did pity them.   (I, iii, 157–67)

Othello seems at least partly aware that his power to win
Desdemona and to hold her love lies not just in his gift for
speaking *for* himself, but in his capacity to *speak himself*:[1]
to manifest what he truly is in his very way of speaking.
When he recounts Desdemona's hint that if he had a friend,
'I should but teach him how to tell my story,/ And that
would woo her', the crucial word is 'how'. And yet, even
here it seems to be Othello more than Desdemona who is
aware that 'how to tell' is as important as what to tell (a
subtler perception than, say, Elizabeth's caustic comment
in *Richard III*, IV, iv, 280 – 'if this inducement force her
not to love,/ Send her a story of thy noble acts'). We may
well already suspect that the seductive iterations and mellow
cadences he attributes to her – 'she swore . . . 'twas strange,
'twas passing strange,/ 'Twas pitiful, 'twas wondrous

[1]Cf. for example the pointed ambiguity of Macduff's remark (*Macbeth*, II,
iii, 72), 'See, and then speak yourselves.'

pitiful' – are more characteristic of his own speech-habits than of hers, as indeed turns out to be the case.

In all of these early speeches, in fact, Othello's language reflects, and also reflects upon, his sense of mastery in and over his world – his power, in particular, to act decisively, to triumph over obstacles, to command admiration and obedience from others. We soon observe that what Eliot called his 'self-dramatizing' habit is also a self-glamorizing habit – a point whose implications I shall return to. But probably the first thing we notice about this habitual story-telling is that, in the early stages of the drama, it clearly satisfies Othello's need to define himself, to fashion and confirm a secure sense of his self in relation to his world.

Later on, under the extreme stress of his delusion about Desdemona's infidelity, Othello's self-dramatizations clearly begin to fail to do this. As we shall see, they no longer manage to effect the self-confirmation they are designed to ensure. More and more starkly, they reveal only his desperate *need* of some stable sense of himself to hold onto amid the disintegrating flux of his experience. As the last three acts proceed, the gap visibly widens between what he rhetorically claims to be, and what his feelings (and denials of feelings) inexorably push him to recognize he actually is. But long before his crisis in Act III, I think, the play implicitly hints at the possible circumstances in which and the possible reasons why such a man naturally attempts, when under stress, to fix and certify a definite sense of himself *verbally*, and to do so all the more energetically as his experience threatens to undermine the self he is accustomed to think he is.[1]

We may put this point slightly differently, and say that from his earliest speeches on, Othello's evident conscious-

---

[1] The potency and danger of Othello's eloquence are discussed in different terms in T. McAlindon's interesting account of the play in *Shakespeare and Decorum* (London, 1973), pp. 80–131.

ness of his own power as a speaker releases rather than impairs his ability to surmount opposition to his will or feelings. Feeling able to tame it with words, his instinctive response to every challenge is to 'out-tongue' it. So long as the challenge remains external (as is Brabantio's charge, for example), he succeeds. But when he so signally fails to meet what he takes as Desdemona's indirect challenge to him as lover, the result profoundly shocks us by its sheer extremity. Yet it cannot take us wholly by surprise. Again and again, even in the first two acts, his speeches have betrayed a man far less secure and 'stoutly-timbered' in his private personal feelings than in his public professional identity.

Our first fleeting glimpse of this comes with his very first long speech (I, ii, 17–27), when he claims to Iago that Brabantio's 'complaints' could never carry sufficient weight to harm his reputation or prove he does not merit Desdemona's love: 'Let him do his spite.' Although he declares that he can quite intrepidly wear his heart on his sleeve, his assurance, we may notice, partly rests on what he has *up* his sleeve:

> 'Tis yet to know –
> Which, when I know that boasting is an honour,
> I shall provulgate – I fetch my life and being
> From men of royal siege, and my demerits
> May speak, unbonneted, to as proud a fortune
> As this that I have reached. (I, ii, 19–24)

He claims, in effect, that he can win hands-down against Brabantio's paltry suit, since he holds two trump-cards – his 'services' and his pedigree. Yet this may already suggest a potential weakness in Othello's inner timbers: his habit – as visible in him as in Iago all through the first two acts – of trusting in and relying on external sanctions and ratifications of his worth, and especially in his habitual assumption that his personal being and his 'reputation' and 'honour' as

a valiant soldier exactly, fully and unquestionably, correspond.

The main sign of this has often been remarked on: the
importance he attaches to reputation, to the reflection of
self in others' eyes. So often does he refer to the significance of others' 'estimation' and 'report' of him, that he
always seems to regard the 'opinion' of others as 'proof'.
(Iago's opening speech had forecast the constant concern
in this play, as in earlier ones, with people's reliance on
'proof': 'I, of whom his eyes had seen the proof . . .'.) For
Othello, 'opinion' is – in the Duke's phrase at I, iii, 222 – a
'sovereign mistress of effects'. He naturally assumes that
any man's good reputation is hard-won, and therefore to
be valued greatly and stoutly defended. This is one reason
why he is so surprised and baffled by others' behaviour in
the drunken brawl in Act II:

> Worthy Montano, you were wont to be civil:
> The gravity and stillness of your youth
> The world hath noted; and your name is great
> In mouths of wisest censure. What's the matter
> That you unlace your reputation thus
> And spend your rich opinion for the name
> Of a night-brawler? Give me answer to it.
>
> (II, iii, 184–90)

As the action proceeds, of course, it takes up the meaning
of 'reputation' and the implications of caring about other
people's judgment, in many other forms than Othello's own.
(Iago and Cassio in particular are always worrying about
how they 'seem' to others, what others must think of them.)
But it is important to notice how much the play underlines
as central in Othello himself the high value he puts on
others' 'estimation' of him, and his habitual reliance on
their estimation to corroborate his own sense of his worth.
His self-esteem is clearly *not* a function of insulated, self-
supporting egotism. Shakespeare's interest in 'reputation',

'honour', 'opinion', and so on goes back a long way – at least as far back as *The Rape of Lucrece*, and it is intensified in such later plays as *Measure for Measure* and *Coriolanus*. But where *Troilus and Cressida*, for instance (the play from which, in this particular respect as in others, *Othello* seems most directly developed), treats this interest rather theoretically – its ethical, military, metaphysical, amatory and other aspects being diagrammatically sketched out or expounded upon, rather than realized in a fully dramatic way – *Othello* treats it with dramatic intensity right from the start. Hardly has the play got under way before we see how much each of the other characters as well as Othello depend, for an image or sense of themselves, on what they see reflected in others' eyes. And we soon see, too, how this dependence naturally increases in proportion as the 'other' is emotionally important – respected, for example, or loved, or feared, whether consciously or not. In Cassio's case, Shakespeare explores some fairly straightforward though painful consequences of these facts. In Act II, and (more interestingly) later on, Cassio equates a tarnished public reputation with a tarnished sense of his personal merit. He not only suffers shame, but feels he has lost his whole *raison d'être* when he loses the job that betokens Othello's 'regard' for him. Desdemona's experience in the last two acts is another case in point, when she finds that for some unfathomable reason she has lost Othello's love and trust and 'rich opinion' of her.

Even before Othello's case is counterpointed by these others, however, Iago's eagerness to recite his story and his 'deserts' to Roderigo (an eagerness which obviously goes hand in hand with his sourness at having been 'denied' the job he wants) has already alerted us to the possible implications of Othello's similar need to have *his* 'worth' publicly rehearsed and acknowledged – his evident need for an audience's attention and approval. For all his consciousness of being a celebrity he seems never really to trust or draw confidence from his own valuation of himself. He needs others to vouch for him – their 'vouchings' are his 'proof': 'how to tell my story' is not a superfluously self-gratifying art for him, but an art vital to his self-respect. And quite early on, I think, we see what this means: that to the very extent that he depends on an audience to ratify his 'merit', he is potentially vulnerable to a world or a person who might deny him the 'yes' he needs.

As far as his soldiership is concerned we harbour no fears that that affirmation will ever be withheld. The history of his heroic feats is on record in others' stories of it as well as his own, and the facts were objectively visible for everyone to see. But of course from the opening lines onwards the play channels our interest in his past as hero into an interest in his present and future as the husband of Desdemona. And in that area we are indeed alerted to the risks attendant on such a man's falling in love in this way and to this degree. For a man obviously so unused to trusting to internal assurances of his own merit, any challenge to his sexual identity is likely to be especially disturbing. For what external measures or guarantees of *that* can anyone appeal to, except the reflection of it one finds (or imagines) in the eyes of the person one loves? – a reflection which in one way or another is notoriously liable to be misconstrued.

Because Othello neither claims nor has any distinct personal identity apart from his professional one, it is naturally the image of himself as soldier that he offers up to Desdemona's approbation and love. I don't think the play gives us any warrant or directive to regard this fact as in itself a disastrous basis for the marriage. But we are a little troubled by what prompts and thus may result from his liberality with the 'varnish', the high-gloss tinting of the ambitious self-portrait he verbally paints for her to gaze upon. We hear him describing to the Senators how he wooed her, but the remarkable fact about his speech is the way it develops: the 'report' turns into what sounds like a full-scale re-recital, the details cascading down, each cadence seeming to mark the end of the rehearsal and yet suddenly the pause giving way again to another luxuriously remembered detail, as if he would enjoy to 'tell his story' again for hours.

> I ran it through, even from my boyish days
> To th'very moment that he bade me tell it:
> Wherein I spake of most disastrous chances,
> Of moving accidents by flood and field,
> Of hair-breadth scapes i'th'imminent deadly breach,
> Of being taken by the insolent foe,
> And sold to slavery; of my redemption thence,
> And portance in my travels' history:
> Wherein of antres vast and deserts idle,
> Rough quarries, rocks, and hills whose heads touch heaven,
> It was my hint to speak – such was the process:
> And of the Cannibals that each other eat,
> The Anthropophagi, and men whose heads
> Do grow beneath their shoulders.   (I, iii, 131–44)

Plainly, Othello enjoys talking about his exploits.[1] And this self-portrait of a veteran hero is clearly the masterpiece of a born autobiographer, a gifted, inveterate toucher-up. It may not contain any 'lies' of the sort Iago alleges are habitual in Othello (II, i, 217) – but we can't help thinking it somewhat 'fantastical'. Splendid it certainly is, and I think we are drawn in by it. Yet considering the excitements it refers to, it sounds oddly tranquil, unexcited. If this was the past Othello has actually lived, 'telling' it seems to transmute it, so that what emerges is as it were the truth, plus and minus a little more besides. More to the point, not only is his round tale also a rather tall one, but

---

[1] It is interesting to note the difference here between Othello and Coriolanus, who can't stand hearing about – let alone speaking about – his prowess and services to the state. In each of them the attitude to self-imaging runs very deep, and is an essential 'cause' of his tragedy.

his eloquence seems so to tame and beautify the things he describes, the pulse of the raw experience is so little registered in the rhythms of the speech, what it presents is so static, *un*agitated, because what it most enjoys (even congratulates itself on) is the image of *himself* as unrufflable, utterly self-composed no matter how dangerous or exotic the circumstances.

Yet what perhaps slightly disturbs us about it is not, I think, the self-consciousness or the glamorizing *per se* but the undercurrent of latent self-doubt it seems at once to betray (to us), to forestall and compensate for, and to which it inevitably lays him open in the future. In so far as we do consider the speech a repeat performance of the wooing-speeches it purports to describe, it is for this reason rather troubling. By recounting so very seductively his outstanding soldierly prowess, his extraordinarily exotic past, and offering these, as it were in full technicolor, as the basis of his sexual attractiveness, he has made it hard (perhaps dangerously hard) for himself ever to rest certain and secure that in his marriage he does and will *measure up* to that self-image.

It is to a suppressed incipient anxiety of this kind rather than complacent egotism that I think we should attribute the otherwise rather dismaying fact that 'in the sixty-one lines in which Othello describes their love, he refers to himself twice as frequently as he does to [Desdemona]'.[1] I say this even though (and partly because) I agree to some small extent with those critics who are worried by 'and I loved her that she did pity [the dangers I had passed]', and who find the whole description of his love in the Senate-scene pretty self-centred. But several things about this scene make it quite inappropriate for us to slide from talking about his rather 'self-centred *description* of love' to judging him a self-centred lover, or, worse, an egotist who is incapable of love. One is the persistently emphasized

[1]Larry S. Champion, 'The Tragic Perspective of *Othello*', *English Studies*, 54 (1973), p. 454.

context in which Othello speaks. He is on 'trial'.[1] The
'trial' indeed turns out not to be very nerve-racking for the
defendant, but this is for the very reason he makes it his
business to keep in the Senators' minds: the (extraneous)
fact of his excellence as a soldier. He is supposed to be
proving that he did not illegitimately coerce Desdemona's
love; what is especially striking is his evident elation in
reminding *himself* that, yes, indeed, she voluntarily fell in
love with him. A related and more important point emerges
if we attend to the tone of the speech, instead of merely
counting its references to himself. Throughout, but
especially in the second half of it, his tone expresses an
exceptionally strong and tender sense of Desdemona, 'her',
'she', as a creature quite other than himself, inhabiting a
household world he knows little about – a 'she' whose
femininity is powerfully magnetic and who seems by some
'strange' and 'wondrous' chance to be magnetized by him.
'She' fills his mind's eye as he speaks of their courtship. But
perhaps the most important factor in our impression of him
as a lover in this scene is the vivid sense we have of Desdemona's love when she arrives to validate his case. The
warmth and womanly decisiveness of everything she says
here convinces us that she is no fool, that she has indeed
fallen thoroughly in love with him, and that she very
evidently feels loved in return. To ignore these facts or
dismiss her sense of being loved as 'misguided' is to belittle
her or sweep her aside as necessarily more ignorant of the
man she loves and has married than we are at this point. I do
not think the action invites us thus to assume our judgment
is so much superior to hers. Rather, I would suggest,
Shakespeare prompts us to take her very assurance as itself a
sort of assurance – even guarantee – of the lovingness, the

[1] For a different view of the significance of this and other trials in the play see
Robert Hapgood, 'The Trials of Othello', in *Pacific Coast Studies in Shakespeare*, ed. Waldo F. McNeir and Thelma N. Greenfield (Eugene, Oregon,
1966), pp. 134–47.

capacity to delight in her, which Othello's self-consciously public speeches here gloss over but which, as I shall suggest in a moment, has already been registered in his earlier speech to Iago and will sound unmistakably in his voice in his speeches by the Cypriot shore.

However, to come back to my main point: all the emphasis on 'story-telling' in the Senate-scene may make us aware of another continuity (which it would be fascinating to examine closely) between one of Shakespeare's interests in *Hamlet* and in *Othello* – and later on in yet another form in (to mention only one obvious case) *Antony and Cleopatra*. In *Hamlet* he had explored the plight of a man who desperately needs to tell his story, express his self, but is constitutionally incapable of doing so. 'Had I but time . . . O, I could tell you –' Hamlet gasps at the end, but we know full well that he never could 'tell', not with all the time in the world. Whereas Othello just before *his* end effectively dictates the version of his life-story he would like to stand as the official record – 'Then must you speak of one that loved . . .', Hamlet characteristically delegates the task to Horatio, to 'report me and my cause aright':

> O God! Horatio, what a wounded name,
> Things standing thus unknown, shall live behind me!
> If thou didst ever hold me in thy heart,
> Absent thee from felicity awhile,
> And in this harsh world draw thy breath in pain,
> To tell my story.   (v, ii, 336–41)

In *Othello*, on the other hand, with its hero who so continually relies on and refers to the importance of speech and verbal self-definition, Shakespeare's imagination is fired by the plight of a man whose very proficiency in self-dramatization may become a stumbling-block – a man who can tell his tale only too fluently. For such a man as Othello may find it virtually impossible to go on living inside the unfolding story of his life once it is complicated by love, since he may not be able to stand the strain of not knowing for sure how it will end or whether he will 'be *found*' to measure up personally to the exotically attractive image of himself which (to his joy and surprise) has won Desdemona as his wife. But this is to anticipate, and my point here is a simple one – that our attention is directed in the opening scenes to the fact and some possible implications of Othello's eloquence, especially his eloquence in delivering stories about himself.

In the Senate-scene, the image of himself as soldier in terms of which he has invited Desdemona to think of him as a man may strike us as slightly glamourized; but it is also substantially true – as we have seen, no one in the scene disputes it. Moreover, as is made clear by the tone and substance of all his speeches to or about her, he has not offered her a mere 'image' of himself at all – he has also, in his own heart, offered her what he simply is, his very self, the man who loves her and longs to be loved in return. And as we perceive that deeper, elemental truth of the matter we also perceive something else – that already, unlike Desdemona, he evidently finds it rather disturbing to adjust to his new sense of himself as the hero who is also a lover, as a man who loves and is loved. Even he, in the very first speeches he makes in the play, seems aware of his difficulty (which we see but no one else does): his loving and being loved not only complicates but causes him to realign his whole perspective on the world. It changes the centre of gravity in his 'life and being':

> For know, Iago,
> But that I love the gentle Desdemona,
> I would not my unhousèd free condition
> Put into circumscription and confine
> For the seas' worth. (I, ii, 24–8)

To find any touch of reluctance in this one would have to be deaf to the tone, and miss the fluent, *un*circumscribed and unconfined movement of Othello's voice. Nothing in it prompts us to see dormant seeds of strife. On the contrary, I think, we hear Othello's quiet, unstressed recognition that love is binding in more ways than one, and that he has freely and gladly chosen his bond.

The Senate-scene reveals a little more of what this choice means for Othello, and in what respects he finds it disturbing: the unprecedented act of opening his heart (and with that, his whole sense of himself) to Desdemona in marriage has inevitably put at stake his old readily sustained source of security.[1] Loving her as he does means now inwardly depending on *her* confirmation of him, not only as worthy and valiant, but also as a desirable lover. He obviously feels impelled to play down his sexuality, publicly at least, and to insist that his old reality as totally dependable soldier remains and will remain unaffected by his change from bachelorhood. In one way, his speech disclaiming sensual motives in wanting her to come to Cyprus is precisely what it seems. And yet his assertions sound a little awkward. It is his very insistence that strikes us as strange. It suggests to us (though not to himself) that love has so subtly but deeply unsettled his former sense of himself that he scarcely knows as yet how his new self will strike others such as the Senators. Unlike Desdemona, he seems not to have properly found his feet again in the ordinary world of public affairs: at least some such uncertainty appears in his eloquent yet faintly embarrassed speech. This is the first time in the play he has bothered at all energetically to justify himself, and his impulse to do so appears all the more significant because for once no justification is even called for. For the first time, I think, there is a defensive note in his protestations:

---

[1] It is interesting to note the similarities here between *Othello* and Conrad's *Victory*: in the cost to each protagonist of daring 'to put his trust in life' ('My life upon her faith!') and of the potential dangers of misrepresentation and 'abominable calumny'.

Vouch with me, heaven, I therefore beg it not
To please the palate of my appetite,
Nor to comply with heat – the young affects
In me defunct – and proper satisfaction;
But to be free and bounteous to her mind.
And heaven defend your good souls that you think
I will your serious and great business scant
For she is with me. No, when light-winged toys
Of feathered Cupid seel with wanton dullness
My speculative and officed instruments,
That my disports corrupt and taint my business,
Let housewives make a skillet of my helm,
And all indign and base adversities
Make head against my estimation!   (I, iii, 258–71)

Since nobody has suggested he 'thinks' anything of the kind we sense a touch of insecurity behind the piled-up denials, the need publicly to trivialize the status of love (to airy 'disports'), the need to relegate sexuality to the periphery of his life, and the heated, challenging insistence that his feelings do not and will not affect his professional reliability. It is as if he as yet scarcely dares trust his capacity to love, dares not fully relax into marriage for fear it might somehow shift the steady *known* ground he has always firmly stood upon as soldier.

In II, i, some such unease as this shows itself again as an edge of fear, a defensive wariness, in his speech of greeting to Desdemona in Cyprus. Here, he seems hardly able to believe, and so is made strangely apprehensive by, his marvellous good fortune in being with her again and having her for his wife. 'O, my fair warrior!' These first words of greeting, as Ruth Nevo has pointed out, 'effectively remind us of the *concordia discors* – Mars and Venus harmonized – which Othello dreamed his marriage might be'.[1]

---

[1] *Tragic Form in Shakespeare* (Princeton, 1972), p. 194. Yet – unsurprisingly – the amatory side of things takes precedence: only after his enraptured reunion with Desdemona does Othello announce the news about the Turks' drowning – news which, in the days before Desdemona came to occupy the centre of his life, would doubtless have been his soul's first business.

The formal, measured movement of his subsequent speech cannot conceal the powerful, unmeasured rush of wonder and joy he feels. Yet no sooner does he acknowledge that joy than his imagination flits to the possibility of losing it, and to the thought of death as perhaps the only way to be really assured that it is 'absolute' – never to be changed or diminished:

> It gives me wonder great as my content
> To see you here before me. O, my soul's joy!
> If after every tempest come such calms,
> May the winds blow till they have wakened death,
> And let the labouring bark climb hills of seas,
> Olympus-high, and duck again as low
> As hell's from heaven. If it were now to die,
> 'Twere now to be most happy; for I fear
> My soul hath her content so absolute
> That not another comfort like to this
> Succeeds in unknown fate.   (II, i, 177–87)

Only in the next act do we grasp just how profoundly revealing this speech was; but even as Othello speaks it, we can hardly miss the clear, troubling signs of a proclivity to fear. His words seem to arise from some wary pessimism, a mistrust of life, an incipient sense that the unknown future may perhaps only erode the 'absolute content' and 'comfort' they hold and share in this present moment. Desdemona, we notice, immediately declares her confidence that their 'loves and comforts' will increase 'even as our days do grow'. For him, only their kiss now can begin to express the love whose full extent and intensity he finds indescribable in words: 'I cannot speak enough of this content;/ It stops me here; it is too much of joy.' And although he now gladly catches up her optimism, he seems able to express it only in wary negatives: '[May] this the greatest discords be/ That e'er our hearts shall make' – a metaphor that Iago instantly snatches up in his famous aside: 'O, you are well-tuned now!/ But I'll set down the pegs that make this music,/ As honest as I am.'

Thus Othello's 'fear' about the possible difference between 'now' and what might be is no sooner uttered than we are made to see it is probably justified. The effect is all the more chilling when Iago's aside is immediately followed by a speech that shows how much Othello's fear is swamped and allayed by his present over-brimming happiness. For once his speech has none of his usual sedate, mellifluous resonance (he himself, we notice, is still sufficiently self-conscious about his speech-habits to observe how uncharacteristic this is – 'I prattle out of fashion'). For once it is simple and relaxed – un'composed':

> Come, let's to the castle.
> News, friends; our wars are done; the Turks are drowned.
> How does my old acquaintance of this isle?
> Honey, you shall be well desired in Cyprus:
> I have found great love amongst them. O my sweet,
> I prattle out of fashion and I dote
> In mine own comforts. I prithee, good Iago,
> Go to the bay and disembark my coffers;
> Bring thou the Master to the citadel;
> He is a good one, and his worthiness
> Does challenge much respect. Come, Desdemona,
> Once more well met at Cyprus!   (II, i, 195–206)

It is not until III, iii, of course, that Iago 'set[s] down the pegs' to turn the lovers' harmonious music into horrible cacophony. But as that crisis approaches we see more and more clearly how everything subtly but ominously paves the way for it. No sooner does Othello leave (after the speech just quoted) than Iago is conspiring once again with Roderigo. No sooner does Roderigo leave than Iago is soliloquizing about 'practising upon [Othello's] peace and quiet,/ Even to madness'. Straight after comes the announcement that Othello has licensed a night's feasting, jointly to celebrate the obliteration – 'mere perdition' – of the

Turks, and his own marriage: a conjunction that (once we notice it) we can hardly not feel as ominous. Even Othello's appeal for caution at the start of the celebrations seems something more than a tactful warning to Cassio, softened by using the plural 'ourselves':

> Good Michael, look you to the guard tonight.
> Let's teach ourselves that honourable stop,
> Not to outsport discretion.   (II, iii, 1–3)

The way this is put – and Othello's tone – seem also to convey his sense that he too, as bridegroom, like Cassio as Lieutenant, should act with caution, honour and restraint, and not be dangerously carried away by his sense of 'full liberty'.

As it turns out, of course, Othello has little chance to 'outsport discretion' in the sense he implies: his first free night with Desdemona is shattered by the premature clanging of a 'dreadful bell' that 'frights the isle/ From her propriety'. As he says after the brawl and the dismissal of Cassio, ''tis the soldiers' life/ To have their balmy slumbers waked with strife'. Yet this remark itself also seems ominous, even before Iago immediately starts making the omen come true. Not only does Iago cynically declare to Cassio, 'Our General's wife is now the General';[1] he then soliloquizes: '–The Moor's] soul is so enfettered to her love,/ That she may make, unmake, do what she list,/ Even as her appetite shall play the god/ With his weak function.' Especially after Othello's words about not outsporting discretion, Iago's inevitably remind us of Othello's persistent anxiety that his personal feelings must be kept safely apart from his professional judgment, and his 'disports' not 'corrupt and taint my business'. In short, even before Othello's private

---

[1] In its spirit and its implications this remark is the exact reverse of Cassio's superficially similar phrase in heartfelt admiration for Othello and 'the divine Desdemona' in II, i, 74: 'She that I spake of, our great Captain's Captain'.

life is violently 'waked with strife' of an internal kind in
Act III, we realize that Cassio's plan (prompted, of course,
by Iago) to 'beseech the virtuous Desdemona to undertake
for me' would be likely to cause trouble even without Iago's
determination to make matters worse:

> Two things are to be done.
> My wife must move for Cassio to her mistress:
> I'll set her on.
> Myself the while to draw the Moor apart,
> And bring him jump when he may Cassio find
> Soliciting his wife. Ay, that's the way.
> Dull not device by coldness and delay.
>
> (II, iii, 371–7)

The crisis is finally ushered in by two brief scenes, both
of which increase still further our tense anticipation of what
is to come. The attempted comedy between Cassio, clown
and musicians is pretty feeble, but it is none the less
inauspicious for that. We can hardly miss the (clumsily
made) point of it. Not only are the musicians, with their
'pegs' slid down, making raucous discord instead of harmony to greet Othello's marriage-morn; Cassio has already,
without 'coldness or delay', asked Emilia (as he puts it to
Iago in another gratingly ironic phrase) to 'procure me some
access' to Desdemona, while Iago, kindly offering to
'devise a mean to draw the Moor/ Out of the way, that your
converse and business/ May be more free', finds his plot
moving on well-oiled wheels. The next brief scene (III, ii)
consists of yet another foreboding little exchange, in which
Othello arranges to meet Iago on the 'fortification' – a word
which by this stage clearly suggests to us a psychological
as well as military meaning (as, for instance, in *Twelfth
Night*, I, v, 137: 'He's fortified against any denial', or,
closer to the mark, the opening scene of *Hamlet* (I, i, 31–2):
'let us once again assail your ears,/ That are so fortified
against our story'). Every minute now 'is expectancy/ Of

more arrivance'.[1] And the central question whose answer we so anxiously await is firm and clear: whether or not Othello's psychological 'fortification' will prove (unlike Cassio's and Roderigo's) stout enough to 'hold the mortise' and withstand Iago's proposed 'molestation'. Will the great defender of Venice in her most vulnerable times prove able to defend himself in his own? Like Cassio's hopes in the storm, our hopes of his survival 'stand in bold cure'. But we fear for him. All the signs are unpropitious. And they become even more so in the opening lines of the scene which, we already realize, will one way or the other prove critical for both the lovers.

---

[1]This is the anonymous gentleman's phrase at II, i, 41–2, at the height of the storm, and like so many others throughout the play (for instance that about Iago, 'whose footing here anticipates our thoughts') is so pointedly apt to describe *our* sense of the unfolding drama that one cannot doubt that Shakespeare had the links between the characters and the audience always in mind.

5

'Alacrity in hardness': Othello's crisis in Acts III and IV

> OTHELLO   I do agnize
> A natural and prompt alacrity
> I find in hardness.   (I, iii, 229–31)

The scene of Othello's crisis (III, iii) is so important in the dramatic design that it demands an especially careful and detailed examination. We come to it, as I have been suggesting, burdened with knowledge and fear – fear especially of Iago's plans, including his specific intention to turn Desdemona's 'goodness' into 'the net/ That shall enmesh them all'. So we cannot look in comfortable ignorance on the opening colloquy between her and Cassio. For any wife to make her husband's bed a 'school', his board a 'shrift', would be a hazardous enough policy were he a weak-kneed or most stolid fellow, neither of which Othello has shown himself to be. And since the particular issue is Cassio's reinstatement, about which Desdemona assures Cassio that 'My Lord shall never rest./ I'll watch him tame and talk him out of patience . . ./ I'll intermingle everything he does/ With Cassio's suit', we hardly share her confidence that a man who (like Montano) scorns any soldier who is 'partially affined or leagued in office' can be so simply out-tongued in the matter. Thus, when Iago and Othello appear, and Cassio ducks off nervously, the exchanges between Desdemona and her husband not only begin to rouse his disquiet but (in another way) begin to increase ours as well.

Judged, as we are prompted to judge it, by the standards of soldiership Othello demanded and himself acted on in dismissing Cassio from office, Cassio's (Iago-prompted) request to Desdemona to plead on his behalf is indiscreet, to say the least, just as her actual intervention is not wholly proper however worthy and generous her motives. Moreover, in discussing the matter with Othello, she adopts a rather femininely wheedling sort of approach, as A. L. French points out.[1] It is this that seems most to unsettle him during and after their conversation. As with everything else in this scene, our attention is held less by what she (or later, Iago) actually says or implies or does, than by the evident effects of it on Othello himself, the way he reacts. In so far as Desdemona needles and pesters him, interfering in what is first and last a professional matter, he withstands her, resolutely refusing to give an inch. He seeks refuge by temporizing, rather than pointing out the hard fact that it is none of her business. To many critics, Desdemona's behaviour here seems winsome, full of feminine charm, and Othello merely stubborn, even boorish, in refusing to comply with her sweetly expressed wishes.[2] The implications of such a view seem to me quite dismaying – partly because of the assumption that women (being so frail) have a perfect right to nag and meddle in their husband's affairs, while the husbands have a marital duty to succumb to such arts of persuasion; and partly because those who assume this (even without realizing their cynicism) are virtually accepting the hair-raising possibility that, for instance, 'our General's wife *is* now the General'. However venial a 'trespass' Desdemona's may be judged, there is no indication in the play either that Othello is happy to let his wife be the General or that Shakespeare wants us to consider wrong his refusal to do so.

Over and above interfering in a professional matter,

[1] *Shakespeare and the Critics* (Cambridge, 1972), pp. 95–100.
[2] Mason, *Shakespeare's Tragedies of Love*, p. 101, is a recent example.

however, Desdemona attempts something worse. She tries to turn the professional issue into a personal one. Most disturbing of all – to Othello, as well as to us looking on – the personal string she tries to pull is not the obvious one of Cassio's love for Othello (though she exploits that too); she converts the issue of Cassio's dismissal into a little matrimonial power-struggle – a test of Othello's love for *her*. 'If I have any grace or power to move you . . .', she begins; and then, having won or rather wrung from him a partial victory, she persists in teasing and trying to manoeuvre him:

OTHELLO   Prithee, no more: let him come when he will;
               I will deny thee nothing.
DESDEMONA   Why, this is not a boon:
               'Tis as I should entreat you . . .
               . . . to do a peculiar profit
               To your own person. Nay, when I have a suit
               Wherein I mean to touch your love indeed
               It shall be full of poise and difficult weight,
               And fearful to be granted.
OTHELLO   I will deny thee nothing.
               Whereon, I do beseech thee, grant me this:
               To leave me but a little to myself.
                                    (III, iii, 75–85)

Those last lines clearly reveal Othello's (understandable) sense of being badgered, yet his tone is neither curt nor aggressive. Rather, I think, he seems to be trying to avoid a real confrontation with her. It is obvious he feels bewildered at finding that his formerly free condition of soldiership has been suddenly put into an unforeseen kind of circumscription and confine. The Desdemona who had always seemed quite compliant has suddenly thrown down a gauntlet, has become a more formidable force to be reckoned with than he had evidently expected her to be, demanding a hearing for herself on a matter that had naturally seemed to him to have nothing to do with their marriage at all. His reply to her here seems to me much more like a plea than a reprimand. As well as asking for some time to himself, his phrase implicitly appeals to her to leave him a little freedom for himself – a little of himself – an area of professional discretion in which he may decide and act as *he* sees fit. It is precisely this that Desdemona has in fact denied him, though she claims both that she leaves him all the power to act freely and that she is merely subject to his whim. More crucially, she has challenged his power to deny her, and disarmed him by raising the spectre of her power to deny *him* ('I wonder in my soul/ What you would ask me that I should deny,/ Or stand so mammering on?'), and raised it by vague, teasing threats ('By'r Lady, I could do much'; '. . . fearful to be granted'). She even – in phrases whose unintentional ambiguities later prove grotesquely ironic – adds further pressure by mentioning that 'so many a time' when she had 'spoken of you dispraisingly', Michael Cassio 'that came a-wooing with you' 'hath ta'en your part'. Her parting shot, still teasing but sharp-pointed none the less, is to assert her power over him by ostentatiously obeying him, mastering him by claiming that she only serves. Wilfully, she 'submits' to a will that has in fact been forced to yield her a *carte blanche* ('I will deny thee nothing'), but which she still implies is capricious, even childish, less yielding than her own:

DESDEMONA Shall I deny you? No; farewell, my lord.
     . . .

     Emilia, come. Be as your fancies teach you.
     Whate'er you be, I am obedient.[1]   (III, iii, 86–9)

As it turns out, 'be as your fancies teach you' is later revealed as a frightful, because quite unwitting, prognostication of what happens in this same scene, when Othello – largely because of a mistaken view of her motives – comes

[1] Her pert echoing of his own phrase in 'Shall I deny you?' ominously foreshadows Iago's tactic of echoing him later in the scene.

139

indeed to be what his horrible fancies teach him, and, ultimately, Desdemona's shocked and bewildered response quite literally crumples into 'Whate'er you be, I am obedient.' As she actually speaks these words, however, we cannot see their future bearing and ironic truth any more than she can. They strike us, as they strike Othello, simply as her last little covert turn of the screw.

It would be a mistake to exaggerate Desdemona's 'error' here, since it is so clearly an error of judgment rather than of feeling, and one based on her own confidence in Othello's trust and goodwill. In her immediately preceding speech with Cassio she is wholly sure that loving ensures generosity, almost apart from *being* loved. She assumes, that is, that love assures prompt alacrity in giving (cf. Emilia's attitude here too), and her own love is clearly as generous as her motives. Although Othello's view of her motives has already been slightly disturbed by Iago's carefully timed suggestion that Cassio appears to have sneaked away, 'guilty-like,/ Seeing you coming', this whole exchange is important not so much because it reveals Desdemona's capacity to engage in emotional skirmishes, but because it reveals Othello's *in*capacity to do so with any ease of mind. Sharp little splinters of feeling perforate the apparently smooth, jocular surface of their dialogue. Where Desdemona goes off unperturbed, Othello is obviously left feeling rather on edge, even if only unconsciously. Superficially relaxed, even perhaps a little amused by her surprising show of spirit ('Excellent wretch!'), he is yet disturbed enough for darker possibilities to flit across his mind:

> Excellent wretch! Perdition catch my soul
> But I do love thee! And when I love thee not,
> Chaos is come again.   (III, iii, 90–2)

That remark has been made much of, and has often been misunderstood. As it actually comes in its context, it is surely not a black prediction, but the very reverse of that.

The first part – up to 'love thee!' – is surely spoken in a tone of warmly outgoing affection, and with a smile in his eyes. Then there is a tiny pause, and the next sentence ('And when . . .') comes with a quieter sobriety and seriousness: it expresses a fleeting yet sharp recognition of what his love for her holds at bay – a slightly troubled and rather fearful recognition, that is, of how she means everything to him now, giving his whole life (his whole self) purpose, cohesion and order, whereas her absence from his heart would mean the disintegration of everything. It is as if, slightly disquieted by their conversation, he is reassuring himself that all is well, yet expressing his confidence, characteristically, in words that betray (to us) his capacity to be shaken to the core. His speech is not a public statement, but a kind of private musing, thinking out loud, addressed inwardly to Desdemona as 'thee', just after she has left. But of course Iago hears what he says, and makes the most of it. Nowhere previously since his marriage has Othello quite so unguardedly worn his heart upon his sleeve as he does in these strange words. Nowhere has he so nakedly expressed his *need* to love Desdemona, the sense that she has become the central rivet that secures his life, without which it would now fall apart. Yet to wear one's heart on one's sleeve (as the ever self-protective Iago had pointed out in the play's first scene) is inevitably to be vulnerable, to expose one's feelings 'for daws to peck at'. So the jack-daw Iago here promptly 'take[s] the safest occasion by the front', to do just that.

Probably few people nowadays would accept (openly, at least) Bradley's and Othello's own professed view of what follows: a man 'not easily jealous', a noble nature, holding out against Iago's villainy longer than most mortals could or would. The facts simply do not support such a view. Cassio's capitulation to Iago's persuasion in II, iii ('I'll do't, but it dislikes me') had seemed precipitate enough.

Othello's collapse here is still more sudden and complete, taking us (and even Iago) by surprise, even though so much that has happened earlier in the play has made us fearfully (and Iago eagerly) anticipate some inner danger. The Bradleyan view of this scene depends on two assumptions: that the swiftness with which a man becomes jealous is a measure of his ignobility, and, conversely, that the capacity to resist jealousy is a clear index of moral strength. I can see nothing in the play itself that endorses or depends upon such neat and simple moral equations as these. Indeed, if we attend to this scene carefully, it gives us no warrant to label Othello simply as 'jealous' and then assess his moral worth according to his capacity or incapacity to hold out against Iago's insinuations. The drama cuts much deeper than that. From the beginning, the scene presses us to attend not only to the shifting current of Othello's feelings, but also to the reasons or 'causes' why he comes to feel in this way: causes that take us far beyond the point at which Othello's behaviour and experience can be adequately pigeon-holed in black-and-white moral terms of 'vice' and 'virtue'.

Moreover, the same also applies to the usual alternatives to the Bradleyan view. Where Bradley stresses Othello's virtue and the slowness of his collapse in this scene, critics such as Leavis – no less moralistic though more sophisticated – stress the swiftness of Othello's fall, and attribute this to vicious egotism. This view – at least, the emphasis on speed – is certainly truer to the dramatic facts than Bradley's, I think; but once again, the moral preconceptions oversimplify and distort what the drama actually gives us. Up to a point, it is indeed plain, as Leavis says, that 'what we should see in Iago's prompt success is not so much Iago's diabolic intellect as Othello's readiness to respond . . .; the essential traitor is within the gates'; and again, 'Othello yields with extraordinary promptness to suggestion . . . [it is plain that] the mind that undoes him is not Iago's but his own'.[1] That way of putting it quite aptly recalls, I think, Othello's own remark earlier when faced with Brabantio's hostile officers: 'Were it my cue to fight, I should have known it/ Without a prompter.' In the crisis-scene Iago is no more than a prompter who provides the cues, and Othello does the rest. As with Cassio, Iago's prompting is necessary to what eventuates, but Iago would have been ineffectual without his victim's proclivity to *take* the particular 'cues' he offers. Like the witches' solicitings in *Macbeth*, Iago's hints and suggestions embody a possibility, an idea of evil, which becomes real only in as much as the hero comes to envisage, then articulate, and finally embrace and act upon it. Like the witches' solicitings, Iago's serve as a catalyst, rather than a sufficient as well as a necessary cause. By the end of the scene we see (as we see in *Macbeth*) that the hero's inflamed imagination replaces Iago as a prompter. From here on, Othello gives as well as takes all the 'cues' himself.

It is of central importance, therefore, that we attend to the play's own 'cues', to the reasons it suggests as to why Othello is so inflammable, why Iago can so easily ignite and fan such an uncontrollable blaze of naked feeling. And the reasons are not only deeper than such terms as 'egotism' or 'self-pride' imply, but because of that, they are crucial to our whole sense of the play as a tragedy. Where Bradley's confused sense of the tragedy prompts him to see Othello as forcibly pushed or dragged into jealousy against his will,

---

[1]"Diabolic Intellect and the Noble Hero', pp. 140–1; 144. Numerous variations and extrapolations of this view – 'the essential traitor is within the gates' – have been advanced (and attacked) since Leavis wrote. J. I. M. Stewart's in *Character and Motive in Shakespeare* (London, 1965 [1949]), pp. 79–110, is a well-known early example; Robert Rogers' 'Endopsychic Drama in *Othello*', *Shakespeare Quarterly*, 20 (1969), pp. 205–15, is a representative recent example of a (dubiously helpful) psychoanalytic version of the argument. Barbara Everett's 'Reflections on the Sentimentalist's *Othello*', *Critical Quarterly*, 3 (1961), pp. 127–39, offers a penetrating and suggestive critique of Leavis's position.

Leavis and many other critics effectively dissolve the tragedy into a nasty tale of brutal egotism by supposing Othello merely plunges into jealousy quite of his own accord. Yet whether such critics say so explicitly or not, they apparently believe (as their contemptuous tone makes clear) that in so far as Othello shows himself ready to believe Iago's insinuations about Desdemona, it must be because in some sense or other he is vile enough to *want* to. Beneath a thin veneer of nobility, Othello – so it is said or implied – is no more than a vicious, self-loving egotist. If that were so, one wonders whether (and for what reasons) anyone would be drawn back to a play that merely exposed its hero as a brute and a blackguard – not to mention other questions, such as whether we are to consider Desdemona a culpable idiot, a foolish romantic, a mere unfortunate, or something else, for having chosen to marry a man so obviously incapable of loving anyone but himself. But to have attended to everything before this scene as well as to everything in it is to find the issues at stake no more simple than in the tragedies to which *Othello* visibly points forward – *King Lear*, for example, and *Macbeth*.

In one way, the moralistic mistake is understandable. From the beginning, as I have suggested, the drama has been concerned, *inter alia*, with the grounds on which people accept what they are told, and the ways their judgment is affected (even, in some cases, effected) by what they feel. Again and again, it shows that the basic reason why some people believe what they do is simply their desire to believe it or their hope that it is true. Roderigo's capacity to be gulled obviously depends on his own desires and hopes; Brabantio's conviction that Desdemona must have been coerced was likewise a kind of wishful thinking; later on (as we shall see) even Emilia and Desdemona show similar tendencies.

As we ponder Iago's alluring strategy in III, iii, we might even be struck by some odd similarities between his tactics and Othello's own courtship of Desdemona, as he described it in Act I. We may recall, for instance, how Othello described how 'it was my hint to speak' of extraordinary events and contingencies, and the way he would tantalize her by dropping vivid alluring snippets of information about his past life as a soldier. He notes that 'this to hear/ Would Desdemona seriously incline', and responding to her 'hint to speak', Othello's prompting led her, he says, to

> . . . come again, and with a greedy ear
> Devour up my discourse; which I observing
> Took once a pliant hour, and found good means
> To draw from her a prayer of earnest heart
> That I would all my pilgrimage dilate
> Whereof by parcels she had something heard.
>
> (I, iii, 148–53)

For all the crucial differences in spirit (which I shall return to in a moment) Iago's tactics are not wholly unlike Othello's wooing: he observes Othello's disposition and, taking a pliant hour, finds good means to deliver 'by parcels' information that Othello devours with a greedy ear and then demands that Iago 'dilate' his story fully. There are other aspects of Othello's courtship that are strikingly apposite as well: 'She swore . . . 'twas pitiful'; she wished she had not heard it, yet she wished . . .'; 'she thanked me'; and so on. As Desdemona was then, so Othello in III, iii is 'half the wooer'.

One would underestimate Shakespeare's art if one supposed that such similarities were accidental (though no one, to my knowledge, has commented on them). But although they may seem to suggest that Othello believes Iago's insinuations because, once offended, he wants to think the worst of Desdemona, the vast differences between the two courtships make us see the second as a visible travesty of the first. The most obvious difference lies in the motivating feelings involved in each, so clearly manifest in the speakers' tones of voice (Othello's and Desdemona's in Act I, Iago's and Othello's in III, iii). Where Othello (like any sensible lover) observed and encouraged Desdemona's readiness to respond to him, and responded in turn to her awakening love and desire to hear all he told her, Iago observes and (like any sensible hater) exploits a readiness in Othello to respond from *fear* of hearing such things as Iago says or implies. This difference is crucial: not to see it is to mistake the source and nature of the tragedy. And for this reason it seems to me high time we gave III, iii a less question-begging name, such as the 'crisis-scene'. Certainly I think we should stop calling it the 'temptation-scene', a phrase whose strongly Edenic suggestions – of being tempted towards and deliberately choosing something forbidden and desired – make it an extremely misleading way to describe what the play shows as Othello's absolute *un*desire, his precipitate involuntary leap from dread to belief.

This kind of leap always fascinated Shakespeare. Indeed, his major exploration of various forms of it in *Hamlet, Othello* and *Macbeth* had their beginnings long before. As far back as *Venus and Adonis* for example (which foreshadows *Othello* in a number of quite striking ways), he had imagined Venus's 'boding heart', and the way 'fear doth teach it divination', rushing her irresistibly from 'alarm', to 'dire imagination', to panic-induced 'certainty' of Adonis's death. Both parts of *Henry IV* (to mention another fairly obvious case – almost any of the comedies might be instanced too) show his developing interest in why and how people leap to false conclusions, and in the influence and potency of 'Rumour' or false report ('Rumour is a pipe/ Blown by surmises, jealousies, conjectures'). Shakespeare's thinking in *Henry IV* and in the other history plays is quite strongly linked with what we find in *Othello*, especially his perception of the way a person's imagination can take fire from what other people hint or say or silently imply. The basic point is that made by Northumberland:

> See what a ready tongue suspicion hath!
> He that but fears the thing he would not know
> Hath by instinct knowledge from others' eyes
> That what he fear'd is chanced.
>
> *(Henry IV* Part 2, I, i, 84–7)

From its very first line – 'Tush, never tell me! I take it much unkindly . . .' – *Othello* traces the ways people react to whatever they are told, the psychic sources of their credulity and the reasons why they so often at first repudiate others' suggestions ('Tush, never tell me!') only to topple into acquiescence by either *mis*taking the point or 'tak[ing] it much unkindly'. Indeed, III, iii is by no means the first occasion in the play where Shakespeare highlights the connection between fear and credulity, the way people are often as quick to believe what they are afraid of as (at other times) they are to believe what they hope for or wish. Iago's behaviour all through the play, for instance, exhibits both propensities, and he everywhere exploits both in other people. His 'timorous accent and dire yell' at Brabantio in the first scene were calculated to achieve exactly this result. Iago had only to shout, 'Look to your house, your daughter, and your bags!', and Brabantio's heart was immediately gripped by its latent fear. Even before searching to see whether or not Desdemona has eloped, he grew alarmed: 'What is the reason of this terrible summons?' Next, he had floundered for a moment in hostile scepticism: 'What, have you lost your wits?'; then he suddenly stumbled on the truth: 'Upon malicious bravery thou dost come/ To start my quiet.' But after a few more stout attempts to resist – 'Thou art a villain' – his assurance was soon swamped by misgivings, then doubts, then a panic-stricken need for support: 'Call up my people!' Significantly, he had added:

> This accident is not unlike my dream:
> Belief of it oppresses me already. (I, i, 143-4)

What Brabantio meant was not necessarily an actual dream he had had just then, but a (perhaps only half-conscious) anxious fantasy in the past that Desdemona would one day abandon him. And thus, because of his lurking fear, a conviction that she has probably gone was seizing his heart and oppressing him with 'belief' even before he could know if it was so. And so it was.

A similar case, we may recall, arose in the Senate-scene, in the discussion about the Turks (I, iii, 1–40). Here again, Shakespeare discloses how fears can father thoughts quite as virilely as wishes can. In the Senators' discussion, feelings move from scepticism to fearful alarm to belief. It is true, of course, that there are some important differences between the manner in which the Senators reach their conclusion, and Brabantio's: they conduct a rational inquiry into the possible grounds for alarm, so the alarm is thereby judged (not merely felt) to be justified. Yet this scrutiny of the threatening reports actually makes it all the more significant that the Duke should nevertheless finally express his alarm in terms so tellingly similar to Brabantio's.

> Nay, it is possible enough to judgement:
> I do not so secure me in the error,
> But the main article I do approve
> In fearful sense. (I, iii, 9-12)

The crisis-scene (III, iii) now presents just such a movement from fearful alarm to belief, though one greatly extended and magnified. For what Iago does (it is all he needs to do) is to thrust at Othello, make him actively envisage, the very possibilities of 'discord' and 'loss' that Othello has already shown himself to be strangely haunted by at times (as in II, i, for example) – the possibilities of 'perdition' and chaos that, coinciding with Iago's onslaught, Desdemona's first teasing threats – 'Shall I deny thee?' – have dimly stirred again and caused to flicker into momentary consciousness. As in Brabantio's and the Duke's cases (though significantly with an even briefer moment of initial scepticism), Iago no sooner alleges what Othello dimly dreads than Othello, despite all his claims that 'I'll see before I doubt', is oppressed by belief of it, not 'securing himself' in the apparent unlikelihood of its truth (given Desdemona's nature) but instantly 'approving' the 'main article' in 'fearful sense'. (The process is succinctly summed up in a later phrase of Desdemona's in the final scene: '*My fear interprets*'.) As the scene proceeds, Othello increasingly becomes – eventually quite literally – prone to fear. His apprehensiveness grows more and more as his alarmed imagination skids uncontrollably from what is 'possible', to 'probable', to 'palpable', until his apprehending mind takes hold of its own fantasies in the conviction that they are 'probal' facts.[1] Whereas both Roderigo and Cassio had each rejected as wholly absurd the aspersions Iago had tried to cast on Desdemona's chastity (and significantly this is the one point on which he is flatly disbelieved by both men, as he is by Emilia too in the final scene), Othello's insecurity is such that he swallows whole, at one gulp, the bait laid on purpose to make him mad. Thus, in some sense, the mind that 'undoes' Othello is, as Leavis says, not Iago's but his own. But this is only part of all that the scene makes us realize. Another part, no less crucial, comprises the dramatically rendered *process* of that 'undoing', the frightful 'how' and therefore the 'why' of Othello's shipwreck: a process that forces us, I think, to reject as distorting any

[1]Thus: 'it is possible enough to judgement' (I, iii, 9); ''Tis probable, and palpable to thinking' (I, ii, 76); 'Judge me the world, if 'tis not gross in sense' (I, ii, 72); ''tis apt and of great credit' (II, i, 278); 'probal to thinking' (II, iii, 328) – and so on. The early scenes of the play continually draw our attention to the dynamics of 'believing' and the grounds on which people draw (or jump to) their 'conclusions'.

account of Othello's state of mind put in such terms as 'angry egotism', 'self-pride', 'ferocious stupidity', and so on.

The initial steps in Othello's collapse in this scene are clear enough. Iago simply exploits Othello's predisposition, which he has noticed (as we have) to be rather anxious, insecure, in matters of personal feeling. Finding the going quite easy, Iago slithers, serpentine, from calling his nebulous allegations 'guesses', to calling them 'conjectures', then 'observances'. Verbally, he shadows forth the dark contours of a possibility, which Othello no sooner glimpses than (as Iago elsewhere says of 'lust') his fear 'conduct[s him] to most preposterous conclusions'.

The crucial little shifts and slides are rendered in vivid and exact detail, which we watch in helpless fascination. At first, we notice, Iago claims that love and duty force him to 'withhold' what he 'thinks': 'Though I am bound to every act of duty,/ I am not bound to all that slaves are free to:/ Utter my thoughts'. When (as he gleefully anticipated) Othello protests that such reticence 'conspires against thy friend', Iago promptly conspires against his 'friend' still further by claiming that 'love and duty' force him frankly to *disclose* what he 'fears' (and no less than Othello are we arrested by that change from 'think' to 'fear'): 'Therefore, as I am bound,/ Receive it from me. I speak not yet of proof./ Look to your wife.' Of course the mere mention of 'proof' suggests (as it is designed to) that 'proof' is to be had. Iago need only 'confide' his 'obscure prologue' to specific allegation, and Othello's nature supplies the exact definition and mentally solidifies it into 'fact'. In other words (which Iago uses in another, related context – II, i, 249ff.), when these flaunted 'mutualities' between two men 'so marshal the way', Othello's proclivity to dread is such that 'hard at hand comes the master and main exercise, th'incorporate conclusion'. Othello swiftly concludes that Desdemona and Cassio must in fact have already come to their sexually 'incorporate conclusion', exactly as Iago so vaguely but terribly hints.

Little else need be said of Iago in this scene; more and more our minds are concentrated in shock on Othello's shocked responses, his panic at the implications of Iago's provocative mimicry:

> OTHELLO What dost thou think?
> IAGO　　 Think, my lord?
> OTHELLO Think, my lord! By heaven, he echoes me,
> 　　　　　As if there were some monster in his thought
> 　　　　　Too hideous to be shown.[1]　　　(III, iii, 103–7)

He is devastated less by Iago's words than by his manner and his *silences*, the preposterous vagueness of his initial hints:

> Nay, yet there's more in this.
> I prithee speak to me as to thy thinkings,
> As thou dost ruminate, and give thy worst of thoughts
> The worst of words.　　　(III, iii, 129–32)

Listening to this we may well be reminded of the terms in which Hamlet questions the Ghost as to why it comes

> Making night hideous, and we fools of nature
> So horridly to shake our disposition
> With thoughts beyond the reaches of our souls?
> 　　　　　　　　　　　(*Hamlet*, I, iv, 54–6)
> Speak; I am bound to hear.　　　(I, v, 6)

It is not long before Othello's need to know the worst becomes as urgent as Hamlet's: 'O, answer me!/ Let me not burst in ignorance, but tell . . .' (I, iv, 45–6). And just as the Ghost who beckoned Hamlet and shook his dispo-

---

[1]On the importance of words such as 'think', 'thought' and 'know' in the play see Paul A. Jorgensen, ' "Perplex'd in the extreme": The Role of Thought in *Othello*', *Shakespeare Quarterly*, 15 (1964), pp. 265–75. Philip C. McGuire's '*Othello* as an "Assay of Reason" ', *Shakespeare Quarterly*, 24 (1973), pp .198–209, also discusses 'the act of knowing and judging' in the play.

sition remarks 'I find thee apt', so Iago finds Othello 'apt', but of course refrains from saying so. It is clear already that Othello's 'disposition' is horridly shaken by thoughts not beyond but within the reach of his frightened soul – thoughts that maim his wits and bring him so preposterously to err. And for us, rather like Messala near the end of *Julius Caesar* ('O, hateful error, melancholy's child,/ Why dost thou show to the apt thoughts of men/ The things that are not?'), the question we keep coming back to is, 'why?' In what terms does Shakespeare prompt us to understand what is happening here?

In describing to the Senate his wooing of Desdemona, Othello had spoken of how she had promised to make him 'dilate' his story. The same word, now in the sense that connects it with pauses, had come up again in Iago's remarks to Roderigo just before the crisis-scene, that 'wit depends on dilatory time'. Iago's wit now depends on 'dilatory' time in a different sense. Significantly the word recurs again here, when Othello says in trepidation that carefully weighed pauses and 'stops' like Iago's must be 'close dilations, working from the heart,/ That passion cannot rule'. The 'dilations' *we* witness, however, are chiefly Othello's own, working from a heart that the passion of fear rules only too tyrannically. Once Iago feigns anxiety so as to arouse it in Othello, he then simply leaves dilatory time for Othello's own imagination to 'dilate' nothings to fearful somethings and thence to terrible 'certainties'. Othello's own 'blown surmises', fostered by fear, not only 'match' but far outstrip Iago's 'inferences'.[1]

---

[1] The terms of Theseus' famous speech near the end of *A Midsummer Night's Dream* are obviously pertinent to the nightmare 'tricks' of Othello's strong imagination, with its 'shaping fantasies, that apprehend/ More than cool reason ever comprehends'. Prompted by Iago and its own fear, it 'bodies forth/ The forms of things unknown', 'turns them to shapes, and gives to airy nothing/ A local habitation and a name' (v, i, 4–22). Shakespeare could see quite clearly that the creative powers of 'imagination' are matched by its destructive ones.

The words 'fear' and 'affright' recur continually through-out this scene, as Othello's capacity for dread begins to grow.

OTHELLO   If thou dost love me,
              Show me thy [horrible] thought.
IAGO   My lord, you know I love you.
OTHELLO   I think thou dost:
              . . .

              Therefore these stops of thine affright me more.
                                        (III, iii, 114–19)

Least of all (as Iago sees) can Othello bear ignorance, uncertainty – the weight of a possibly infinite fear. As we had glimpsed in II, i (183ff.), the 'unknown' terrifies him. So of course it is just this spectre that Iago raises:

IAGO   O, beware, my lord, of jealousy!
              It is the green-eyed monster, which doth mock
              The meat it feeds on. That cuckold lives in bliss
              Who certain of his fate loves not his wronger,
              But O, what damnèd minutes tells he o'er,
              Who dotes yet doubts, suspects yet fondly loves!
OTHELLO O misery!   (III, iii, 163–9)

This appalled whisper seems to me appalled precisely because (*pace* Kenneth Muir, for instance), far from missing the personal application of Iago's carefully general remarks, Othello is only too well convinced that it is he who has 'good cause' to 'doubt' and 'suspect' he is a cuckold.[1] Indeed, so potent are his doubt and suspicion that he quickly begins to grow 'certain of his fate'. This is why Iago can thrust still closer to his heart, in a speech that again recalls (to us at least, and perhaps to Iago too) Othello's

[1] Cf. Muir's comment in his New Penguin edition, p. 202: 'Othello is not referring to himself.' I think the shock and misery in these two words shock *us* just because they make us see that for Othello (in Donne's words from 'A Lecture upon the Shadow'),
              Love is a growing, or full constant light;
              And his first minute, after noone, is night.

own words in II, i, about his 'fear' that 'unknown fate' will make him poorer than the richly absolute 'content' and 'comfort' of the present:

IAGO Poor and content is rich, and rich enough;
    But riches fineless is as poor as winter,
    To him that ever fears he shall be poor.
    Good God, the souls of all my tribe defend
    From jealousy!   (III, iii, 170–4)

It is immediately plain how little Othello's heart can absorb such shocking suggestions. Flustered, he denies their applicability to himself, defensively clings to his multiple negatives; yet the positive account of himself he tries to elicit out of all his exclamatory denials – the self-confident, judicious and decisive man he is in other matters – sounds more and more shaky:

  Why, why is this?
 Think'st thou I'd make a life of jealousy,
 To follow still the changes of the moon
 With fresh suspicions? No, to be once in doubt
 Is once to be resolved. Exchange me for a goat,
 When I shall turn the business of my soul
 To such exsufflicate and blown surmises,
 Matching thy inference. 'Tis not to make me jealous
 To say my wife is fair, loves company,
 Is free of speech, sings, plays, and dances well:
 Where virtue is, these are more virtuous.
 Nor from mine own weak merits will I draw
 The smallest fear or doubt of her revolt,
 For she had eyes and chose me. No, Iago,
 I'll see before I doubt; when I doubt, prove;
 And on the proof, there is no more but this:
 Away at once with love or jealousy! (III, iii, 174–90)

Once again, although the speech is ostensibly addressed to Iago, Othello's mind seems turned inward, and by the end his words are a kind of semi-soliloquy, self-communing.

And as we (along with Iago) observe, he protests too much.[1]

It is not long before we realize the weight of all the ironies of this speech – ironies we feel all the heavier because Othello naturally does not feel them at all. As Iago proceeds, in the way any reasonably adept anxiety-monger would ('I am much to blame . . . For too much loving you'), he elicits yet another unwittingly ironic reply from Othello: 'I am bound to thee for ever.' It is Iago's cue to pretend 'fear' and 'concern' in himself, to push Othello consciously to pretend he is less upset and less concerned than he knows he is, and thereby make him that much less self-confident.

IAGO   I see this hath a little dashed your spirits.
OTHELLO Not a jot, not a jot.
IAGO   In faith, I fear it has.
          . . .
          I do see you're moved.
          I am to pray you, not to strain my speech
          To grosser issues, nor to larger reach
          Than to suspicion.   (III, iii, 212–18)

Since Iago's aim is of course precisely to entice Othello to strain his speech to grosser issues, he does so by pretending to retract, thereby forcing Othello to advance:

IAGO   But, pardon me, I do not in position
          Distinctly speak of her, though I may fear
          Her will, recoiling to her better judgement,
          May fall to match you with her country forms,
          And happily repent.   (III, iii, 232–6)

It is the same sort of tactic the Turks had used in order to confuse their enemies. Like them, Iago pretends to withdraw, then 'restem[s]' his 'backward course'.[2] He even

---

[1] Cf. for example the deeply shaken tone of Othello's 'I'll see before I doubt', with Horatio's far calmer speech (*after* he has actually 'seen'): 'Before my God, I might not this believe/ Without the sensible and true avouch/ Of mine own eyes' (*Hamlet*, I, i, 56–8).

[2] Alvin Kernan also remarks on this similarity in his suggestive (if self-admittedly over-schematic) introduction to the Signet *Othello* (New York, Toronto and London, 1963), p. xxxii.

pretends physically to withdraw, allowing time only for his 'friend' to recognize how much is still unknown but to be feared: 'Why did I marry? This honest creature doubtless/ Sees and knows more, much more than he unfolds.' By now Othello's heart (as he said of others' hearts in the brawl-scene) is 'brimful of fear'. And like the dreadful clanging alarm-bell in that same scene, Iago 'frights' Othello from his 'propriety' (II, iii, 169–70, 208). Everything he does and says aims further to excite Othello's alarm and certainty by insisting that nothing is certain: 'I would I might entreat your honour/ To scan this thing no farther. Leave it to time.' For a frightened man, 'time' is always 'dilatory time'; so of course nothing faster excites Othello's belief that he has 'worthy cause' to fear Iago's 'fears' are justified:

IAGO   In the meantime,
    Let me be thought too busy in my fears,
    As worthy cause I have to fear I am,
    And hold her free, I do beseech your honour.
             (III, iii, 250–3)

Othello's assertion here that fear is not necessary is precisely what confirms *our* fear: 'Fear not my government', he says – meaning, fear not my lack of government. Yet that lack is exactly what his immediately following soliloquy (III, iii, 255ff.) reveals to us with appalling vividness. This speech marks the most critical development in the scene so far: alone, in a state of violent inner turmoil, Othello's imagination dives from one panicky thought to the next, until his nerve snaps altogether.

The reasons for his collapse are clearly suggested in the process by which it happens – but here, once again, we come up against the inadequacies of the standard views of the play, especially the Leavisian. One of Leavis's particular statements expresses a judgment common to virtually all anti-Othello critics:

It is plain, then, that [Othello's] love is composed very largely of ignorance of self as well as ignorance of her . . . It may be love, but it can be only in an oddly qualified sense love of her: it must be much more a matter of self-centred and self-regarding satisfactions – pride, sensual possessiveness, appetite, love of loving – than he suspects.

This comes out unmistakably when he begins to let himself go; for instance, in the soliloquy that follows Iago's exit . . .[1]

There are several things to question in this, I think. One is the assumption that 'love' must necessarily express itself in 'positive', wholly benign feelings, and that violent revulsion, vindictiveness, destructive curses, crude self-pity, and all such negative feelings, must indicate a *lack* of real 'love'. Anyone who tried to come to terms with, say, *King Lear* on this assumption would find it hard to explain why Lear can truly be called a tragic hero rather than a chronically wilful, unloving, vicious egotist. The problem there is usually 'solved' by claiming that Lear 'learns through suffering' to become a truly loving father who thus merits Cordelia's love and forgiveness – a view of the play that manages only to turn it into something much more like a cosy moral fable than a tragedy whose greatness lies in its power to make us radically re-think and re-feel our usual comforting assumptions about human 'needs' – in particular the needs to love and be loved. Just because the tragedy of *Othello* resembles and points forward to *Lear* in precisely this kind of power, I think the Leavisian view of it needs to be challenged at its foundation. Its basic assumption, that 'real' love must be a matter only of 'positive' feelings, does not seem to me one that the play, *Othello*, simply endorses. On the contrary, it explores it, deeply and daringly. It shakes the ground beneath that very assumption in us – or rather, that hope and expectation in us – by showing

[1]'Diabolic Intellect and the Noble Hero', p. 145. Cf. John Holloway, *The Story of the Night* (London, 1961), pp. 155–65, who criticizes Leavis's argument on grounds rather different from mine.

just such hope and expectation in both Othello and Desdemona tragically shaking their love and splintering their
lives.

To put my point another way, I believe the assumption
Leavis makes in the passage I have quoted is important
because it is made by all the chief characters in the play. It
is gradually revealed – to us, that is – as both profoundly
natural, because based on a natural human need of comfort
and security, and yet also false, sometimes tragically false,
to actual human experience of love. In fact, one of the
central concerns of the play is the power of quite genuine
and profound love to release destructive energies as naturally as positive ones; and the play traces that power through
the development of Othello's and Desdemona's separate
but intimately related crises, and especially in those moments when 'negative' feelings well up most potently and
uncontrollably in Othello's heart.

Othello's soliloquy just after Iago's exit (III, iii, 255ff.) is
just such a moment, and it is interesting that the flow of
Leavis's comment (above) displays a mental process not
unlike Othello's own here. The first sentence I have quoted
from Leavis, 'It is plain, then . . .', presents the general
conclusion that is then further explained and specified in
the sentence beginning, 'It may be love . . .'. Basically,
Leavis's argument is structured thus: 'It may be . . ., but
it can be only . . .: it must be . . . more than he suspects;
. . . it is plain, then . . .'. One need not be much of a logician
to see the holes in such an argument. Yet the speech of
Othello's then cited in evidence ('This comes out unmistakably . . . in the soliloquy that follows Iago's exit') is one
whose very point in the drama is surely to reveal the terrible
speciousness of Othello's logic as he contemplates Iago's
'evidence' of *Desdemona's* supposed lack of love. In effect,
he makes the same slide from 'it may be . . .', to 'it can be
only . . .', to 'it must be . . . more than [I] suspect . . .',
'it is plain':

This fellow's of exceeding honesty,
And knows all qualities with a learnèd spirit
Of human dealings. If I do prove her haggard,
Though that her jesses were my dear heart-strings,
I'd whistle her off, and let her down the wind
To prey at fortune. Haply, for I am black
And have not those soft parts of conversation
That chamberers have; or for I am declined
Into the vale of years – yet that's not much –
She's gone: I am abused, and my relief
Must be to loathe her. O, curse of marriage!
That we can call these delicate creatures ours
And not their appetites! I had rather be a toad
And live upon the vapour of a dungeon
Than keep a corner in the thing I love
For others' uses. Yet 'tis the plague of great ones . . .

(III, iii, 255–70)

On any count, this is very ugly indeed. For that very
reason, of course, it prompts us to stand off from it, to
distance ourselves from such hideous feelings by rejecting
them with moral censure and indignation. Yet moral indignation is no substitute for moral imagination; and it is
the latter more than the former that Shakespeare challenges
in us here. Since Othello's words reveal to us not only his
emotional conclusions, but also what brings him to them,
we are enabled to grasp why his mind finds and plunges
into that vile image of himself as a toad in a dank dungeon,
and why he is driven to imagine that that sort of existence
would be preferable to his present (supposed) predicament.
To see *that* is to find our impulse to condemn him qualified
by other feelings – feelings that contribute to and yet
painfully complicate our recognition that these rampant
fantasies virtually preclude any chance of Desdemona's
ever disproving or dispelling them.

In several significant ways the process of Othello's mind
here resembles, indeed echoes, that of Brabantio in the
play's opening scene. Once convinced of injury, Othello

instantly reaches for the nearest form of 'relief' and
exorcism:

> She's gone: I am abused, and my relief
> Must be to loathe her. O, curse of marriage!
> . . .
> Yet 'tis the plague of great ones . . .

Brabantio's response had been very similar, if rather less
sudden:

> Gone she is,
> And what's to come of my despisèd time
> Is naught but bitterness.
> . . .
> Who would be a father? –
> . . .
> O treason of the blood!
> Fathers, from hence trust not your daughters' minds
> By what you see them act.
> . . .
> Get weapons, ho! (I, i, 161ff.)

Othello's imagination seeks relief in subjunctives ('though
that her jesses were my dear heart-strings'), asserting his
power to hurt Desdemona every bit as violently as she
seems to have hurt him. Just so had Brabantio tried to
relieve the pain of Desdemona's rejection by imagining a
matching, hypothetical violence of his own – violence that
might cancel the emotional hurt he now has to suffer
helplessly:

> For your sake, jewel,
> I am glad at soul I have no other child,
> For thy escape would teach me tyranny
> To hang clogs on them. (I, iii, 193–6)

The imagined 'tyranny' betrays Brabantio's need to deny
what her rejection has forced him to realize about love:
that since it must be freely given, one can never securely

imprison and 'fetter' it or insure oneself against its 'escape'. Trying to deny this fact, Brabantio asserts his power to '*bind*' a child to him by force; Othello, for just the same reasons, violently asserts his power to *un*fetter, *un*bind, 'sever' the 'strings' that tie him to Desdemona, and 'let her down the wind'. Desperately, he claims the power to do to her exactly what he is terrified (and now convinced) she has done to him. Once again, the brutality of the claim betrays to us the violent, disintegrating fear that she has cast him out of her heart.

But Othello's process of mind here also differs from Brabantio's in some quite crucial ways, which are equally revealing of how and why he feels as he does. The main difference emerges if we consider what seems at first a similarity between the two men's reactions to feeling cast off. To Brabantio's mind, we remember, it was 'impossible' that Desdemona should have married Othello voluntarily. That would be 'unnatural': 'For nature so preposterously to err . . ./ Sans witchcraft could not'; 'perfection' could not so 'err against all use of nature' unless under some spell. Just before Iago leaves Othello in III, iii, he reminds him of Brabantio's view: Desdemona, he says, 'did deceive her father, marrying you . . ./ She that so young could give out such a seeming,/ To seal her father's eyes up close as oak –/ He thought 'twas witchcraft'. As this begins to sink into Othello's mind, he (Othello) muses, 'I do not think but Desdemona's honest . . . And yet, how nature erring from itself – '. Iago adroitly interrupts before Othello's thought can articulate itself, and he turns the issue into a general principle: that it is 'unnatural' in *any* woman not to prefer to marry one of her own countrymen. What he intends, of course, is that Othello should draw from this a very particular conclusion (the one Brabantio had self-consolingly drawn): that it would have been much more natural for Desdemona to have fallen in love with some-one else (implication: someone not black). Othello does promptly draw that conclusion; and his doing so is perhaps the most significant fact in the scene so far. It is the clearest demonstration of that capacity for personal self-doubt we have glimpsed in him from time to time, and a demonstration that it is also far stronger than we had ever foreseen or supposed.

Indeed, just before his soliloquy we might have been alerted to this fact by noticing how Iago, having put Othello in a state of total confusion and distress, can so easily and fearlessly insult him on just these grounds:

> I may fear
> Her will, recoiling to her better judgement,
> May fall to match you with her country forms,
> And happily repent.   (III, iii, 233–6)

Othello, we notice, does not protest, 'What do you mean, "recoiling *to* her *better* judgement"?' By seeming not to notice the insult he tacitly concedes Iago's implication. This is precisely what he does again here in his soliloquy. His response is the reverse of Brabantio's. Brabantio's beliefs that it would have been 'unnatural' in Desdemona to choose Othello and that she could not possibly have been 'half the wooer' sprang from his need to reassure himself that her 'escape' did not reflect any failure in him nor any demerit as a father worthy of her complete 'obedience' and loyalty. His beliefs, in short, were both self-consoling and self-excusing, prompted by and temporarily satisfying his need to think the situation was not really as bad as it seemed. Othello's creeping belief (that it would have been more 'natural' in Desdemona to prefer one of 'her country forms') is also an attempt to console himself – but by convincing himself that all painful 'maybe' and 'haplys' are 'musts': convincing himself that the whole situation is doubtless *worse* than it seems from Iago's account. The savage, punishing bitterness against Desdemona ('I'd whistle her off, and let her down the wind/ To prey at fortune') accompanies – is indeed the only way he can allow himself to articulate – a savage, bitter fear of some personal insufficiency in himself. It is the fear that some demerit or failure on his part 'must' have compromised his claim to her love, obedience and loyalty.

This is surely why he slides with such shocking speed from 'if' – 'If I do prove her haggard' – through all those highly revealing subjunctives, which take the sting out of the facts by treating them as mere hypotheses: 'Though that her jesses were my dear heart-strings, I'd . . .' Of course they *are* his heart-strings, which is precisely why he needs to sheer away from the fact and speak as though it were only a possibility. From there, in growing despair, his imagination veers to fleeting speculations about why she may have been 'haggard' until it suddenly precipitates the conviction, 'she's gone'. It seems as if he can endure the thought that Desdemona may have 'repented' of her choice of him only by collapsing into the certainty that she must have: 'She's gone.' If we remember the way Iago in his self-fortifying soliloquy in I, iii (38off.) had also slid from the rumour to the avowed belief that he has been cuckolded by Othello ('I know not if't be true/ But I, for mere suspicion in that kind,/ Will do as if for surety'), the echo makes us even more sharply aware of how little Othello's slide here from hypothesis to certainty is a deliberate 'pluming' of the will. He plummets headlong from 'suspicion' to 'surety', not because it suits him to do so, but because he is totally unable to sustain a doubt, unable to hang suspended over the chasm of 'if'.

Nor is there any great mystery about the underlying causes of that incapacity: his soliloquy clearly betrays his emotional (and by now also racial) insecurity.[1] Where

---

[1]Mainly for the reasons outlined earlier I agree with Gareth Lloyd Evans (*Shakespeare IV, 1601–1605* (Edinburgh, 1972), pp. 45–8) that Othello's race is not such a major issue in the play as many twentieth-century critics have claimed. A recent example of what Evans calls grafting 'specifically

Brabantio had asserted that Othello must be entirely to blame, Othello does not assert that Desdemona's defection must be because of *Cassio's* witchcraft or wooing-power. Significantly, the speculations prompting him to conclude that Desdemona 'must' have gone are not concerned with Cassio's attractions – in that sense, Othello (except at odd moments) is not jealous at all. He thinks rather of his own likely unattractiveness to Desdemona: 'Haply, for I am black/ And have not . . .'; 'or for I am declined/ Into the vale of years'. Although he tries to shrug off or deny such causes – 'yet that's not much' – it is actually these self-critical musings that abruptly precipitate his certainty, 'she's gone'.

It is equally significant that in his speech a little earlier (III, iii, 174ff.), where he had rather shakily denied being a doubting, shakable or indecisive man, he crowned his argument by denying something Iago had not explicitly mentioned at all:

> Nor from mine own weak merits will I draw
> The smallest fear or doubt of her revolt.

What he does in his soliloquy is draw the greatest fear of her revolt from his own feared 'weak merits'. What the soliloquy also makes clear is that (as he had claimed with unconscious irony) for him 'to be once in doubt/ Is once to be resolved'.

---

twentieth-century notions about colour' onto the play is Sanford E. Marovitz, 'Othello Unmasked: A Black Man's Conscience and a White Man's Fool', *Southern Review*, 6 (1973), pp. 108–33. Marovitz ignores the two key points, both made by Evans, that only Othello's adversaries (specifically Iago and Roderigo) associate his vices with his colour and that Othello is not a pariah but a celebrity in Venetian society. No 'racial prejudice' is held by Desdemona, Cassio, Emilia or the Duke, for instance; even Desdemona's father (as Othello publicly reminds the assembly) had formerly 'loved' and 'oft invited' Othello. Brabantio's paternal hysteria about miscegenation, aroused and exacerbated by Iago's gross shouts about how 'an old black ram/ Is tupping your white ewe', is inextricably muddled with other, non-racial issues and is certainly not the prevailing view in the Senate-scene or at any other point in the play.

From this soliloquy onwards Othello's speeches betray his complete lack of anything like 'negative capability' to cope with himself or his world, his total incapacity to 'remain content' and live with questions or half-knowledge, and, above all, his incapacity to sustain doubts about his own worthiness to be desired and loved. In the absence of 'surety', he is compelled to invent it. Thus (to borrow a phrase from one of the Sonnets), 'Incertainties now crown themselves assur'd'.[1] The drama gives us to see what Othello himself is in no condition to realize at all – that he assumes the worst so as not to have to wait in suspense, not to have to endure the terrible rack of wondering and *then* to have to suffer the devastation of learning he has indeed been 'cashiered' as he fears. He assumes his loss is total in order to insure himself against the shattering discovery of it. Rather like Edgar in *King Lear*, that is (IV, i, 1–4), he assumes the worst in order not to be reduced to it by circumstances; but of course where Edgar's psychological stratagem is deliberate, a calculated act of self-preservation, Othello's is an instinctive reflex of self-protection, so extreme that it denies all possibility of 'esperance', since any hope is for him only a ground of fear. As we realize this, we also glimpse something of how this play develops from and extends the concerns of earlier ones such as *Hamlet*: 'Haste me to know't', Hamlet says to the Ghost, 'that I with wings as swift/ As meditation or the thoughts of love,/ May sweep to my revenge' (I, v, 29–31); and the Player Queen remarks (III, ii, 165ff.) that 'as my love is siz'd, my fear is so./ Where love is great, the littlest doubts are fear;/ Where little fears grow great, great love grows there.' And we glimpse too, how *Othello* points ahead to later works such as *Cymbeline* – for example, the scene in which Imogen pleads with Iachimo:

---

[1]Sonnet 107. It is interesting how many phrases in this sonnet foreshadow the concerns and language of *Othello*.

> . . . pray you –
> Since doubting things go ill often hurts more
> Than to be sure they do; for certainties
> Either are past remedies, or, timely knowing,
> The remedy then born – discover to me
> What both you spur and stop. (I, vi, 93–8)

Shakespeare was obviously very alert to the relations between doubt and the need for 'certainty', insurance against shock and pain, as well as the relations between doubting and self-consciousness; and in Othello he presents a man whose need to assume that the worst is a fact, rather than reckoning with it as a possibility, arises from his absolute need of some firm, clear, finite sense of his identity. With that, Othello can face the world, since he at least has a clear role he can play in it. He can be, for example, the abused victim, a member of a well-known and accepted category – those unfortunate 'great ones' whose meritorious position causes rather than prevents this kind of fate. Seeing himself as 'fated' to be victimized in this way partly frees him from having to feel that Desdemona's betrayal reflects some failure in him, and allows him to suppose that probably no one could hold her interest for long. It also allows him the comfort of having something he can 'justly' *do*: he can (in Hamlet's phrase) 'sweep to my revenge'. Assuming the worst at least enables him to wrap himself up for a while in the consolations and reassurances of philosophic self-pity.[1]

> Yet 'tis the plague of great ones;
> Prerogatived are they less than the base.
> 'Tis destiny unshunnable, like death:
> Even then this forkèd plague is fated to us
> When we do quicken. Desdemona comes . . .
> (III, iii, 270–4)

---

[1] As the Second Lord puts it in *All's Well* (IV, iii, 62), 'How mightily sometimes we make us comforts of our losses!'

As always, the chief attraction of a fatalist philosophy is to free one from responsibility – and, equally, from self-appraisal, self-blame and self-contempt.

Desdemona's entrance at this point is so deeply disconcerting to Othello just because it pushes him back from his new-found 'certainty' to another 'if': 'If she be false, O, then heaven mocks itself!/ I'll not believe't.' Her manifest innocence prompts him again to hard, direct self-scrutiny: 'I am to blame.' When he complains of 'a pain upon my forehead here', he is surely not referring (as is sometimes claimed) to his cuckold's horns. He seems rather to be talking half to himself, in renewed bewilderment. The 'pain' is that of hardly knowing what to think, or how much to trust himself to her evident sense (implied in her manner and tone) that nothing has changed between them and that their bond is quite secure. Hence, of course, as G. R. Elliott remarks, 'the intensely symbolic quality of the conversation here'.[1] For one brief moment, reconciliation is perhaps possible. So we cannot miss the significance of the dialogue in which that flickering possibility of restoring their 'bond' is snuffed out, for ever, by Othello's self-mistrust:

DESDEMONA Why do you speak so faintly?
           Are you not well?
OTHELLO I have a pain upon my forehead here.
DESDEMONA Faith, that's with watching: 'twill away again.
           Let me but bind it hard, within this hour
           It will be well.
OTHELLO   Your napkin is too little.
           [*He puts the handkerchief from him,*
           and she drops it]
           Let it alone. Come, I'll go in with you.
DESDEMONA I am very sorry that you are not well.
                         (III, iii, 279–86)

Desdemona naturally assumes his pain to be physical: 'Faith, that's with watching' – and she naturally offers him

[1] *Flaming Minister* (New York, 1965 [1953]), p. 126.

comfort and sympathy. As we realize, of course, the hurt
is from 'watching' in another way altogether; and the only
'remedy' that might bind, soothe and heal the pain in his
heart and mind is her embracing love. But his lingering
fears and doubts and self-doubts are such that he rejects
the proffered napkin – a token and assurance of her love –
as inadequate, 'too little' for the full extent of his need.
(The most terrible irony is that this same 'too little' handkerchief later proves so momentous that it leads to the
destruction of them both.)

The ominous fact of his being unable to accept and be
restored to ease by the particular 'remedy' she offers is
underlined for us by Emilia's first comment when the
lovers depart:

> I am glad I have found this napkin:
> This was her first remembrance from the Moor.
> . . .
>
>   he conjured her that she should ever keep it.
> (III, iii, 287ff.)

We (unlike Emilia) can have little doubt about the motives
behind Iago's 'wooing' of her to steal this vital little token
of Othello's and Desdemona's love. The exchanges between
Emilia and Iago that follow are typical of their own relationship in more ways than we realize as yet, since our attention
is fastened on that of Othello and Desdemona, and on Iago's
gleeful confidence (in his soliloquy after he has packed
Emilia off) that he can distil from the handkerchief a
'poison' so toxic that no 'medicine' will ever cure Othello.

The poison of doubt and self-doubt indeed proves un-
'med'cinable' in Othello: his sudden reappearance at this
point leaves us in no further hope of reconciliation. He has
plunged back once more into believing the worst:

> Ha, ha, false to me!
> . . .
> Thou [Iago] hast set me on the rack.

> I swear 'tis better to be much abused,
> Than but to know't a little.
>
> IAGO   How now, my lord!
> OTHELLO   What sense had I of her stolen hours of lust?
> I saw't not, thought it not, it harmed not me.
> . . .
>
> He that is robbed, not wanting what is stolen,
> Let him not know't, and he's not robbed at all.
>
>   (III, iii, 330ff.)

To us, this marks yet another significant step in the drama. It simply never enters his mind that the reason why he 'found not Cassio's kisses on her lips' and had no sense of 'her stolen hours of lust' might be that these never existed. The point here is precisely what he tries to deny, for he does not 'know' at all. His desperation is his uncertainty; and now he oscillates in a kind of frenzy between needing to know everything and asserting that he would rather know nothing. His next speech, so self-exposing in its wail of self-pity, points to the same fundamental anguish, which he cannot endure. Nostalgia is the only opiate he can find to dull the questions of the present: hence the querulous lament he bursts out with for his glorious and (above all) secure past. Nevertheless, however nasty and self-gratifying his rhetoric is, and his elaborate pathos, there is a real *cri de coeur* in it. There is not only nastiness and self-pity to be heard, but also the savage pain which the self-pity and the savage defilement in his mind try to master by exaggerating:

> I had been happy if the general camp,
> Pioneers and all, had tasted her sweet body,
> So I had nothing known. O, now, for ever
> Farewell the tranquil mind! Farewell content!
> Farewell the plumèd troops and the big wars
> That make ambition virtue – O, farewell!
> Farewell the neighing steed, and the shrill trump,
> The spirit-stirring drum, th'ear-piercing fife,

The royal banner and all quality,
Pride, pomp and circumstance of glorious war!
And, O you mortal engines, whose rude throats
Th'immortal Jove's dread clamours counterfeit,
Farewell! Othello's occupation's gone.   (III, iii, 342–54)

This is indeed an extraordinary outburst. By now, we cannot believe for a second that crazily self-deluding assertion in the first three lines, though we can certainly see what prompts it. The iterations and the turgid rhetoric of the 'farewell' sound like a strangely magnified echo of Cassio's plaintive cry in Act II:

Reputation, reputation, reputation! O, I have lost my reputation! I have lost the immortal part of myself, and what remains is bestial. My reputation, Iago, my reputation!   (II, iii, 255–8)

The reminder is made sharper by Iago's observation (at ll. 158ff.), just before Othello's speech, that 'he that filches from me my good name/ Robs me of that which not enriches him/ And makes me poor indeed' (a remark exactly contrary to what he had said to Cassio earlier in reply to the latter's outburst about his lost reputation). Once again, the echo of a previous moment underlines the causes of Othello's acute anguish. Unlike Cassio, Othello has no real reason to assert that his occupation's gone.[1] Desdemona's supposed infidelity in no way disqualifies him or incapacitates him as a soldier in the way Cassio's dismissal disqualifies *him*. Othello is voicing not a literal truth, but an emotional one: he cannot command others if he cannot command himself, and to feel he no longer has Desdemona's love is to feel personally negated in every respect. Robbed (as he thinks) of what most ratified his worth and manhood, he feels that the bottom has dropped out of his whole world.

[1] Although 'occupation' certainly had sexual connotations in Elizabethan times, I can see no element of lewd joke either in Othello's mind or Shakespeare's at this point.

As the scene develops, it becomes more and more plain that what is tested, frayed and snapped in it is not – *pace* Leavis and others – Othello's love for Desdemona, but his assurance of both her love for him and (more crucial still) his worthiness to win and keep it. It is as if he secretly fears he deserves to be spurned. Loving Desdemona as he does, he has (like all lovers) given her the power to affirm him, and therefore to 'deny' and negate him, to the very extent that he has committed himself in that love. To have committed all is to be open to lose all, however; and uncertain as he is of whether he has really lost her love, his fear is without limit. A prominent speech of Cassio's in the very next scene (III, iv) is as clearly relevant to Othello's case as his own, although Cassio (his predicament being less extreme and less complicated) can obviously articulate the point in a way Othello cannot. 'I do beseech you', Cassio says to Desdemona,

> That by your virtuous means *I may again*
> *Exist* and be a member of his [Othello's] love,
> Whom I, with all the office of my heart,
> Entirely honour. I would not be delayed.
>
> (III, iv, 107–10; my italics)

And he goes on to say that if nothing

> Can ransom me into his love again,
> But to know so must be my benefit.

For us, every word of this speech when it comes has a most pointed application to Othello, and, as we shall see in turning to Acts IV and V, to Desdemona too. Indeed, the careful dramatic positioning of this speech, between the scenes rendering Othello's condition and those (straight after it) that render Desdemona's, expressly alerts us to its application to both of them. Like Cassio, only more acutely, Othello plainly feels that he does not 'exist' except in being 'a member' of Desdemona's love. We see now that his reply to Brabantio in the Senate-scene was both a confident challenge and a statement of fact: 'My life upon her faith'. This is indeed the risk Othello has willingly dared to take in committing himself to Desdemona, consecrating his 'soul and fortunes' to her (just as she has done in loving him): he has staked his whole life and being upon her faithfulness to him and – more to the point – upon her faith *in* him as her chosen husband. 'Soul' (like 'heart', as well) is a crucially recurrent word all through the play ('these fellows have some soul'; 'you have lost half your soul'; 'my perfect soul'; 'perdition catch my soul'; and so on, continually). 'I durst, my lord, to wager she is honest,/ Lay down my soul at stake', Emilia declares in the brothel-scene (IV, iii, 11–12). And by that point in the drama we have come to realize the sense in which true loving always means this: to commit oneself and entrust one's love to another's keeping, *is*, in effect, to dare lay down one's soul at stake. At the centre of the play lies a truth about love – a truth explored in Desdemona's case (and others too, in smaller ways) as well as Othello's own: to the extent that any person loves another, he bestows the power to hurt, and in the fullest love, the power to hurt totally, irremediably, beyond any possibility of cure. It is not simply that, as the motto on Portia's casket in *The Merchant of Venice* puts it, 'who chooses [love] must give and hazard all he hath'. In *Othello*, Shakespeare explores the much more radical insight, that 'who chooses love must give and hazard all he *is*'.

To sum up, then: by the middle of III, iii, Othello is clearly overwhelmed by the fear that everything he has staked on Desdemona's love – 'she had eyes, and chose me' – is lost. Her teasing words at the start of the scene, 'Shall I deny thee?', had provoked unease. The 'smallest fear or doubt of her revolt', pushing him back upon his need of her love and upon his 'own weak merits', has (with Iago's malice) pushed him towards the abyss: to be not only rejected, but betrayed at his most vulnerable point. He had freely chosen his bond with her, just as she had freely chosen to love him; but such 'full liberty' is frightening for Othello, for whom (to adapt Kierkegaard's phrase) 'dread is the dizziness of freedom'.[1] The possibility that she has chosen to 'repeal' her bond is, for him, the anguish of being strung on an 'if' over a total void. For Othello it seems less dreadful to be, as Iago puts it, a cuckold 'certain of his fate' than to have to endure the misery of one who 'dotes yet doubts, suspects yet fondly loves' – a misery so great that every nerve strains for the relief of any securing rivet, anything definite, on which his centre might hold. For us, his position seems like an extreme instance of something suggested by Iago's otherwise oddly cryptic remark in the next act (IV, i, 72–3): 'No, let me know;/ And knowing what I am, I know what she shall be';[2] for in Othello's case here this works in reverse: he doesn't 'know' what he is nor what he shall be, except by knowing what Desdemona is and has been – whether she is 'chaste' (and he still loved) or 'foul' (and he spurned). No wonder, then, that he grows so hot for certainties. The rest of the scene shows him shaking himself to pieces between hope and dread, and violently demanding 'proof':

> Villain, be sure thou prove my love a whore;
> Be sure of it: give me the ocular proof . . .
> . . .
>
> Make me to see't: or, at the least, so prove it
> That the probation bear no hinge nor loop
> To hang a doubt on – or woe upon thy life!
> . . .
>
> By the world,

[1] *The Concept of Dread*, trans. Walter Lowrie (Princeton, 1973 [1944]), p. 55: the whole passage forms a suggestive gloss on the kinds of 'dread' Shakespeare examines in Othello and Macbeth.
[2] I quote the (admittedly puzzling, but usually accepted) Folio and Quarto reading, 'what she shall be', in place of Muir's emendation, 'what shall be'.

I think my wife be honest, and think she is not.
. . .

I'll have some proof. Her name that was as fresh
As Dian's visage is now begrimed and black
As mine own face. If there be cords or knives,
Poison or fire or suffocating streams,
I'll not endure it. Would I were satisfied!

(III, iii, 356ff.)

Like Gloucester in another context in *King Lear* (I, ii, 96), Othello is so desperate that he would virtually 'unstate [him]self to be in a due resolution'.

Thus the need to *know*, to have 'surety' proved and confirmed, becomes a hideous self-consuming appetite in Othello – a hunger of the imagination whetted to unendurable sharpness by the insinuations Iago mockingly feeds it: 'You would be satisfied? . . . How satisfied, my lord? . . . Where's satisfaction? . . . If imputation and strong circumstance . . . will give you satisfaction, you might have't.' Anything will now do; and to the preposterous tale of Cassio's sleep-talking, Iago needs only to add the lie about the handkerchief, to prod Othello to rush maddened beyond any return. To goad him to the limit Iago has only to urge the impossible: 'Yet be content . . . Patience, I say: your mind perhaps may change.' By now Othello can hold himself together in only one way: 'Never, Iago . . .'. Having now seized upon a sense of himself that is at least single, unshameful and definite, a version of the decisive *doer* he has always been as a soldier, he commits it in a mutual vow that reflects only too clearly the inner and outer destruction it ratifies.

The ugly violence in Othello's feelings increases in the following scenes; it is indeed as shocking and abhorrent as Leavis claims. That does not mean, however, that the play invites us to cashier him. Our moral position is much more difficult than that. In showing us (all the more nakedly in Act IV, as we shall see) the nature and the depth of Othello's inner, self-inflicted wounds, the play compels us to enter imaginatively into his feelings at the same time as it also compels us to stand aside and see how the extreme and frenzied reactions of his fear engender the very situation he dreads: the loss of the trust, the mutual 'joys and comforts' in which his and Desdemona's lives had seemed to consist. Of course, part of the play's complexity lies in the recognition it forces on us, that some of the ugly feelings in Othello are indeed like some of Iago's (and, potentially at least, our own); it certainly underlines the 'bond' between the two men. But to claim that Othello's craven behaviour demonstrates mere Iago-like egotism and a lack of love for Desdemona is to miss the *tragic* power of the play. For Shakespeare also underlines the radical differences between Othello and Iago, which arise from and reflect the central, obvious and essential fact that Othello is also, and 'for ever', deeply 'bound' to Desdemona. As Othello himself comes to realize in the final scene, Iago – to whom he has bound himself – is unlike himself *and* unlike the other person to whom he has bound himself, in that Iago cannot be psychologically destroyed by anyone but Iago himself. Othello and Desdemona are able, all too readily, to be killed emotionally and physically just because neither can seal himself off from the other in an impenetrable fortress of egotism. At the play's centre, indivisibly, are Othello's terrible (Iago-like) capacity to destroy Desdemona, *and* his terrible (Desdemona-like) capacity to *be* destroyed by her (imagined) rejection of his love.

The play's deepest challenge, I am suggesting, is to make us realize both the co-existence of and the connection between the power to hurt and the power to be hurt; and because both these aspects of its subject are equally important and everywhere shown to be inseparable, 'the essential traitor within the gates' of Othello's self, as Leavis puts it, can be likened to, but certainly not simply identified with, Iago. In other words, if Iago 'represents' something that is in Othello, so equally does Desdemona; and hence it is perhaps less misleading to say, rather, that Iago presents (makes present) to Othello's consciousness something that usually lurks below it – the shadow of a fear that momentarily surfaces whenever Othello's heart is deeply stirred, as Desdemona alone (or the thought of her) can stir it. In III, iii, the instantaneous result of Iago's deliberately vague 'presentment' is Othello's false and terrified *presentiment* of perdition and chaos: his imagination is caught, then mesmerized, then totally dominated by the vast dark shapes his fear projects on the screen of his fantasy. From this moment until the end of the play, he becomes (in a manner quite unlike Iago's) incapable of distinguishing what is from what is not. He succumbs helplessly to the treachery of his own heart. Objective facts – such as Desdemona's offer to bind his aching 'head' with her handkerchief, a gesture of love from which, if he were not so deeply shaken, he might 'receive such balms as else cure everything' – only aggravate the compulsive force of his imagination. Like the lover in Donne's 'Twicknam Garden' –

> But O, selfe traytor, I do bring
> The spider love which transubstantiates all,
> And can convert Manna to gall –

Othello's treacherous self-doubt transubstantiates reality so thoroughly that, under stress, he indeed does convert manna to gall: the benefits and blessings of Desdemona's love are transformed in his mind into injuries and curses. He is at once the source and the prey of the fears that now engulf his whole world. Time and again the play forces us to recognize that, as for those who harbour desire (like Roderigo), so for those who harbour dread: 'trifles light as air' (a handkerchief, or a phantasmal nothing) are 'confirmations strong/ As proofs of holy writ'. Gall is turned to manna, and manna to gall, with the same astonishing ease and speed.

176

This, then, is the central paradox of Othello's state: the remarkable forwardness with which he responds to what he most dreads to hear. In Acts III and IV, he is so preoccupied with everything that seems to confirm his fears that he can see nothing for what it is; in his panic, he judges everything in a manner that least favours his own quiet, and inevitably manages to envelop everything in the web of his fantasies. His fears of suffering loss and chaos are so extreme that they eventually 'credit' and realize themselves. Iago stands on the other side of the fine border between extreme fear and extreme desire: his desire to inflict anguish and chaos on others' lives grows so extreme that it becomes the addictive habit of his own. Both men thus become bondslaves to their most exigent passions, self-enslaved men whose most chronic delusion is to suppose themselves free. All of the other characters' lives are ranged as it were between these two poles. Every one of them, we notice, in his own peculiar way and to his own peculiar degree is either very quick to *be* (or to feel) hurt and even to embrace the injury as somehow unavoidably fated to be his, or – on the other hand – very quick to inflict hurt on others (or himself) in order to relieve or cancel his own real or imagined wounds.

Not only does the play reveal the naturalness of both these habits of feeling; it constantly underlines the vital connection between them. The pattern they form, and the nexus between them, is best summed up, I think, in Shakespeare's own phrase for it – a phrase he gives to Othello himself (significantly enough) in the Senate-scene in Act I – a potently suggestive phrase, whose full significance and irony only gradually become clear to us as the drama develops, though never clear to Othello or anyone else within the play:

> The tyrant, custom, most grave Senators,
> Hath made the flinty and steel couch of war
> My thrice-driven bed of down. I do agnize

A natural and prompt alacrity
I find in hardness; and do undertake
This present war against the Ottomites.

(I, iii, 227–32)

In the immediate context (I, iii – a significantly early stage, when Shakespeare is still establishing and signalling what the play's major concerns are to be), Othello's conscious meaning is quite straightforward: he is a tough fighting man by nature and inclination as well as by repute. To us, however, his phrase, 'a natural and prompt alacrity I find in hardness' may well – even in Act I – begin to assume a sharper edge of meaning than any Othello himself can 'agnize'. For in another sense his phrase is uncannily apposite to what Shakespeare has just shown us in Braban-tio, for instance: *his* alacrity (born of fear) to feel a 'hardness' has been inflicted on him, and his consequent alacrity to inflict 'hardness' on those he thinks have victimized him. The same twin forms of 'alacrity in hardness' are there in Roderigo as well. In a different way they appear in Cassio's drunken behaviour, and – differently again – in Iago's dealings with his world. Desdemona (as we shall see), once she has recognized Othello's 'hardness' to her, shows a very prompt alacrity to suffer and accept it, though a significant unwillingness to inflict injuries, even in self-defence. Emilia too – both like and yet unlike Desdemona – is ready enough to accept Iago's 'hardness' as an inevitable condition of her marriage, even if she is theoretically ready (as she explains to Desdemona in the willow-scene) to claim a woman's 'right' to repay a husband's hardness with her own.

The most extreme case of alacrity to *suffer* hardness is, of course, Desdemona; in her it is human vulnerability we are most acutely aware of. Correspondingly, the most extreme case of prompt alacrity in being hard and inflicting hardness is Iago; in him it is human culpability we are most acutely aware of. In this respect, *they* mark the two poles between which all the other characters are ranged – including Othello, in whom we see the Desdemona-extreme and the Iago-extreme inextricably fused.[1] Being what he is – or, rather, in his uncertain sense of what he is – Othello shows a terrifyingly prompt alacrity to imagine, believe in, and suffer a 'hardness' in Desdemona's heart, and a consequent prompt alacrity to turn the 'soft' comfort of their marriage-bed into a 'flinty and steel couch of war'. However wrong Iago is about the cause, his prediction in Act I (iii, 343ff.) that 'the food that to him now is as luscious as locusts shall be to him shortly as acerbe as the coloquintida', proves, very 'shortly' indeed, all too true.[2] For Othello, to be 'once in doubt' is instantly 'to be resolved': if Desdemona may not be absolutely pure, she must be a whore. For him there can be no relative degrees of rich or poor. Having committed himself to her 'faith', he can see only two absolute alternatives: 'angel' or 'devil', 'bliss' or 'hardness', all or nothing. From 'absolute content' he plunges headlong to absolute despair, ducks 'as low as hell's from heaven'. A natural fear prompts and engenders the prompt alacrity to believe he has been 'abused', cashiered; for that, he can find no remedy except an alacrity to *be* 'hard' and to inflict injuries as deadly as those he feels he has been dealt. His increasingly desperate gropings for 'comfort' and 'remedy', and their final, inevitable failure, dominate the second half of the play.[3]

[1] The double meaning of the phrase 'alacrity in hardness' is of course also very apposite to what Shakespeare explores again in such later plays as *King Lear*, *Macbeth* and *The Winter's Tale* – not just in the protagonists, but (as in *Othello*) in all the subordinate figures as well.

[2] It is interesting that the First Quarto version of Brabantio's warning to Othello very aptly points ahead to Othello's subsequent 'alacrity' and promptness to suppose Desdemona has deceived him:

> Look to her Moor, *have a quick eye to see:*
> She has deceiv'd her father, may doe thee.

[3] Once again, one of the Sonnets (144) offers a suggestive analogue to Othello's psychological state by the end of Act III. His bond with Desdemona and his sense of her as 'fair' might well be said to have given him a sense of

himself as 'a man right fair'; his capacity to love her might well be said to be his 'better angel'; his 'worser spirit', his capacity to enter into the bond with Iago – the bond which, because it 'colours her ill', tempts all that is best in himself to be corrupted by fear and suspicion, and leaves him in a state of violent despair and uncertainty. Indeed, the psychological state which the sonnet is trying to wrestle with, where the mind's despair is at once caused by and expressed in its starkly polarized vision of the world – 'comfort'/ 'despair', 'fair'/'ill', 'angel'/'devil' – is precisely one of the things Shakespeare is exploring, with much deeper and firmer insight, all through *Othello*. (Given what we are shown of Othello's 'desperate turns', Gratiano's remark that Desdemona's death would have made Brabantio 'do a desperate turn' and 'curse his better angel from his side' (v, ii, 206–8) is obviously applicable to Othello as well.)

6

The 'hollow hell' of vengeance: Othello's attempted remedies

OTHELLO   Arise, black vengeance, from the hollow hell!
                                                    (III, iii, 444)

OTHELLO   But there where I have garnered up my heart,
           Where either I must live, or bear no life,
           The fountain from the which my current runs,
           Or else dries up – to be discarded thence . . .
                                                    (IV, ii, 56–9)

Of Othello's last long speech in the play, Eliot remarked that he did not believe 'any writer has ever exposed this *bovarysme*, the human will to see things as they are not, more clearly than Shakespeare'.[1] I am not sure exactly what Eliot meant by 'exposed' here, but if we take it as suggesting, not censorious rejection, but rather the kind of moral judgment inseparable from profound and inward understanding, the remark does point to something dramatized not just in this speech of Othello's but all through the play, and most piercingly from the crisis-scene (III, iii) onwards.

I have outlined some of the different forms such evasiveness takes in the other characters – in Iago, for instance, or Brabantio, or differently again, in Roderigo, or even in Cassio. In the second half of the play it appears in Emilia and Desdemona too. But mostly, of course, it is still central in Othello. Indeed, Othello's is at once the most varied and urgent form of it, yet (as I have been arguing) one

[1]'Shakespeare and the Stoicism of Seneca', p. 131.

sign of Shakespeare's intensely coherent imagination is that at different moments throughout the action Othello's behaviour shows striking and highly significant resemblances to that of other characters in their particular crises.

From III, iii onwards, Othello's 'will to see things as they are not' – the will that binds him to Iago – becomes much more a *need* to see and feel things as they are not, a need which links him in more subtle ways with Desdemona. And the source and counterside of this need, as we see with fearful clarity in Acts III–V, is a no less desperate need in him not to see and feel things as they are.

Both needs express themselves, and reveal themselves to us though not to Othello himself, in the shrill denials of his capacity to be hurt or even to feel – specifically, of course, in his denials that he loves Desdemona.

> O, that the slave [Cassio] had forty thousand lives!
> One is too poor, too weak for my revenge.
> Now do I see 'tis true. Look here, Iago –
> All my fond love thus do I blow to heaven:
> 'Tis gone.
> Arise, black vengeance, from the hollow hell!
> Yield up, O love, thy crown and hearted throne
> To tyrannous hate! Swell, bosom, with thy fraught,
> For 'tis of aspics' tongues!¹   (III, iii, 439–47)

Of the many critics of *Othello* who argue that Shakespeare's chief impulse in the second half of the play is to present the moral case against its hero, some cite this speech as an example of Othello's viciously vengeful nature. Some, however, choose not to mention it. One's first impression

---

¹At line 444 Muir, for reasons he does not explain, accepts the Quarto reading, 'thy hollow cell'. I have remained with the more commonly accepted Folio version, 'the hollow hell'; apart from anything else, the juxtaposition of 'heaven' (l. 442) with 'hell' seems more consistent with Othello's characteristically polarizing turns of mind. However, the difference between the two readings does not affect my argument below.

is that they may be wise not to, for the most obvious and dramatically most significant qualities of this expression of vengefulness are surely its spuriousness, feebleness and artificiality. 'Hatred' and 'black vengeance' declaimed as histrionically as this hardly strike us as authentic or convincing. They seem more like conventional cardboard notions of vengeance – 'hollow' indeed. The very exclamatory style of the rhetoric gives it away: so flailing that it may well remind us of Iago's remark about Othello's habit of uttering mere 'bombast circumstance', speeches 'horribly stuffed with epithets'. By contrast with Othello's powerfully assured speeches to Brabantio in Act I, for instance, or his speeches in the brawl scene, this sounds so empty that it betrays the very impulse to 'revenge' (rather than just the scope for it) as itself 'too poor, too weak'. It is 'hollow', that is, not because it cannot be substantiated by actual facts or deeds; on the contrary, Othello's rhetoric leads all too directly to vengeful action of the kind he promises. Its hollowness lies rather in the very evident gap between the feelings of vulnerability that give rise to it, and the feelings of sternness and invulnerability it asserts. It lays claim to a spontaneous 'hatred' of Desdemona which its stiff, willed rhythms and histrionic tone do not support, and indeed seem positively to belie.

This is only one of many such strained, over-rhetorical speeches Othello makes from this point on, and of course many critics have noted how his language often sounds rather artificial. But what this artificiality signifies is another matter. I think its *dramatic* import has usually been missed or misunderstood; and since it is crucial in our estimate of the play's greatness or alleged 'limitedness', it needs close consideration.

The account that more perhaps than any other in the last thirty years has influenced critical thinking about the play's language and related issues is Wilson Knight's description of what he calls 'the Othello music': –

Images in . . . Othello's poetry . . . are concrete, detached; seen
but not apprehended. . . This detached style, most excellent in
point of clarity and stateliness, tends also to lose something in
respect of power. At moments of great tension, the *Othello* style
fails of a supreme effect. Capable of fine things . . . it nevertheless sinks sometimes to a studied artificiality, nerveless and
without force. For example, Othello thinks of himself as:

> . . . one whose subdued eyes . . .
> Drop tears as fast as the Arabian trees
> Their medicinal gum . . .   (v, ii, 347)

Othello's lines here . . . [as in] the 'Pontic sea' passage . . . use
the typical *Othello* picturesque image or word; both [speeches]
compare, by simile, the passion of man with some picture
delightful in itself, which is developed for its own sake, slightly
over-developed – so that the final result makes us forget the
emotion in contemplation of the image . . . Othello's slightly
over-strained phraseology . . . deliberately refuses power in the
level prolixity of simile, and searches always for the picturesque.
The *Othello* style is diffuse . . . At the most agonizing moments
of Othello's story . . . there is apparent weakness: we find an
exaggerated, false rhetoric . . . [The speech] that begins ['Behold,
I have a weapon . . .'] degenerates finally to what might almost
be called bombast . . .

> O cursed, cursed slave! Whip me, ye devils . . .

These lines lack cogency because they exaggerate rather than
concentrate the emotion.[1]

Much of this seems to me finely and truly said. On the
other hand, it does not at all follow, as Wilson Knight (and
many others) seem to suppose, that the play *Othello*
therefore falls below Shakespeare's greatest art. The 'studied artificiality' is there – but this does not make the play
ipso facto a failure on Shakespeare's part adequately to

[1] *The Wheel of Fire*, 4th rev. edn (London, 1960 [1949]), pp. 99–102.

184

realize his hero's inner state. If we examine the play carefully, I think that now-famous label, 'the *Othello* music', can be seen to be a most unfortunately blurring and misleading one. It encourages the easy but crucially muddling slide from talking about 'Othello's style' to talking about 'the *Othello* style'. The former is the medium in which Shakespeare dramatically presents his hero in the play. The latter is a descriptive and potentially critical judgment about the play. Wilson Knight and those who cite him tend to ignore or fail to see any such distinction.

Despite the fact that other characters – Cassio, for instance, in the storm scene – occasionally speak in the 'heroic mode' usually associated with Othello himself, it is important not to confound the function of this quasi-choric 'music' with that of Othello's own particular habits of language. *His* have to be taken as dramatically revealing: as realizing and defining what he personally feels and values and is. His speeches, in short, 'demonstrate, in complement extern', the 'native act and figure' of his unique, particular self. The quasi-choric eloquence of the other characters' descriptions of the storm, for instance, has a different purpose and effect: to establish, impersonally, the kind of world they all inhabit, or to express a sense of what Othello represents to Cassio, for example, or the reality, import and significance of the storm as Cassio and others perceive this. Sometimes these 'choric' speeches work very economically to establish a physical atmosphere that (as we see it) mirrors a psychological one. At other times they seem rather slack and facile. Nevertheless, this slackness is too minor and insignificant to interest or trouble us much; at such moments (and they occur more or less often, and more or less significantly, in all of Shakespeare's plays) it is easy enough to grasp the general points that Shakespeare seeks to make. When Othello's *own* speeches reveal the qualities Wilson Knight points to, however – 'artificiality', a phraseology that is 'slightly over-strained' – these qualities are dramatically important, and they surely prompt us (before we rush to conclude that Shakespeare was incompetent) to ask what, if anything, they reveal of the hero's particular nature.

Many critics who agree – whether implicitly or explicitly – with Wilson Knight's account of Othello's language discuss it in terms of what Eliot called Othello's way of 'dramatising himself against his environment'. Leavis, for example, rightly claims that 'the essential function of . . . the "Othello [*sic*] music" . . . [is] to express Othello's sense of himself and make us share it'[1] (though we may notice that this way of putting it blurs the distinction between Shakespeare's purposes and those of his character, Othello). Yet since it is by no means as obvious as Leavis seems to think just what Othello's 'sense of himself' is, and how it changes and why it matters in the play, we need to be patient enough to ask, as we ponder particular speeches, exactly what 'sense of himself' does this or that speech express? And why? Does Othello's expression (or that of other characters too, for that matter) itself exhibit – perhaps unintentionally – anything about his state that seems to belie or to undermine his overt claims about it? These questions are rarely considered by critics, however. Those who actually discuss Othello's tendency to self-dramatization usually assume, with Leavis, that its dramatic point is to expose Othello's 'egotism'; and, like Leavis again, they usually move directly from 'self-dramatization' to more heavily loaded terms such as 'self-centredness', 'self-idealization', 'self-regard', 'self-pride', 'complacent self-esteem', and the like.[2] Yet it seems to me that this easy

---

[1]'Diabolic Intellect and the Noble Hero', p. 143.
[2]See for example Derek Traversi, *An Approach to Shakespeare*, 2nd rev. edn (New York, 1956 [1938]), pp. 128–50; Heilman, *Magic in the Web*. The unwarranted and misleading slide from 'self-dramatizing' to terms that have a censorious moral edge has led many other critics to reject the whole notion of 'self-dramatizing' in this or any play (some even claim that it is as fallacious as the absurd old notion that characters who speak poetry are poets). This is

slide, made without stopping to reconsider the dramatic evidence or the moral distinctions involved, also leads many usually alert and scrupulous critics to miss or distort what Shakespeare subtly reveals. Even a moment's thought might suggest that people often wish, or need, to indulge in rhetorical self-dramatization in order to compensate for their sense of weakness, rather than gratuitously to express their self-esteem: people secure in their sense of worth and greatness do not need to resort to self-aggrandizing rhetoric. If we actually listen to Othello's speeches, without assuming that such inflated language and picturesque self-idealizations must signal an inflated ego and unshakable complacency, it does not seem hard to detect the unacknowledged (indeed, unacknowledgeable) needs that prompt him again and again to project these elaborate, idealized images of himself. Moreover, it is surely important that these self-images are far more strained, exaggerated and urgently rhetorical in the second half of the play than any in the first. (All of Wilson Knight's examples of the 'slightly over-developed' quality in Othello's style, we may notice, are drawn from Acts III–V.)

By an odd irony, some of the shrewdest and most subtly suggestive of Wilson Knight's remarks about *Othello* are those he himself followed up least and that subsequent critics who take up the catch-phrase 'Othello music' have passed over. One example is Knight's observation that '*at moments of great tension*, the *Othello* [*sic*] style fails of a supreme effect'; or, '*at the most agonizing moments* of Othello's story . . . there is apparent weakness: we find an exaggerated, false rhetoric' [my italics]. To come back to the play's text from these comments is to find them fully

---

an overreaction and a mistake: as a neutrally descriptive term 'self-dramatizing' is very useful and even necessary, for in plays as in ordinary life we can and do distinguish between those moments when a person is simply 'being himself' and those when he is posturing, or role-playing, or 'dramatizing himself' in some more subtle way.

confirmed (though in the first quotation 'the *Othello* style' should in my view read 'Othello's style'). Othello's rhetoric indeed seems most false and exaggerated when the tension in him is most acute. So the obvious question arises: is this just a coincidence, or does increasing stress actually *produce* a tendency in Othello to rely increasingly on rhetoric?

Wilson Knight himself seems to suggest the latter is far more likely (though again he blurs the issue by blurring the distinction between the play and its hero) when he says in another acute phrase that Othello's style (or as he misleadingly puts it, 'the *Othello* style') '*deliberately refuses power* in the level prolixity of simile, and searches always for the picturesque' [my italics]. That strangely ambiguous yet illuminating phrase 'deliberately refuses power' is one we do well to ponder, for on whose part is it 'deliberate' (and why is it deliberate?) – Shakespeare's or Othello's? (It is the same question we need to ask of Knight's phrase 'apparent weakness'.) Even at a quite simple level, it is clear that a speech like the one about 'black vengeance' quoted above, which Othello utters near the end of the crisis-scene (III, iii), comes at one of the most 'agonizing moments' of his 'story', and equally clear that it shows just those stylistic qualities Wilson Knight observed as characteristic: it is 'overstrained', for example, and 'sinks . . . to . . . artificiality, nerveless, without force'. 'Arise, black vengeance, from the hollow hell! . . . Swell, bosom, with thy fraught.' This is a representative case where we need to decide if the weakness is Shakespeare's – an unhappy collapse (at a critical moment) into the flabby rhetorical style of, say, *Titus Andronicus* – or if it is not rather Othello's, and revealed as *his* 'weakness' by a Shakespeare fully cognizant of what he is doing.

As I see it, the rhetorical strain here not only can but certainly should be taken as Othello's. For what Shakespeare dramatically reveals is Othello's struggle to convince himself of what he says – that he can simply 'blow' all his fond love to heaven, and thus, by an act of will, successfully command 'tyrannous hate' to replace love in his heart. As we are soon made to realize (though Othello himself continues to deny it), this is exactly what the dramatic action reveals he cannot do. In an earlier speech, we recall, he had asserted how simply he could dispose of feelings: 'I'll see before I doubt; when I doubt, prove;/ And on the proof, there is no more than this:/ Away at once with love or jealousy!' Now, when he actually tries to do 'away at once with love', he manages to do so no more successfully than he had actually 'seen' before he doubted, or actually 'proved' his doubts. In his 'black vengeance' speech he asserts what his manner and his language signally fail to *show:* that he has doubted, seen, proved, and can thus blow all his love to heaven – as if he could remove it simply by wishing and willing to do so. As with so many of Othello's subsequent speeches, Shakespeare here prompts us to realize that, exactly to the degree that Othello's rhetoric actually becomes forced and strained, it betrays, as this speech patently does, not conviction or self-assurance but the lack of it. In short, it is Othello himself, as Shakespeare conceives and projects him, whose speech exhibits a peculiar artificiality and inflatedness of language here. The drama is exploring and 'placing' the psychic conditions that lead him to rely so heavily on declamatory and histrionic speech. Here, as throughout the play, the strain in the language marks the strain in Othello trying to believe he is what he claims: for instance, a man truly worthy of Desdemona's unchanging love, but unjustly wronged and therefore justly loathing her and seeking 'revenge'.

To complain, therefore, as many critics implicitly or explicitly do, that the 'literariness' and 'remoteness' of such speeches as this betray Shakespeare's 'failure' to realize his hero's inner state, that this 'weakness' of expression therefore prevents us understanding and feeling for Othello in his 'jealousy' (as we can with Leontes, for

instance), and that consequently *Othello* is rather 'more
limited' an achievement than we might expect of the mature
Shakespeare: all this seems to me to miss the crucial
dramatic point. The failure to realize the feelings of 'hatred'
and 'vengeance' Othello claims to have is Othello's own
failure. What is more, once we see this, we can appreciate
how profoundly and subtly Shakespeare understands and
portrays it. Othello's rhetoric dramatically exhibits how
little he himself can *afford* to understand or acknowledge
what he really feels or really is. His rhetoric is the noise of
floundering desperation; and we come fully to understand
why this is so later in the play. When Othello does open
himself to the full brunt of what he really feels, he utterly
disintegrates.

In this 'black vengeance' speech, and in subsequent and
more famous ones, I would argue, we are shown Othello's
effort to slough off everything that causes pain, and to
reshape both the situation and his own feelings so as to
make them somehow more tolerable. They are efforts, we
might say, to 'cheer himself up'; and the dramatic point is
that they all visibly fail. His very next speech after the 'black
vengeance' one is a case in point, revealing precisely because
of the self-bolstering, picturesque language with which he
replies to Iago's suggestion that his 'mind perhaps may
change':

> Never, Iago. Like to the Pontic sea,
> Whose icy current and compulsive course
> Ne'er feels retiring ebb, but keeps due on
> To the Propontic and the Hellespont,
> Even so my bloody thoughts with violent pace
> Shall ne'er look back, ne'er ebb to humble love,
> Till that a capable and wide revenge
> Swallow them up. Now, by yond marble heaven,
> In the due reverence of a sacred vow
> I here engage my words.[1]
> > [*He kneels*]   (III, iii, 450–9)

[1] There is a particularly fine commentary on this and related speeches in

The dramatic ironies could hardly be more richly terrible – all this, all these assertions of steadiness and self-command, coming from the man whom Iago has with such ease been mentally manipulating precisely as he wants. The very iterations of this speech, the self-flagellatory denials ('never', 'ne'er feels', 'ne'er look back', 'ne'er ebb') betray far more feeling than they manage convincingly to deny or control.

To notice this, in fact, is to notice too that in effect (though quite unconsciously of course) Othello is trying the same 'remedy' for 'torment' that the arch self-deceiver Iago so prides himself on being a master of, and which he sneeringly advocated to Roderigo in Act I, when that desperate 'lover' had to 'confess it is my shame to be so fond, but it is not in my virtue to amend it'. According to Iago, we remember, nobody who knows 'how to love himself' need endure feelings he does not want; the 'power and corrigible authority' over our feelings 'lies in our wills'. But in Othello's 'Pontic sea' speech it is precisely the violent straining of will that shows how little 'authority' over his feelings he really has. The self-compulsive quality of the speech is unmistakable if one sets it beside, say, the analogous speech in which Lady Macbeth summons *her* powers of 'direst cruelty' (*Macbeth*, I, v, 40ff.). Othello's attempt to 'stop up th'access and passage to remorse' and eradicate his love has nothing of the thrill – the spontaneous, *un*willed voluptuous excitement – of Lady Macbeth's 'Come . . . Come . . . Come . . .' In short, his language here (and in subsequent speeches) reveals to us just what it is subconsciously designed to conceal from himself – that his will cannot master his heart, cannot 'weed up' the love he feels nor 'sow' hatred in its place. However much he tries to deny them, potent currents of feeling for Desdemona

---

Michael Black's discussion of *Othello* in *Poetic Drama as Mirror of the Will* (London, 1977), pp. 78–92.

keep welling up in him, so that (like Brabantio) he most vehemently asserts his power to control his feelings at precisely those moments when he is most impotent in the face of them. The 'compulsive course' of vengeance he speaks of is neither 'compulsive' nor 'icy' at all – it is hotly pained and trying to force itself to unfeeling coldness. As Cassio remarks in the scene following this, if there is really no hope of a reprieve from pain, then merely

> . . . to know so must be my benefit:
> So shall I clothe me in a forced content
> And shut myself up in some other course
> To Fortune's alms.   (III, iv, 115–18)

Othello cannot any longer contemplate such 'ifs' as Cassio can, nor can he sustain or think of 'hope'; but his remedial effort is at once like and unlike Cassio's – like, in that the 'course' he tries to adopt is that of calmly accepting and acting on what he 'knows' (though of course he doesn't 'know'), and unlike, in that the only 'forced content' he can manage to 'shut [himself] up in' is a 'compulsive', *willed* 'hardness' and a correspondingly hollow lust for vengeance. He attempts to seem and be what he is not – unconsciously trying, as it were, to 'show out flag and sign' of hate (as Iago had quite deliberately sought to 'show out flag and sign of love' in Act I), but without being able to realize or admit (as Iago could) that 'it is indeed but sign'. His speech shows that his 'hatred' of Desdemona here has no more substance than has Iago's professed 'love' for *him*.[1]

Othello's self-protective stratagems are not peculiar to him, of course. And it is by dramatically revealing their affinities with those of the other characters in their crises

---

[1] Othello's state, revealed through his trappings of 'revenge', is at once more acute and less self-aware than Hamlet's. The latter is able to say what Othello cannot begin (nor afford) to recognize: 'I have that within which passes show –/ These but the trappings and the suits of woe' (*Hamlet*, I, ii, 85–6), though Hamlet cannot accurately *name* 'that within which passes show' any more than Othello can.

that Shakespeare explores and 'places' them. There is a telling parallel between Othello's behaviour in these scenes and that of the drunken Cassio in Act II, for instance, when his 'devil', drink, had stolen away *his* brains:

Drunk! And speak parrot! And squabble! Swagger! Swear! And discourse fustian with one's own shadow!

(II, iii, 272-4)

The sharpest pathos of such speeches of Othello's as that about 'black vengeance', or the 'Pontic sea' one, lies in the similar condition they show in him. He of course cannot recognize what he is doing (as Cassio retrospectively can) because his condition is so serious that it does not bear thinking on. Whatever he himself thinks he is determining on and achieving, we see that he is managing to do no more than 'speak parrot', and deluding himself, just as the drunken Cassio did, about his condition and his capacity to master and to deal with the world that 'mocks' him. To fortify himself, he too 'discourses fustian with his own shadow', as a way of holding at bay the threat lurking everywhere and in everything.[1] Or, to use another suggestively parallel term, his language, like the defensive stratagem of the Turks, is a psychological stratagem, 'a pageant to keep us in false gaze': more crucially, his language creates a 'pageant', a large, clear and pathetic but false 'shadow' of himself to keep *himself* 'in false gaze' and so divert his attention from the actual but insufferable state of his heart.[2] Wilson Knight's description comes very near and yet misses the truth: 'the final result [of Othello's speeches] makes us forget the emotion in contemplation of

[1] The most betrayingly turgid and melodramatic of all his pieces of 'fustian' is his speech in the penultimate scene about Desdemona's 'lust-stained' bed (v, i, 31-6).
[2] For a different view of Othello's language and behaviour in the last three acts see Derick R. C. Marsh's account of the play in *Passion Lends Them Power* (Manchester, Sydney and New York, 1976), pp. 89-140.

the image'. It is not *we* who 'forget'. The final result is rather that we are able to see Othello himself struggling to 'forget' his real emotions 'in contemplation of the [picturesque] image' of other emotions he tries to sow in place of those growing in his heart. By the end of the crisis-scene (III, iii), his extravagant language and the act of kneeling with Iago 'in the due reverence of a sacred vow' clearly represent a will straining toward power – power not only over his feelings, but over his very capacity to feel. He tries, we might say, to give birth to and institutionalize a 'new' self, finalize it in a new bond the very sealing of which constitutes a willed rejection of his own unacknowledgeable vulnerability.

Watching the two men in this scene we can see how much Othello's self-mistrust impels and is then dispelled by his trust in Iago. He trusts Iago because Iago seems to respect and trust in him as a General, a soldier, a man of 'honour' – in short, as a source of decision and (above all) of power. Their sacred 'vow' of vengeance affirms the power of his own will to control life; it also enables him to re-establish and reconfirm the secure reality, the entire (as he thinks) self-sufficiency, the 'hardness' of his self. What all this betrays in him, of course, is what it betrays in Iago too – a knot of profound and pervasive self-contradictions, although in Othello we find it far more painful to witness because they are so visibly destroying a self whose needs spring from positive capacities. Although the real deficiency in him is to fear that some deficiency in himself has caused Desdemona to defect, he can only suffer that fear, but he cannot admit it even to himself. Instead, he masks it behind another sort of deficiency, which he can envisage just because it is not inherent in his self, and therefore not something he is responsible for: he sees himself as the helpless victim, not of his own insecurity and fears, but of 'fate', of the abuse many 'great ones' are liable to because of their position, because of *other* people's betrayal. The advantage of this sort of attitude, as we have seen many times, is that it allows him to place responsibility for his feelings and behaviour on to others, or on to some impersonal agency or value. In seeing himself as a powerless victim, he can also see himself as a just avenger of wrong, able to master all his feelings, able – indeed, required – to make himself invulnerable to any personal feeling. Once again, it is the familiar consolation of dressing oneself up now as a helpless victim, now as a righteous agent, and thereby blunting the intolerable pain of being, in a quite different way, both and neither. One reason why we find Othello's vow with Iago so painful is that he so obviously needs the bond as a sort of security against the abysmal 'hollow' left by Desdemona's supposed betrayal. The vow is itself the very betrayal it seeks to compensate for. It reveals his natural 'alacrity in hardness' in every sense of the phrase: his capacity to be hurt, his readiness to be hurt, and his capacity to deny both and yet inflict hurt upon others. The grandiose polysyllables of the vow, mockingly mimicked in Iago's fraudulent offer of faithful service, clearly betray to us not a man firm and coherent and determined, not a new self, but the same defenceless Othello trying to will the denial of the 'humble love' still alive and rawly exposed but concealed in his heart.

The rest of the play charts the inevitable drastic collapse of Othello's effort to spurn and alter his deepest feelings – his struggle (which is, as we shall see, dramatically compared and contrasted with Desdemona's) to keep the real 'monster' of desolation, 'mere perdition', from his mind. The successive breaks in his fabric are many, violent and dreadful; and through and in them we glimpse the raging despair behind the barely maintained façade. For obvious reasons, Desdemona's presence shakes and unnerves him more than anything else, as in the scene immediately after his 'vow'. 'O hardness to dissemble!', he cries – a cry whose ambiguity inter-relates her (supposed) 'hardness' in dissembling love, and his own difficulty in dissembling calm and holding his heart in a corresponding 'hardness'.

The relationship between experiencing and giving pain is now appallingly clear – to us, that is. As he feels tormented himself, Othello begins to torment her, threatening her with precisely what he has feared and now feels, though he cannot properly admit it. His word for it is highly revealing: 'such perdition as nothing else could match'. His tale about the history of the handkerchief is grotesquely cruel; yet again the terms he uses betray to us what prompts the cruelty: the handkerchief, he claims, had the power to make his mother 'amiable' and 'subdue my father/ Entirely to her love', while 'if she lost it', his 'father's eye/ Should hold her loathèd, and his spirits should hunt/ After new fancies'.[1] His violent anger, which so alarms and bewilders Desdemona – 'Is't possible? Indeed! Is't true?' – is the other side of his own anguish and bewilderment. He speaks 'startlingly and rash', incoherent in his panic and dismay, for even now he scarcely knows whether he can be 'certain'. Could she produce the handkerchief now it might allay his fears. But when she equivocates and hedges, his conviction of her guilt rises to overwhelm and break one floodbank of his heart and mind: 'Fetch't . . . Fetch me the handkerchief: my mind misgives . . . The

[1]The discrepancy between this story and what he says about the handkerchief in v, ii, 215–16 – 'It was . . . an antique token/ My father gave my mother' – has been the subject of much debate, conveniently documented by Michael C. Andrews, 'Honest Othello: The Handkerchief Once More', *Studies in English Literature*, 13 (1973), pp. 273–84. My own view – a common one, which Andrews challenges but doesn't convincingly refute – is roughly that of Steevens (cited in the Variorum *Othello*, p. 317): 'The first account . . . is purposely ostentatious, in order to alarm [Desdemona] the more', whereas in Act V 'the truth was sufficient to his purpose'. However, what I think is at issue here is not Othello's 'honesty', nor his 'primitivism', nor his capacity to 'dissemble', but his emotional state *vis-à-vis* Desdemona at this point – the aching need, and barely suppressed despair, which are as visible in his language as in his face. *Our* attention is surely arrested by what arrests and frightens Desdemona here.

handkerchief! . . . The handkerchief! . . . The handkerchief! . . . Zounds!' [*Exit*].

Inevitably, most of the crises in Act IV involve the
handkerchief, for it has become for Othello the physical
symbol and evidence of Desdemona's 'honour' – a fact
which itself betrays to us how much his mind now 'mis-
gives' the world to him. In IV, i, Iago thrusts the fact of the
handkerchief at Othello's attention, although Bradley and
a number of other critics suppose that Othello has forgotten
the matter and needs to be reminded. I cannot think that
this is really so. It seems rather as if Othello desperately
wishes he *could* forget it, along with everything it now
means to him:

IAGO   But for the handkerchief –
OTHELLO   By heaven, I would most gladly have forgot it!
          Thou said'st – O, it comes o'er my memory
          As doth the raven o'er the infected house,
          Boding to all! – he had my handkerchief.
IAGO   Ay, what of that?   (IV, i, 18–23)

Othello's heart is of course already fatally 'infected': his
mind harbours bodings so terrible that he cannot disbelieve
them. The 'raven'-handkerchief is the main such 'sign', so
oppressive that he 'approves' it 'in fearful sense'. The
movement of his recollection here – 'Thou said'st – . . . he
had my handkerchief' – is literally arrested as the appalling
shadow of what this means 'comes o'er [his] memory',
dislocating his syntax. He seems for a moment shudderingly
transfixed. Indeed, his sense of threat and disaster, associated here with the terror of the plague, so overwhelms him,
that the raven's cry of doom even seems to half-echo
weirdly in his own doleful cry: 'O, . . . o'er . . . o'er . . .
boding to all': the tale of Cassio with the handkerchief now
has this extraordinary potent significance, boding to all he
had ever dreamed his love could be.[1] And this, of course, is

[1] It was a bold stroke on Shakespeare's part to cast Othello's misery here in

why Iago's next announcement – about Cassio's alleged 'confession' – excites in him such a literally insupportable rush of emotion. For all his inability to stand doubt and uncertainty, this apparent certainty is altogether more than he can take. The storm within him now lashes and 'enchafes' him so violently that it effects yet another, even worse break in his fabric. He literally founders on the 'guttered rocks and congregated sands' of his own treacherous imaginings. Just as the high-wrought tempest in Act II had let 'nothing at all' be clearly 'discerned', and had so 'quenched the guards of th'ever-fixèd pole' that human sight failed even to 'descry' a sail or 'distinguish' sea from sky, so too here, in Othello's inner 'molestation', the 'fixed marks' from which he might take his bearings on reality are 'quenched':

Handkerchief – confession – handkerchief! To confess and be hanged for his labour. First to be hanged and then to confess! I tremble at it. Nature would not invest herself in such shadowing passion without some instruction. It is not words that shakes me thus! Pish! Noses, ears, and lips! Is't possible? – Confess? Handkerchief! O devil! (iv, i, 37–43)

One effect of this speech is to make us painfully aware that 'it is precisely words that *have* shaken him thus . . . with all their symbolical import';[2] his very denial of it is a clear sign that Iago's words have staggered him. The frightful strain of confused 'realities' and shaken feelings literally floors him. He falls. Doubt and self-doubt have grown insupportable, as Iago gleefully sees; no sooner does

---

terms so close to those Marlowe had used, to such splendidly comic effect, in Barabas's loudly self-consoling lament as he waits to recover his hidden bags of gold (*The Jew of Malta*, ii, iff.). Certainly I think the almost physical sense of Othello's sickened apprehension here is realized more powerfully in these lines than Shakespeare had managed with, say, Juliet's comparably momentous recollection of Romeo's banishment: 'I would forget it fain,/ But, O, it presses to my memory/ Like damned guilty deeds to sinners' minds' (iii, ii, 109–11).

[2]Proser, *The Heroic Image in Five Shakespearean Tragedies*, p. 133.

Othello recover (physically, but not mentally) from his 'epileptic' collapse, than Iago openly mocks him for his weakness, his 'unmanly' failure of will: 'Would you would bear your fortune like a man!'; 'be a man . . .'; '. . . a passion most unsuiting such a man'; '. . . nothing of a man'.

It is just this humiliated sense of himself as 'nothing of a man', abused, powerless, exposed to others' scorn – especially Desdemona's – that so enrages Othello in the eavesdropping incident that follows in the same scene. In some respects this incident is one of the most perfunctory in the whole play – Shakespeare's conception of Cassio in it, for instance, seems pretty makeshift – and on the page, as we read it, it may seem rather heavy and melodramatic. It may be relevant that it is derived fairly wholesale from Cinthio, though it is also worth remembering that Shakespeare had written many such scenes of misapprehension before, in the comedies especially, and the incident obviously has affinities with the remarkable eavesdropping scene (v, ii) in *Troilus and Cressida*. On stage, however, it is extraordinarily powerful, as many critics attest. Granville-Barker, for example, calls it a 'painfully grotesque pantomime', with Othello 'craning his neck, straining his ears, dodging his black face back and forth like a figure in a farce';[1] and as another reader has observed, Othello is now 'in the same position as Iago was [in the quay-side scene – II, i, 165ff.] – standing off to a side, casting hate-filled glances and phrases at Cassio. (Thus Shakespeare uses stage-movements and groupings to reinforce dramatic meanings . . .)'[2]

Certainly, there is no missing the key-point of the incident. The effect on Othello of his eavesdropping emer-

[1] As is obvious from my account, I disagree with Granville-Barker's over-all view of the play, but his local comments are often fresh, vigorous, and very much to the point. For the quoted comment see *Prefaces to Shakespeare*, Fourth Series, *Othello* (London, 1945), p. 82.
[2] Ephim Fogel, in *Teaching Shakespeare*, ed. Arthur Mizener (New York, Toronto and London, 1969), p. 201.

ges with terrible force. He has reached a stage where his mind
'mis-gives' and 'mis-takes' everything (including nothing)
entirely in accordance with its own tumults of feeling. His
suggestibility is virtually boundless now, maniacal.

A common view of his state and behaviour from III, iii
on is that they reflect only loathing for Desdemona. When
he says of his love ''Tis gone', many critics seem (rather
credulously) to take him at his word. And if this were the
case, the play would certainly be a more limited affair than
Shakespeare's other great tragedies. But it seems to me a
falsifying oversimplification of the facts. Throughout Acts
IV and V, the most vivid feature of every incident concerning Othello – the most distressing (for us as well as for him) –
is the wild ambivalence of his feelings about Desdemona.
From moment to moment he zigzags uncontrollably
between nostalgic longing for her and hysterical fury
against her – 'a tortured mixture of longing and loathing'
(to use Bradley's phrase).[1] At times his violent urge to
destroy is all too atrociously real. Like Emilia in her sudden
outbursts of punitive rage against anyone who has abused
Desdemona, Othello sometimes hankers for a whip to lash
his wrongers naked through the world, longs, that is, for
any means of destruction that would soothe his own sense
of being emotionally tortured and mutilated, by torturing
and mutilating those who did it to him: 'I would have him
nine years a-killing'; 'I will chop her into messes! Cuckold
me!' There is nothing willed about these execrable flashes
of bloodlust, nor about those in Act V: 'Had all his hairs
been lives, my great revenge/ Had stomach for them all.'
(These, we may notice, are related to his eventual, though
less hideous, longing for punishment on Iago: 'Are there
no stones in heaven/ But what serve for the thunder?')
Nevertheless, the feelings that prompt the vindictive
outbursts against Desdemona also keep stifling his capacity,

[1] *Shakespearean Tragedy*, p. 144.

and even his urgent desire, to kill her. The thought of her enrages him only to seduce him, 'unman' him again. And, as so often happens in the play, we are brought to see that both the reason for and the pattern of these wild veerings was foreshadowed earlier, in IV, i, in his immediate intuition when he first decided to kill her: 'I'll not expostulate with her, lest her body and beauty unprovide my mind again.'

All through the last two acts, every time he thinks of her or sees her, Othello flounders in powerful currents of longing for her, which threaten to drown his will and 'unprovide' his mind and heart. A 'chaos of Thought and Passion, all confus'd;/ Still by himself abus'd, or dis-abus'd', he struggles and barely manages *not* to 'ebb to humble love', *not* to think of his pain so as not to feel it. He has to strain to make his heart completely insentient: hard, 'flinty and steel'. The effort of will is of course not a consciously deliberated one; in fact, it is comparable with the one Chaucer's Troilus found himself unable to adopt on losing Criseyde:

> Thow farest ek by me, thow Pandarus,
> As he that, whan a wight is wo bygon,
> He cometh to hym a paas, and seith right thus,
> 'Thynk nat on smert, and thow shalt fele non.'
> Thow moost me first transmewen in a ston,
> And reve me my passiones alle,
> Er thow so lightly do my wo to falle.
>
> (Troilus and Criseyde, Bk IV, 463–9)

Because his anguish is so extreme, Othello tries – un-consciously and unsuccessfully – to 'reve' himself of all his passions, to turn his heart to stone. The effort to stamp out all human weakness in himself only creates further prob-lems (as in a different way it does for Coriolanus). He feels that the only 'remedy' for his pain is to kill 'the cause' of it, Desdemona; yet he can only preserve that impulse to do violence on her by also preserving the very pain he seeks

to heal. He cannot bring himself to the pitch of going
through with the 'remedy' except by realizing and suffering
to the full the anguish of the wound. He cannot think of
her in hatred without still feeling his love; because he loves
her and wants her, the thought of her keeps disarming him,
'singing the savageness' out of him. All his denials that he
loves her or that he suffers keep betraying themselves by
Freudian slips that reveal the very feelings he claims
freedom from. His expressions of loathing pull always back
to love (and vice versa); declarations of flinty imperviousness disclose and aggravate the raw wound:

OTHELLO I would have him nine years a-killing! – A fine woman,
a fair woman, a sweet woman!
IAGO Nay, you must forget that.
OTHELLO Ay, let her rot and perish, and be damned tonight, for
she shall not live! No, my heart is turned to stone:
I strike it, and it hurts my hand. – O, the world hath
not a sweeter creature! She might lie by an emperor's
side and command him tasks.
IAGO Nay, that's not your way.
OTHELLO Hang her! I do but say what she is: so delicate with her
needle, an admirable musician! O, she will sing the
savageness out of a bear! Of so high and plenteous wit
and invention!
IAGO She's the worse for all this.
OTHELLO O, a thousand, thousand times! – And then of so gentle
a condition.
IAGO Ay, too gentle.
OTHELLO Nay, that's certain – but yet the pity of it, Iago! O,
Iago, the pity of it, Iago!
IAGO If you are so fond over her iniquity, give her patent to
offend, for if it touch not you, it comes near nobody.
OTHELLO I will chop her into messes! Cuckold me! (IV, i, 177–99)

This is one of the moments when it is hardest to govern
our loathing of Iago for the stone-hearted ease with
which he keeps injecting poison exactly where Othello's
heart is most deeply 'touched'.

All through these scenes, as we should expect, Othello's most violent and brutal declarations of his power to hurt come at precisely those moments when he feels most helpless, impotent in the face of his own wounded feelings. His lack of 'government' over himself is compensated for by an increase in his bullying commands to her, assertions both of his right and of his capacity to control her. The more overwrought he feels, the more domineering he becomes. This, clearly, is why he is driven to strike her in IV, i, the scene so sharply contrasted with the Senate-scene (I, iii) in which the calmly dignified Othello had respectfully petitioned for Desdemona's presence with him in Cyprus. Now, in Act IV, in this the next 'official business' scene ('The Duke and Senators of Venice greet you'), Othello is boiling with desperate rage – 'Fire and brimstone!' – and Desdemona seems careless of it ('What, is he angry?'). In her capacity as the General's wife she keeps heedlessly babbling on to Lodovico about Cassio. For Othello, it seems as if she is publicly mocking him, and the 'indignity' is one that 'patience could not pass'.[1] Blindly, he hits out, unable either to contain his feelings or express them in any other way but by forcing himself upon her, forcing her to reckon with the fact that he will not, cannot, endure it. Similarly, when Lodovico remarks on her submissiveness and 'obedience', Othello tyrannically demonstrates his power and right to rule her by ordering her back, having just ordered her 'Out of my sight!'[2] She obeys him, and – split apart by the emotional trap he is in – Othello flares out at Lodovico: 'What would you with her, sir?'

LODOVICO Who? I, my lord?
OTHELLO   Ay, you did wish that I would make her turn.
           Sir, she can turn, and turn, and yet go on,

[1] Iago's terms in II, iii, 239–40.
[2] The terrible alteration in the lovers' relationship is epitomized in the difference between 'Out of my sight!' and the tone of his earlier speech (III, iii, 84–5): 'I do beseech thee, grant me this:/ To leave me but a little to myself.'

And turn again. And she can weep, sir, weep.
And she's obedient; as you say, obedient,
Very obedient – proceed you in your tears –
Concerning this, sir – O, well-painted passion! –
I am commanded home – get you away!
I'll send for you anon. – Sir, I obey the mandate,
And will return to Venice. – Hence, avaunt!

(IV, i, 253–62)

The virulent sarcasm is savage to the very extent that
Othello stands close to the brink of collapse. Of course,
his main impulse here is to lash out at Desdemona's supposed lasciviousness, fickleness and promiscuity: he
bitterly uses the word 'turn' in its sexual sense. But in its
ordinary sense, 'turn, and turn, and yet go on,/ And turn
again' is exactly what we have been seeing as the ungovern-
able, exhausting fluctuation of his own feelings about her,
all through the second half of the play.

As Othello oscillates between scarcely controllable
longing and the uncontrolled revulsion which is the other
face of longing, both feelings emerge again and again in
sexual terms. The most obvious and extreme case is in the
next scene (IV, ii) – a scene ushered in by another ominous
remark of Iago's:

LODOVICO What! Strike his wife!
IAGO   Faith, that was not so well: yet would I knew
          That stroke would prove the worst!   (IV, i, 274–6)

Significantly, IV, ii is the first time in the play so far that
we have seen Othello and Desdemona alone together.
Half-maddened with rage and pain, he treats her as a
whore, declaring she's as 'honest'

. . . as summer flies are in the shambles,
That quicken even with blowing. O, thou weed,
Who art so lovely fair, and smell'st so sweet
That the sense aches at thee, would thou hadst ne'er been born!

(IV, ii, 65–8)

The very violence of the attempt to spurn her betrays the inner failure of the attempt, and the source of his need and despair: 'so lovely fair . . . that the sense aches at thee'. (It is interesting that it is just at *this* point that the play should recall the ambivalences of Shakespeare's Sonnet 94, just as Emilia's remark in v, ii about the 'power to do harm' and 'to be hurt' recalls the same sonnet.) In his speech about the 'summer flies' it is Othello's imagination that festers, spawning fantasies that 'quicken even with blowing' in the shambles of his own infected mind. The fecund corruption in these imaginings is like an intensified version of the phantasmal torture of Brabantio that Iago's imagination had hatched at the start of the play: 'though he in a fertile climate dwells,/ Plague him with flies'.

The central speech in this scene (IV, ii) – Othello's anguished reply to Desdemona's question, 'Why do you weep?' – is one of the most crucially revealing speeches in the whole play. It gathers and brings to a focus lines of imagery that run through from the first act to the last: images of filth and purity, poverty and richness, captivity and freedom, affliction and joy.[1] And in bringing these images together the speech traces the extraordinary shifting process of Othello's sense of utter loss and degradation. His grossly self-pitying sense of himself as a long-suffering Job emerges in the catalogue of afflictions he declares he could have borne:

> Had it pleased heaven
> To try me with affliction, had they rained
> All kind of sores and shames on my bare head,
> Steeped me in poverty to the very lips,
> Given to captivity me and my utmost hopes,
> I should have found in some place of my soul
> A drop of patience. (IV, ii, 46–52)

[1]Michael Black brings out very finely the force of these images, in his discussion of this and connected speeches in *The Literature of Fidelity* (London, 1975), p. 16ff., especially (for this speech) pp. 28–9. See also his comments in *Poetic Drama,* pp. 87–8.

The extremity of these imagined trials vividly reflects the
extremity of his feeling that 'they' *have* rained sores and
shames on his bare head, that his self and his utmost
hopes *have* been 'given to captivity'. Once again, the resort
to subjunctives, the need to project a merely hypothetical
situation, reveals both how naked and 'unhoused' he feels
himself and how little he can bear to acknowledge the fact.
He edges a little nearer to acknowledging what he really
feels – only then to slide away towards self-pity again:

> But alas, to make me
> A fixèd figure for the time of scorn
> To point his slow unmoving finger at!
> Yet could I bear that too, well, very well.
>
> (ll. 52–5)

It is a sense of himself as the utterly helpless object of
others' malignant wills, an object of searing mockery
being mercilessly exposed by time's 'slow' finger, the
horrible finger that stops moving altogether when it reaches
him and so drags out his anguish interminably. He is the
'fixed' figure who cannot escape but must endure being
pointed at, relentlessly, for ever. Earlier, he had spoken
of how 'my soul hath her content so absolute . . .', but here
his soul is on its own rack, and his cry of near-hysterical
self-pity expresses a correspondingly absolute misery – a
scarcely tolerable sense of constriction and imprisonment,
epitomized by the oppressively locked-in, self-scorning
quality of the images ('figure'/'finger', 'fixed'/'unmoving').
Clearly, to our view at least, the cruelly jeering exposer and
the pitiably defenceless victim are twin aspects – inner and
outer – of a single projection of himself. Caught inside the
dungeon of his mind, the toils of his fantasy cramp and
deform; his 'free and open nature' (as Iago once called it)
can scarcely endure this 'circumscription and confine' of
an existence – so he takes it – entirely without love. 'Yet I
could bear that too, well, very well'; his 'yet' strives to

resist his admission that he cannot bear it 'well', or even at all. And then at last he brings himself – or, rather, his feelings bring him – to the most central, most direct and most agonized acknowledgment of what is really at stake for him. It is a unique moment in the play, and it exposes the very heart and fountain of the entire dramatic action – exposes it as precisely that of Othello's own life and love:

> But there where I have garnered up my heart,
> Where either I must live, or bear no life,
> The fountain from the which my current runs,
> Or else dries up – to be discarded thence . . .
>
> (IV, ii, 56–9)

Brief though this is, it has a poetic simplicity and power that stamp it quite unforgettably in our minds. It is one of those moments that only Shakespeare's genius could command, and command with such apparent ease and naturalness that moral imagination is visibly one with creative insight. For it comes to us as the crucial *truth* in everything we have seen. Being what he is – a mature and yet in many ways an emotionally innocent, insecure and disarrayed man – Othello has indeed garnered up his whole heart in Desdemona; without her sustaining love, her bounteous fruit-fulness, he now simply has nowhere to go, no way of living as himself.[1] That is what he has risked, and the supposed 'loss' is of course what he has been fearing all along.

Even now, at this crisis, alone with Desdemona, he lacks the emotional strength to dwell on the truth for more than a moment. The syntax of his speech breaks off, he cannot complete his thought, and his mind abruptly twists back on itself, sliding away to envisage the vile lust of toads – just as, at an earlier moment of horror and panic, he had imagined *being* a 'toad', living on 'the vapour of a dungeon', claiming that he would rather be that 'than keep a corner in the thing I love/ For others' uses' (III, iii, 267–70). Here

[1] Cf. his question in the final scene: 'Where should Othello go?'

in IV, ii, his imagination plunges even further: he sees his own life as a cistern in which *other* foul toads go to't:

> . . . to be discarded thence
> Or keep it as a cistern for foul toads
> To knot and gender in! (ll. 59–61)

To us, these 'foul toads' that 'knot' are obviously gendered in his own mind, and his mind is itself the sewer-cistern, the dank breeding-ground of these hideous phantoms of his own degradation and denial.

Even so, this long speech is strikingly unlike most of his earlier speeches since the crisis-scene in Act III: quite unlike the flailing rhetoric of his 'black vengeance' speech, for instance, or the self-bolstering, tightly willed force of his elaborate analogy between himself and the Pontic sea. Only in the speech just before his collapse in IV, i, and in some of his half-hysterical, menacing speeches to Desdemona in this same scene, does he burst out in this kind of spontaneous, authentic, unwilled, uncontrolled passion. Both the image of Desdemona as his very life-spring, and the consequent image of his 'current' as degenerated into a fetid cistern for others to gender in, rush directly from his heart. Repulsive as his own craven repulsion is, it is nevertheless a naked and terrible indication of the depth of his sexual need and longing for her alone. 'There where I have garnered up my heart – . . . to be discarded thence . . .': this is not the kind of language that has usually come to the lips of this man who so well knows 'how to tell my story'; it is unrehearsed, uncomposed, rawly self-exposing. (In some ways, its qualities are not unlike the monumental grief, self-pity and emotional prostration of Heathcliff's sobbing speeches about being discarded by Catherine, in *Wuthering Heights*.) The very word 'discarded' is important in itself. It comes up in other Shakespearean plays too – in *Henry IV* Part I (I, iii 178), for instance, in a speech of Hotspur's concerned, in fact, with a matter not unlike this in *Othello*: 'And shall it, in more shame, be further spoken/ That you are fool'd, discarded, and shook off,/ By him for whom these shames ye underwent?' The word comes up later, too, as in *Lear*, which *Othello* anticipates in so many ways, and once again in a scene (III, iv, in the hovel) concerned with the nakedness of 'unhousèd', 'unaccommodated' man exposed to the to-and-fro conflicting elements in a storm likewise 'too rough for nature to endure':

LEAR Is it the fashion that discarded fathers
      Should have thus little mercy on their flesh?

More unguardedly than at any moment so far, and despite his slithering off into self-pity and panicking horror, Othello reveals in this long speech his basic sense of being not just maimed but *mortally* injured by Desdemona's betrayal. It is at once a cry of despair, a cry of protest which turns into hysterical disgust and loathing, and a cry for cure or remedy or solace – but for solace that *we* see as plainly impossible for Desdemona or anyone else to give him, since the 'affliction' is, in every sense, 'begotten on itself'. Othello's mind now clearly mis-gives him too much; its last life-lines to objective reality have become so frayed that even Emilia's and Desdemona's explicit testimony of her innocence only serves to strengthen his conviction of her guilt. As he founders, anything that suggests that he has been discarded is intolerable; yet *not* to be convinced – still to have a 'hinge to hang a doubt upon' (III, iii, 363) – is equally intolerable. Thus he rushes from conviction to suspicion and back again, hurling now the word 'committed' in Desdemona's face ('What committed! . . . Committed? . . . What committed! . . . What committed? . . . Impudent strumpet!'), and now, when she still denies it, clutching at the word 'possible' (What! Not a whore? . . . Is't possible?').

To envisage Desdemona's betrayal as only a 'possibility' always undermines Othello's rage and overturns his resolution, his desire to 'do', to *act*. It forces him back to

the abyss of an 'if' that renders everything except passive
suffering impossible. Hung over that dread-filled chasm,
cut off from all 'content' or life, his reactions at once
horrify and compel us. Even though many readers recoil
into complete moral rejection of him, I think the play no
less strongly urges us not to 'discard' him, by making us
recognize his humanity in his very inhumane bloodlust,
his very panic and collapse. We surely cannot fail to see
how close he is to his breaking-point, the limit (to adapt
Gerard Manley Hopkins's word) of his 'durance':

> O the mind, mind has mountains; cliffs of fall
> Frightful, sheer, no-man-fathomed. Hold them cheap
> May who ne'er hung there. Nor does long our small
> Durance deal with that steep or deep.[1]

All through these dreadful scenes the stress (in both
applications of the word) falls on durance – on how much
of reality, even a supposed 'reality', a man can bear. We are
brought face up against the fact, which Othello can only
fleetingly realize, that although a man can endure some
kinds of loss or suffering, some losses are literally a matter of
life and death. And although we are intensely aware that
Othello has virtually lost his wits and not (as he thinks)
Desdemona's love, we also see that he is so irretrievably
lost in his delusion about having lost her that the consequences may well be as dire as if this were indeed so. By the
end of Act IV, Othello is nearing the limit of his capacity
even to think about that kind of loss. Several times, and
very clearly, the play makes the point that human endur-
ance has limits. Emilia, for instance, in this same scene
(IV, ii, 116) speaks, apropos of Desdemona, of such a degree
of pain and grief 'as true heart cannot bear'. Even Roderigo
reaches his limit: directly echoing Othello's words earlier

[1]Hopkins's phrases (from 'No Worst, There is None') are reminiscent of
Othello's words in the final scene: 'Wash me in steep-down gulfs of liquid
fire!'

('I'll not endure it . . .') he declares to Iago that he has
borne all he can – 'I will indeed no longer endure it' (IV,
ii, 178). For Othello, as for Desdemona, it becomes less and
less a matter of what he will or will not endure but of what
he can or cannot. Gradually, we are brought to realize
about Othello what I think Desdemona comes to realize
about herself: a truth put very simply in Isaac Rosenberg's
'The Amulet' (part of *The Unicorn*) in the passage to which
D. W. Harding drew attention:[1]

LILITH I think there is more sorrow in the world
       Than man can bear.
NUBIAN None can exceed their limit, lady:
       You either bear or break.

As Act IV proceeds, then, it grows increasingly clear that
Othello (and Desdemona) have passed the point where
either could, in this storm, ever be safely 'ensheltered and
embayed' in the other's love. As with the Turks in Act II,
'it is impossible they bear it out' (II, i, 17–19). The irony
is grim if we recall the terms of Othello's wooing-speeches
('the dangers I had passed', etc.), for by now this 'imminent
deadly breach' between the lovers seems indeed too
'deadly' to leave alive in them or us the expectation of any
even 'hair-breadth scapes'. Desdemona's intuition is right:
she must die.

Othello's struggle to find and sustain the resolution to
commit the murder he sees as his only 'remedy' also forces
his 'heart' to concentrate on its own state. His impulse to
kill her, which has now become a desperate need, is thus
(as we see it) the need to *kill in himself* the capacity to love
and thus to feel pain. The only way to 'provide his mind'
lies in trying to turn his heart to stone – and then to
extinguish his suffering once and for all by making *her*

---

[1]Leavis took this up in 'Tragedy and the "Medium" '. It should be said tha
the strength of the passage depends on its being extracted from its by and
large disastrously Shelley-like context.

dead as stone. We can scarcely miss the dramatic relevance to Othello of Iago's words to Roderigo at the end of IV, ii, about the proposed murder of Cassio:

Come, stand not amazed at it . . . I will show you such a necessity in his death that you shall think yourself bound to put it on him. (IV, ii, 237–40)

As the last act begins, Roderigo and Iago's comments about the murder of Cassio again point us to Othello's sense of the murder *he* is trying to 'think [him]self bound to put on' Desdemona:

IAGO   Quick, quick; fear nothing: I'll be at thy elbow.
        It makes us, or it mars us; think on that,
        And fix most firm thy resolution.
        . . .
        Be bold, and take thy stand.
                                    [He retires]
RODERIGO I have no great devotion to the deed,
        And yet he hath given me satisfying reasons.
                                (V, i, 3–9)

By this time Othello has fixed most firm his resolution (as we see when he next appears). He too has evidently found 'satisfying reasons', an incontrovertible 'cause' for killing Desdemona – one that (as he has to delude himself in order to make it incontrovertible) depends not on his personal feelings, but on an impersonal 'necessity'. When the final, fatal scene opens, he seems at last calmly 'provided' to go through with the deed – but only by thinking of it as a 'sacrifice', not a murder, and thus thinking of himself not as a murderer but as a hard, flinty, resolute and disinterested instrument of impersonal 'justice'. Claudius's pat remark in *Hamlet* (IV, iii, 9–11) that 'Diseases desperate grown/ By desperate appliance are reliev'd,/ Or not at all' seems pertinent here, for in *Othello* as in *Hamlet* Shakespeare realizes that even the most desperate appliances often do turn out 'not at all' to relieve desperate diseases. Even before Othello's 'appliance' of murder is put to the test, we have been brought to see that, for *his* kind and degree of 'disease' and sickness at heart, 'revenge' will not be in the least 'satisfying': it will worsen his anguish a thousand-fold, not relieve or 'cure it' at all.

7

Self-charity and self-abnegation: the play's women in love

MONTANO . . . nor know I aught
By me that's said or done amiss this night,
Unless self-charity be sometimes a vice,
And to defend ourselves it be a sin
When violence assails us.   (ii, iii, 194–8)

DESDEMONA A guiltless death I die.
EMILIA O, who hath done this deed?
DESDEMONA Nobody – I myself – farewell.
Commend me to my kind lord – O, farewell!
[*She dies*]   (v, ii, 123–6)

One of the oddest things about criticism of *Othello* is how little usually gets said about Desdemona. She is often considered as a necessary element in the drama only because she is a necessary element in its plot – the woman with whom Othello just happens to be in love – rather than a major dramatic figure conceived in relation to everyone else. There is a strong tendency in critics of all persuasions to take her as a helpless, hapless victim – like one of those ideal Victorian heroines in whose mouths not even margarine would melt. As Marvin Rosenberg points out, 'Desdemona has been in grave danger of being canonized',[1] with the result that the play is made to seem much simpler than it is – much as similar conceptions of Cordelia, for instance, have a similar result with *King Lear*. As Rosenberg also points out, however, the same result follows from the (not

[1] *The Masks of Othello*, p. 108.

uncommon) alternative view of Desdemona, which sees her not as an innocent victim but as the culpable agent of her fate, or as someone whose 'flaws' or 'indiscretions' are such that she partly 'deserves' what happens because she 'brings it upon herself'.

It seems to me that Rosenberg is right: neither of these views of Desdemona will do. Not only is she a more interesting and complex character, but she also emerges as a crucial and complex element in the dramatic design.[1] To miss or distort what she – and Emilia and Bianca, the play's other women in love – represent in the world of *Othello* is to miss an essential element in its tragic power. What Leavis, for instance, asserts but nowhere explains is true: 'the tragedy is inherent in the Othello–Desdemona relation'.[2]

In a general way, of course, the shape of Desdemona's married life is largely determined by that of Othello's. His crisis entails hers, and it affects both the nature and degree of what she suffers. Nevertheless, the significance of the play is deepened by what it shows her individual inner experience to be – especially what it shows in her love for Othello and her ways of responding to him throughout the action. She is clearly not a sort of conventional villainess in disguise, but neither is she a conventional heroine, a saintly, 'ill-starred wench' to whom we must accord absolute, unquestioning admiration and pity; and to suppose either that Iago succeeds because he is vicious-and-therefore-powerful or that Desdemona dies because she is virtuous-and-therefore-powerless is to accuse Shakespeare of a sentimentality as ludicrous as the opposite

[1] There is a good account of Desdemona's character in Katherine S. Stockholder, ' "Egregiously an Ass": Chance and Accident in *Othello*', *Studies in English Literature*, 13 (1973), pp. 256–72. Julian C. Rice, 'Desdemona Unpinned: Universal Guilt in *Othello*', *Shakespeare Studies*, 7 (1974), pp. 209–26, also makes some interesting points about her, although I cannot agree with his over-all argument.
[2] 'Diabolic Intellect and the Noble Hero', p. 141.

sort that Miss Prism pinpricks in *The Importance of Being Earnest*: 'The good ended happily and the bad unhappily. That is what Fiction means.'

Shakespeare's moral insight and thinking in *Othello* are not sentimentally pessimistic, nor do they feed on hopeful fantasies. Indeed, as I have been suggesting, the play is largely *about* the implications and consequences of fear-begotten pessimism and wishful thinking. Desdemona is made to mean much more to us than a conveniently touching murderee for the nastier elements in Iago and Othello to practise on and set off by contrast. Shakespeare does not see the world in terms of clear-cut guilt and innocence, bad agents and good victims. In *Othello*, as we come to realize, no one is entirely master of his fate (not even Iago); equally, no one is merely a victim (not even Desdemona – despite the derivation of her name from a Greek word for 'ill-fated'). Her death is catastrophic – a 'monstrous act', as Montano says (v, ii, 187); but we respond to it as a tragic (not merely an unfortunate) event because we have come to see how her fate too is largely – and yet not wholly – defined and shaped by her particular disposition. Othello kills her because he loves her in the ways he does; but the play also makes us realize that Desdemona is murderable because she has staked her life upon *his* faith and love. Being the particular woman she is, who loves him in that way, her responses to him unwittingly add fuel to the spreading fire of his fear and rage. Having done that, she is yet unable to quell, escape or even much resist – let alone extinguish – the blaze in his feelings, which finally consumes them both. All through, Desdemona's nature, her sense of herself, and her ways of responding to her husband, are dramatically compared and contrasted with those of others. And with her, as with them, the moral perceptions and discriminations *we* are led to make are much more complex than the kind of neat computations of praise and blame, of 'fairness' and 'foulness', that she and Iago jocularly toss to and fro on

the Cypriot shore in Act II, and that *Othello*'s critics have
been tossing to and fro ever since.

Quite early in the play it becomes clear that, just as Othello
has an ideal conception of Desdemona, so too she has an
ideal conception of him. John Bayley's account of Othello's
arrival in Cyprus catches this nicely:

> Desdemona's love for Othello is also of course wildly romantic –
> he personifies for her all the romance she has discovered to
> exist in life – but committing herself to this vision is for her a
> more matter-of-fact business than it could be for him.[1]

Yet if her commitment to this romantic image of Othello
is more intrepidly 'matter-of-fact' than his, it is shown as
no less perilous. That neither of them really 'knows' the
other is hardly surprising, given the circumstances of their
courtship. More importantly, however, as we grow alarmed
by the possible consequences of that ignorance we also see
that it is persisting: neither of them seems able to notice,
let alone adjust to, what the other actually is. With deepen-
ing unease we observe Desdemona holding to her ideal
conception of Othello more staunchly, not less so, even
when – from III, iii, onwards – he keeps 'cashiering' his
ideal sense of her. Her passionate tenacity and his passionate rejection are shown to be mutually reinforcing, in ways
that prove utterly disastrous for them both.

Desdemona's ideal, romantic image of Othello, like his
of her, does to a considerable extent correspond with reality.
He is indeed a valiant soldier, a man of real substance and
experience, who has given all of himself to her admiration
and love. 'She loved me for the dangers I had passed',
Othello declares, 'And I loved her, that she did pity them'
(I, iii, 166–7). Even as early as this we may well have a passing doubt about the soundness of admiration and pity as
foundations for a marriage – not so much because we have

[1] *The Characters of Love*, p. 160

reason to question their love for each other, as because we
may wonder about their capacity to avoid collisions and
misunderstandings.[1] When things do begin to jar between
them, we realize that the way Desdemona described her
love for Othello before the Senate was as revealing as
Othello's way of describing his love for her:

> That I did love the Moor to live with him,
> My downright violence and storm of fortunes
> May trumpet to the world. My heart's subdued
> Even to the very quality of my lord.
> I saw Othello's visage in his mind
> And to his honours and his valiant parts
> Did I my soul and fortunes consecrate.
> So that, dear lords, if I be left behind
> A moth of peace, and he go to the war,
> The rites for which I love him are bereft me,
> And I a heavy interim shall support
> By his dear absence. Let me go with him.
>
> (I, iii, 245–56)

This is certainly not the tone of a timid, selfless hero-
worshipper. In context, the immediate effect of this speech
is to reveal both the bold, unqualified frankness of Desdemona's commitment to Othello, and her beautifully relaxed
acceptance of it. Yet Othello's own speeches to the Senate
have already suggested to us that there is more to him than
her terms – 'honours' and 'valiant parts' – acknowledge.
We begin to see, long before she does herself, that her sense
of his 'very quality' stops short of the more obscure, less
controllable and less simply admirable emotional potentialities of his nature, which are naturally engaged and stirred
by the marriage he makes rather late in life. In the event,
this matters only because her conception of him *remains*
so narrow. She proves quite unable to recognize or acknowledge any of his less than honourable and valiant parts

---

[1] We very quickly see and believe that they are bound by more than (as Iago
puts it so as to encourage Roderigo) 'sanctimony and a frail vow' (I, iii, 384).

until (largely because of her non-recognition) they have already corroded the man she thought him – the 'all-in-all-sufficient' noble Moor whom neither fear nor passion could shake. The play pushes at *us* the fearful truth not only that fear and passion certainly can shake Othello, but that Desdemona's view of him as unshakable is itself disastrously unshakable. So closed is she to doubt, in fact, that not until IV, i does his behaviour impinge on her sufficiently to make her question or adjust her sense of him at all. As the first three acts continually suggest, it is precisely her naïve, loyal devotion to her adored ideal Othello that blinds her to his reality until it is too late. Her responses to him are the mirror image of his to her. The more she 'appears' to be fair, the more obdurately does he hold to his notion that she must be foul; the more plainly he 'appears' to differ from her romantic notion of him, the more tenaciously she defends and clings to the ideal. She asserts (because she needs to believe) that he cannot 'really' be what he seems – he cannot be 'foul', he must be fair.

Like Othello, of course, Desdemona herself 'errs in ignorance'; yet, as we see again and again, ignorance can be fatal, and innocence can incur guilt. Neither the best of motives nor the most pressing of 'causes' can undo or even mitigate the actual consequences of 'error', and the results of mistakes of judgment and feeling can be equally devastating whether the mistake was ignorant, or 'cunning', or a mixture of both. In IV, ii, Desdemona, by now utterly bewildered, asks Othello, 'Alas, what ignorant sin have I committed?' It is a question that all the main characters (except Iago) come implicitly or explicitly to ask; and as with her, the 'ignorance' of the error does not make it any the less 'committed', nor the damage any easier to undo or repair.

With Desdemona, as with the others, our interest is directed to the peculiar nature, effects, and implications of her 'ignorant errors' of judgment and feeling. The first three acts concentrate on what Dr Johnson in his Notes on the play nicely described as her 'slowness to suspect that she can be suspected' – the opposite of Othello's 'alacrity in hardness' in suspecting *her* of hardness. In the last two acts her belated recognition that she is suspected leaves her dazed, miserable and withdrawn – the opposite of Othello's dazed, miserable, aggressive response to his 'recognition' of her falsehood. In the first three acts she seems active, resolute, confident – as decisive as Othello at the beginning. (Compare, for example, his speech ''Tis yet to know . . .' (I, ii, 19ff.) with hers – 'My downright violence . . . may trumpet to the world . . .' (I, iii, 245ff.).) She is daring enough, for example, to reject the suitors her father has selected, to elope with Othello, to defend her actions before the Senate, to accompany him to a theatre of war and to challenge his judgment over Cassio. If anything disturbs us about her behaviour in the first half of the play, it is her *un*hesitating self-assurance and energy. But from IV, i onwards, it is the reverse, her peculiar passivity, that is most disturbing. Quite suddenly, she seems to lack both the power and the will to challenge or resist anyone. She seems stunned into apathetic submission, and quite incapable now of such confident and proper wifely presumption as, for example, Portia shows towards *her* husband in *Julius Caesar* (II, i, 237ff.), imploring Brutus to 'make me acquainted with your cause of grief', and quietly refusing to be fobbed off by claims that he is ill: 'No, my Brutus;/ You have some sick offence within your mind,/ Which by the right and virtue of my place/ I ought to know of.' Such efforts as Desdemona makes to find out what is wrong or to defend herself against Othello are so nervous, so recessive and so disastrously ambiguous that he takes them as implicit admissions of her guilt.

There is more to this than a simple switch from vigorous activity to passive inertia, however. Were that all the play gave us, we might fairly conclude that Shakespeare treated

Desdemona's 'character' merely as an expedient device to suit the 'plot': the first part of it requiring a woman capable of getting herself into awkward situations, the second a frail, timid one to suffer her fate with due pathos. But this is to do much less than justice to the intensity and coherence with which Shakespeare conceives the dramatic design as a whole. Desdemona is an essential element in that whole, and if we examine it carefully we can see how and why she is – both in herself, and in relation to everyone else, especially Iago and Othello. The tiny and the momentous changes that occur within Othello are dramatized with no lack of interest in the minor and major alterations that simultaneously and consequently occur in Desdemona. Much as Chaucer does with Criseyde, for example, Shakespeare portrays Desdemona's inner experience and her responses to the world around her in a way that discloses the psychological *process* of her change from bold self-assertion to frightened recessiveness. He reveals, that is, both the difference and the continuity between her self in Act I and in Act V.

The early acts show her as buoyant, determined and naïve – buoyant and determined largely because naïve. Nothing more plainly reveals her slowness to suspect that she can be suspected than her innocent persistence in urging Cassio's suit – the persistence which so ironically confirms Othello's suspicions of her infidelity.[1] Not less because of the all too plainly harmful effects on Othello, Desdemona's unsuspecting persistence is for us the surest index of how very far she is from doing the harms he misconstructs upon it. From the first, we are convinced of what he doubts and fails to recognize: it is her deep *trust*

---

[1] Iago's gloating over this easily exploitable conjunction of Othello's fearful credulousness and Desdemona's unsuspecting goodness may again remind us of Edmund's phrases in *King Lear* when he congratulates himself on having 'A credulous father! and a brother noble,/ Whose nature is so far from doing harms/ That he suspects none; on whose foolish honesty/ My practices ride easy' (I, ii, 170–3).

in his love for her that prompts and enables her so warmly to take up Cassio's 'cause' in defiance of Othello's will, just as it previously gave her the bold energy to elope with him despite her father's will. As we see it, her friendly support for Cassio is a clear sign of her assurance that her love for Othello and Cassio's love for him imply Othello's trust and goodwill towards them both, and that this will naturally prevail over any other consideration. Hence, with her trusting assurance goes a failure or ignorant error of tact and understanding. She loves Othello for his honourable soldiership but she neither has nor acquires any real sense of what this soldiership means to him and demands of him, nor of how it must therefore impinge on their marriage. In effect, she tries to make their marriage impinge on his job – which is of course exactly what Othello (in his speeches to the Senators while she was present) had so anxiously insisted would *not* happen. The Duke, we remember, promptly put this claim to the test:

DUKE   Th'affair cries haste,
           And speed must answer it. You must hence tonight.
DESDEMONA Tonight, my lord?
DUKE   This night.
OTHELLO   With all my heart.
                                    (I, iii, 273–5)

This is a telling little moment. Desdemona's surprise and (understandable) disappointment that official business can so peremptorily sweep aside her personal wishes is sharply juxtaposed with Othello's prompt alacrity in accepting this as a fact. His next speech likewise accepts the fact, and leaves her no room for protest: when professional matters call, he says, 'we must obey the time'.

Subsequent events not only give *us*, they also give Desdemona, opportunity enough to observe Othello's habitual assumption that military matters must necessarily take precedence over private wishes – the main such event being, of course, Cassio's dismissal. But Desdemona completely fails to take the point. We first learn of her support for Cassio in a speech of Emilia's to him, telling him to cheer up (III, i, 40–9). It is a speech that has sometimes been taken – by those who see Desdemona as entirely flawless, and those who assume that Emilia, being the wife of a chronic liar, must therefore be a chronic liar herself – as mere fabrication. There seems to me no dramatic reason at all to suppose that Emilia here is speaking anything but the simple truth, and the following dialogue between Desdemona and Cassio fully corroborates it. What Emilia says, moreover, is surely given to her to utter just because it is both true and significant. Cassio, we recall, has come to ask her to arrange an interview with Desdemona, so that he can persuade the latter to intervene on his behalf. Emilia tells him that Desdemona has already, unprompted, taken up his cause, evidently not having needed Cassio's 'cue'.

EMILIA Good morrow, good Lieutenant; I am sorry
For your displeasure: but all will sure be well.
The General and his wife are talking of it,
And she speaks for you stoutly. The Moor replies
That he you hurt is of great fame in Cyprus,
And great affinity; and that in wholesome wisdom
He might not but refuse you; but he protests he loves you
And needs no other suitor but his likings
To take the safest occasion by the front
To bring you in again.   (III, i, 40–9)

The crucial fact Emilia so 'stoutly' reports here is surely Othello's statement that he 'needs no other suitor but his likings': he himself would personally be happy to reinstate Cassio, but politically it would as yet be improper and inexpedient to do so. His reply to Desdemona, had she listened and understood, should have silenced her plea and led her to trust the matter to Othello's own competence. Likewise, Emilia's report of it should have silenced Cassio.

It does neither. And when Desdemona promises Cassio to continue his suit, she actually gives a guarantee of her success:

> Before Emilia here,
> I give thee warrant of thy place. Assure thee,
> If I do vow a friendship, I'll perform it
> To the last article. My lord shall never rest.
> I'll watch him tame and talk him out of patience;
> His bed shall seem a school, his board a shrift;
> I'll intermingle everything he does
> With Cassio's suit.   (III, iii, 19–26)

Her subsequent deeds prove as good as her words. Intermingling everything with Cassio's suit, she talks Othello 'out of patience' in ways she never foresaw, watching him wild, not 'tame'. As Othello had done with Brabantio, she tries to 'out-tongue' Othello's 'complaints'. I have already suggested (see above, pp. 136ff.) that in her conversation with him early in III, iii (immediately following her colloquy with Cassio) we notice, with a sense of alarm that soon overtakes Othello too, how deftly she resorts to a kind of emotional blackmail, demanding in effect that he show his love for her by allowing her to be the General. Denying his freedom and rejecting his judgment, she forces him to deny her power and reject her feelings. And of course the result is to make him all the more conscious of her power over his heart – so much so that, egged on by Iago, he takes the fact of her intervention as the sign of her having already exerted her power to reject him.

Dr Johnson spoke of Desdemona's 'artless perseverance' in urging Cassio's suit. If at first it does strike us as 'artless' in some ways (though dangerously artful in others), her perseverance soon strikes us as also rather imperceptive as well as tactless. For the extraordinary fact is that even as late as IV, i we find her still continuing to press Cassio's case, evidently not having noticed (or being determined to ignore) how disastrous a topic it is with Othello, who by now finds Cassio's very name anathema. So numerous and so violent are the explosions about this subject that they sharply emphasize the blindness to Othello that allows Desdemona to persist, just as his persistent misunderstanding of her persistence reveals his desperate blindness to her. Yet blindness (or imperceptiveness) is not quite the right word for what her behaviour shows. It is progressively revealed rather as a kind of desperation that is both like and unlike Othello's own in relation to her. Her apparent imperceptiveness is shown to be really more like a nervous *refusal* to acknowledge – even to herself – that Othello could possibly be jealous or suspicious. As Brabantio had done with her (insisting, for example, that she is 'a maiden never bold'), she seems with Othello almost wilfully to ignore the reality and the implications of his behaviour, implicitly insisting that he is a man never suspicious. Her romantic sense of him tightens into a need – a self-preservative need – to believe his strangeness is caused by anything except some change or breakdown in her relationship with him. She insists that he is neither more nor less than the same husband to whose 'honours and valiant parts' (as she said in I, iii) she has 'consecrated' her 'soul and fortunes'.

It is in order further to alert us to this – the closedness of Desdemona's image of Othello and its growing necessity to her as a self-protective 'art' by which to steal her thoughts away from his present state (and her own) – that Shakespeare gives us, straight after the crisis of III, iii, the pointed little dialogue between Desdemona and Emilia about the handkerchief (III, iv, 23ff.). Desdemona, having just discovered that her precious token is missing, remarks that 'I had rather have lost my purse/ Full of crusadoes.' For us, her remark merely underlines how much more grievous her 'loss' may be than, say, Roderigo's loss of all his money. But Desdemona herself, we notice, even though she cannot know the significance of her loss, is quick to see its theoretically possible consequences: it would be enough, she says, to upset a lesser man. It is *she* who first mentions the possiblity of jealousy here. Yet – with an irony accentuated by later developments – she makes her suggestion only to discount it, in much the same way as, early in III, iii, Othello's mind had flitted to the possibilities of 'perdition' and 'chaos', only to discount them. She instantly confirms – for her own assurance it seems, as much as Emilia's – her belief that Othello is not an ordinary erring mortal at all. His noble nature, she declares, contains no trace of 'baseness':

DESDEMONA Believe me, I had rather have lost my purse
Full of crusadoes; and, but my noble Moor
Is true of mind, and made of no such baseness
As jealous creatures are, it were enough
To put him to ill-thinking. (III, iv, 25–9)

Though evidently surprised by Emilia's gentle query, 'Is he not jealous?', she dismisses it at once, without allowing it a second's thought – fondly, and with a touch of complacency:

DESDEMONA Who? He? I think the sun where he was born
Drew all such humours from him.
EMILIA Look where he comes. (III, iv, 30–1)

In the dialogue that follows here Othello's wild behaviour proves wild enough to bruise but not to shatter her assurance. His extraordinary, brooding remarks about her hand –

Hot, hot and moist. This hand of yours requires
. . .
Much castigation, exercise devout;
For there's a young and sweating devil here
That commonly rebels – (III, iv, 38, 41–3)

are met only by her refusal even to attend to what he is saying, let alone to what it implies:

DESDEMONA I cannot speak of this. Come now, your promise
[about Cassio].

When she cannot produce the handkerchief Othello shrilly
demands to see, he bursts out with his fabulous tale about
its origins; but once again, although the tale betrays to us
the raw emotional state behind it as clearly as if Othello
had announced it directly, Desdemona still manages not to
see it. Even when his threatening tone prompts her to ask,
'Why do you speak so startlingly and rash?', she only asks
him the question, but never presses it on herself nor tries
to answer it. On the contrary, she declares he is only using
'a trick to put me from my suit'. While he works himself
into an absolute frenzy about the handkerchief, she still
goes on and on trying to push the conversation back to
'Cassio', until in desperate anguish he storms away to be
alone.

Every detail of this scene is revealing – even the rather
uncomic 'comic' dialogue between Desdemona and the
clown with which it opens. As in the play's other 'comic'
scenes, Shakespeare's muse seems to labour here, though,
as Robert A. Watts points out,[1] the incident is obviously
pertinent to the play's main concerns, not a mere diver-
sionary caper or a piece of light refreshment before the
going gets really tough. It is plain enough that Shakespeare
includes it in order to deliver the clown's (albeit rather
heavy) puns on 'lying':

I dare not say he [Cassio] lies anywhere . . . He's a soldier, and
for one to say a soldier lies is stabbing . . . I know not where he
lodges, and for me to . . . say he lies here, or he lies there, were
to lie in mine own throat.   (III, iv, 2ff.)

The pun is a commonplace, of course; but one effect of it
here is simply to consolidate our sense of Desdemona's

[1]'The Comic Scenes in *Othello*', *Shakespeare Quarterly*, 19 (1968), pp.
349–54.

innocence.[1] Like the clown, she has not the faintest idea
where Cassio lies. But the larger dramatic import of it
emerges clearly enough in the lovers' subsequent dialogue
about the handkerchief – dialogue which ironically repeats
in a more frightening form the same sequence of misunderstandings as those in the clown's banter with Desdemona.
Lies about lying (or false accusations of others for lying
about lying) are the stuff of most comedies and tragedies
about sexual relations, of course, and *Othello* is no exception. Thus in IV, i (35ff.), for example, Othello madly
juggles both parts of the pun in his mind: 'Lie with her?
Lie on her? We say lie on her when they belie her. Lie with
her! Zounds, that's fulsome!' In III, iv, the clown's puns
serve to accentuate Iago's lies about lying in the previous
scene, for instance, but also to pave the way for the lovers'
conversation that follows immediately after: Othello lies
about the handkerchief's magical provenance because he is
sure Desdemona lies when she says she has not lost it –
sure she lies, because (so he thinks) she has lain with
Cassio and has given the handkerchief to him. The result
of Othello's threat is to frighten her into a lie – or at least
a half-lie (for she thinks she has only mislaid the handkerchief, not lost it). She lies, in short, because she is innocent,
and yet in doing so manages only to convince him of the
lie that she is not. It is a dreadful vicious circle.

What keeps it in motion, however, is not Desdemona's
lie to Othello *per se*, but the fact that the whole incident
exacerbates her need to lie to *herself* about the possible
meaning of Othello's extraordinary conduct. She is frightened into lying by Othello's mistrust and implicit accusation that she is lying. To Emilia's gently repeated question after Othello has stormed off (for Emilia does not view
Othello through romantic spectacles) – 'Is not this man
jealous?' – Desdemona's answer shows how little she can

[1]For a very interesting general discussion of the pun on 'lie' see Christopher
Ricks, 'Lies', *Critical Inquiry*, 2 (1975), pp. 121–42.

even yet acknowledge that something is indeed seriously wrong: 'I ne'er saw this before./ Sure, there's some wonder in this handkerchief.' Desdemona subtly side-steps the real wonder, which she dares not contemplate: that *she* more than the handkerchief or its 'charm' is causing Othello's 'strange unquietness'. Having just (in Othello's presence) evaded the point of his tale about the token's magical properties she now (just as Brabantio had done about her own behaviour in Act I) anxiously asserts that some spell or charm must have caused his rashness. It is Emilia who keeps quietly insisting on what Desdemona needs to evade or deny: the fact that her marriage is collapsing.

When Cassio enters, Desdemona makes what is surely one of the largest understatements in the play, and one of the most ironical in its unwitting use of Iago's metaphor:

> My advocation is not now in tune:
> . . .
> You must awhile be patient.
>
> (III, iv, 119, 125)

There is a welling but still unacknowledgeable bewilderment in that. She can explain her distress only in terms of the consequences for *Cassio* of her failing in her suit despite having 'stood within the blank of [Othello's] displeasure/ For my free speech!' This makes it all the more dismaying for us (and cheering for Cassio) to learn that she proposes to continue. Her misapprehension of Othello's state by now seems at once wilful and emotionally necessary to her. In her effort to explain his angry recalcitrance (or, rather, to explain it away), for instance, we recognize the same move as everyone in the play has taken in their attempts to make tolerable sense of their perplexities: she tries to ascribe it to some comfortingly impersonal, objective 'cause':

> Something, sure, of state,
> Either from Venice, or some unhatched practice
> Made demonstrable here in Cyprus to him,
> Hath puddled his clear spirit.   (III, iv, 136–9)

Not the least chilling of the ironies here is that produced by her metaphor of an 'unhatched practice/ Made demonstrable'. For us (in ways she of course is wholly unaware of), it is both an accurate phrase for Iago's foul calumnies and a clanging reminder of his characteristic metaphors of conception and pregnancy: 'Hell and night/ Must bring this monstrous birth to the world's light' (I, iii, 397–8); 'There are many events in the womb of time, which will be delivered' (I, iii, 364–5); 'my muse labours,/ And thus she is delivered' (II, i, 126–7); 'this granted – as it is a most pregnant and unforced position' (II, i, 229); and so on (metaphors which we are to hear again in another ironic context, on Othello's lips in the final scene). Moreover, like everyone else in the play, Desdemona next tries to cheer herself up with philosophic generalizations, implicitly claiming that her troubles are both ordinary and easily explicable:

> . . . and in such cases
> Men's natures wrangle with inferior things,
> Though great ones are their object. 'Tis even so.
>   (III, iv, 139–41)

Nothing betrays her unconscious need to reassure and calm herself more than her implicit assertion that her problems are negligible because Othello's condition is no more serious than a hurt finger:

> For let our finger ache, and it endues
> Our healthful members even to that sense
> Of pain.   (III, iv, 142–4)

As this scene proceeds, it becomes more and more clear that Desdemona is doing the reverse of what Othello does

throughout the whole latter half of the play. Where he
clings to his conviction that all must be ill in their marriage,
she clings to her belief that all must 'really' be well, despite
the increasingly obvious signs that it is not. Consequently,
we can no longer respond to her responses as if these were a
mark simply of naïvety, or a lack of gumption, or some kind
of insensitivity to Othello. Whereas earlier her persistent
harping on Cassio had seemed rather tactless and imperceptive, it is now more as if a fear is stealing over her – the
fear that something is changing, or perhaps has already
changed, in Othello's sense of her. Her imperceptiveness now
seems to reflect a *need* to remain oblivious to the change
whose implications are so frightening. I think we begin to
recognize in her a positive will not to see things as they are –
a will which, while it is the reverse of Othello's need to see
things as they are not, nevertheless springs from a very
similar cause: the fear of having to recognize that perhaps
(and perhaps through some suspected fault or 'demerit'
of her own) she has lost his love. From this scene on, her
behaviour strikes us as involving delusions as well as illusions – self-preservative delusions whose cause and emotional function are too pathetic for us to pass any clear-cut
disparaging judgment on her. We are distressed and
apprehensive, not censorious, that she should disclaim any
right to just such 'observancy' as she has every right to
look for from the man she has just married:

> Nay, we must think men are not gods,
> Nor of them look for such observancy
> As fits the bridal. (III, iv, 144–6)

Nor is this merely self-consoling. It also seeks to protect
Othello from blame or disapprobation. So we can hardly
not be touched and dismayed by the difference between
Othello's shocking 'unkindness' towards and denigration of
her in the previous scene with Iago (III, iii), and her self-
chiding for having momentarily thought unkindly of *him*:

DESDEMONA Beshrew me much, Emilia,
I was – unhandsome warrior as I am –
Arraigning his unkindness with my soul;
But now I find I had suborned the witness
And he's indicted falsely.   (III, iv, 146–50)

Even as Desdemona utters this last speech, however, we realize only too forcefully that it is she herself who has been 'indicted falsely'. And although she of course does not realize that, she now begins to grow more and more uneasy. To Emilia's 'Pray heaven it be state matters, as you think,/ And no conception nor no jealous toy/ Concerning you', she now implicitly seems to concede that the latter is more likely: 'Alas the day, I never gave him cause.' Now, the penetration of Emilia's unhappy reply clearly troubles both of them (as it further troubles us):

EMILIA   But jealous souls will not be answered so;
They are not ever jealous for the cause,
But jealous for they're jealous. It is a monster
Begot upon itself, born on itself.
DESDEMONA Heaven keep that monster from Othello's mind.
EMILIA   Lady, amen!   (III, iv, 155–60)

Because we know that the monster is already begot and born on itself we suspect, even here, that dismay, regret and appeals to heaven are not going to cut much ice with Othello. We already sense that such responses are likely to nourish and strengthen the monster, not tame it into submission; and indeed it turns out to be the case that the submission will now be all on Desdemona's side.

It is very obvious that all through *Othello*, as in so many of his plays – *Much Ado* and *As You Like It* are two obvious cases; so, in a more closely related way, is *King Lear* – Shakespeare is centrally concerned with the dynamics of mutual misapprehension in various kinds of human relationships. What this particular scene (III, iv) stresses more sharply than any so far is the process whereby Desdemona's unconscious attempts to evade the meaning of Othello's conduct actually aggravate in him the very condition whose existence she strives to deny. Simultaneously, it shows the same process working in reverse.

It is clearly significant, for instance, that Othello and Desdemona's exchanges about the handkerchief are immediately juxtaposed with those of Bianca and Cassio on the same topic. Here it is not Othello but Bianca whose 'mind misgives'; unlike him, however, she and Cassio both speak out directly in accusation and countercharge. Each claims to know the 'cause' of the other's behaviour, Bianca declaring that Cassio lies to her because he lies with someone else, and Cassio retorting that her jealousy is absurd:

BIANCA This [handkerchief] is some token from a newer friend.
　　　　To the felt absence now I feel a cause.
　　　　Is't come to this?
CASSIO　　　　　　　　Go to, woman!
　　　　Throw your vile guesses in the devil's teeth
　　　　From whence you have them. You are jealous now
　　　　. . .
　　　　No, by my faith, Bianca.　　　　　　(III, iv, 177–83)

Plainly, the Bianca who accuses Cassio so boldly and heatedly (and falsely) is to be contrasted with Othello, who is still too choked with conflicting emotions to accuse Desdemona directly. Equally, Cassio, who dismisses the allegations as 'vile guesses' and scornfully exculpates himself, is to be contrasted with Desdemona, who as yet scarcely dares even to suspect, let alone acknowledge, that she is suspected of falsity. The similarities and differences between the two couples here are quite simple (for Bianca's and Cassio's relationship is not dramatized very fully or consistently), but they do underline the reasons why it is now virtually impossible for Othello and Desdemona to convert *their* discord into any sort of harmony. Unlike Bianca's and Cassio's, their responses to one another have grown dangerously oblique. And we notice further that, even though Cassio's and Bianca's exchanges are open and direct enough for some sort of reconciliation to be possible for them, the 'cure' – the mutual understanding – they achieve is in fact only temporary. (How much harder, therefore, is it likely to be for Desdemona and Othello to arrive at any kind of remedy.) Once the seeds of false doubt about Cassio are sown in Bianca's mind, even his explicit and scornful rebuttal cannot effectively weed it out. By the very next scene (IV, i) Bianca has lapsed again into hurt and angry disbelief of Cassio's fidelity:

What did you mean by that same handkerchief . . .
I was a fine fool to take it . . . There, give it
your hobby-horse, wheresoever you had it.

(IV, i, 148ff.)

Perhaps more than anything else, however, Bianca's and Cassio's angry charges and countercharges (like Emilia's and Iago's in the final scene) highlight Desdemona's evident inability to charge Othello – in public or even in private – with making contemptibly false charges against her. It becomes clearer and clearer that she *shirks* the recognition that he mistrusts her – shirks it not because she is still heedless of his state, but rather because she cannot face what such mistrust of her would imply about *him*. What she seems to shrink from is any shade of disloyalty to Othello – even to the extent of never allowing herself to question either of the two (rather Bradleyan) moral assumptions on which she responds to him: that jealousy and 'ill-thinking' are the definitive marks of a vicious nature (rather than, in less rigidly absolute terms, the marks of a frightened and confused one); and that Othello, being a noble and honourable man, 'therefore' cannot possibly be jealous. Hence she is able to see every reason but the real one for Othello's 'unquietness': matters of state; the 'unkind breach' with Cassio; the official document that 'commands him home, deputing Cassio in his government' –

anything, in short, except a cause that she dare ask him about or one that might call in question his 'noble' nature.

It is not until Othello has so far broken apart as to hit her, and in public, that Desdemona's delusions also begin to break (IV, i, 240ff.). It is now impossible for her to ignore or deny what he has become. The sudden physical blow is far more painfully a psychological one, which knocks her terribly off balance. At last, inescapably, his actual reality strikes her; and the judgment of him it forces upon her has much the same effect as her own publicly delivered blow to her father's delusions had had on him: she is stunned ('I have not deserved this'), and crushed into silence ('I will not stay to offend you').

Inevitably, it takes time for her to grasp what has really happened and what it implies. After the blow, her next conversation with Othello (IV, ii) is so painful (for us as well as for each of them) because even now she still clutches a shred of hope that perhaps, despite everything, he is not really jealous after all. (It is a hope that, naturally, Iago strives to encourage in her as long as possible: 'I pray you, be content: 'tis but his humour;/ The business of the state does him offence,/ And he does chide with you' (IV, ii, 164–6).) Even when Othello openly challenges her to 'be double-damned:/ Swear thou art honest', her anguished answer, affirming their unity and capacity to *share* sorrows, reveals her trying for the last time to believe their marriage may still be salvaged:

DESDEMONA Alas, the heavy day! Why do you weep?
   Am I the motive of these tears my lord?
   If haply you my father do suspect
   An instrument of this your calling back,
   Lay not your blame on me. If you have lost him,
   I have lost him too
   . . .

   I hope my noble lord esteems me honest.

(IV, ii, 41–6, 64)

It is during this scene that some vital string breaks in Desdemona. Her bewilderment deepens into sheer dismay. From now on, she wavers between rare moments of quite firm self-assertion – 'By heaven, you do me wrong' – and more and more frequent moments of something that seems very like self-abandonment. Grief, shock and fear make her more and more recessive: 'Alas, the heavy day!'; 'O, heaven forgive us!'; 'It is my wretched fortune.' And as things grow from bad to worse, we notice how she seems to become not only less and less capable of asserting herself against Othello, but strangely less and less impelled to try:

> Do not talk to me, Emilia:
> I cannot weep; nor answers have I none,
> But what should go by water. (IV, ii, 101–3)

From this point on, I believe, our attention is continually drawn to Desdemona's strange passivity in the face of the violence that assails her – a passivity that is juxtaposed against the violent means by which others in the play seek to defend themselves and to remedy the 'ills' done to them by repaying them blow for blow. There is the sharpest contrast, and the most revealing comparison, between Desdemona and Othello in this. But the action also stresses the similarities and differences between Desdemona and Emilia, and it is these perhaps more than anything that raise questions about the morality of self-preservation which have been implicit right from the start of the play and which Montano had explicitly mentioned in Act II:

> . . . nor know I aught
> By me that's said or done amiss this night,
> Unless self-charity be sometimes a vice,
> And to defend ourselves it be a sin
> When violence assails us. (II, iii, 194–8)

In the last two acts, Desdemona likewise knows not aught that's said or done amiss by her – 'Alas the day, I never gave him cause'; 'I do not know'; 'I know not how I lost him'. She knows only that she *has* 'lost him', and that she loves him still. Unlike Montano, however (or Iago or Othello), she does not respond to abuse with counter-aggression: she acts – or seems to act – not from any impulse of 'self-charity', but in a spirit of self-abnegation.

I think it is this distinction – between 'self-charity' and self-abnegation – that the play now most pushes us to question and re-think, especially in our response to Desdemona's and Othello's responses to each other. (I would be pleased to have found a still accurate but less clumsy term for what I call 'self-abnegation' here. Bradley's remark in *Shakespearean Tragedy* that 'the Hamlet of the Fifth Act shows a kind of sad or indifferent self-abandonment' (p. 119) reminds us that Shakespeare had pondered this sort of state before. His interest in it goes back many years – to *The Rape of Lucrece*, for example; but I think that from *Julius Caesar* onwards his explorations of it become increasingly subtle and various, greatly extending his earlier sense of the distinction between what the Dauphin in *Henry V*, II, iv, calls 'self-love' and 'self-neglecting'.)

Significantly, the distinction between self-abnegation and self-charity is basically what Desdemona and Emilia discuss in their conversation about marital relations at the end of the willow-scene (IV, iii).[1] Othello's accusations prompt Desdemona there to wonder if *any* woman would choose to commit adultery, since (in her own view) no possible benefit could come from such an injury. In the face of Desdemona's gentle idealism and her assertions that good and bad are absolute, exclusive opposites, the more worldly-wise Emilia replies that losses and gains are always

---

[1]This dialogue between the women is certainly important, but I doubt whether it is important for the reasons Ralph Berry advances, or to the degree he suggests ('Our whole response to the play should be conditioned by [it]') in 'Pattern in *Othello*', *Shakespeare Quarterly*, 23 (1972), pp. 14ff.

relative, and that if the end-result of adultery were vastly beneficial this would enable one to justify and rectify the injurious means:

> Why, the wrong is but a wrong i'th'world; and having the world for your labour, 'tis a wrong in your own world, and you might quickly make it right. (IV, iii, 79–81)

She goes on to argue feelingly that abuse is fair exchange for abuse – indeed that, for self-respecting women, repayment 'in gross kind' is the justly self-charitable defence against husbands who 'strike us' or break out 'in peevish jealousies':

> Why, we have galls, and though we have some grace,
> Yet have we some revenge.
> . . .
> Then let [men] use us well: else let them know
> The ills we do, their ills instruct us so.
> (IV, iii, 91–2, 101–2)

Emilia's heated argument has often been taken as an admission of what she actually practises. I cannot see why it needs to be taken so at all. In fact, the feelings and thoughts she expresses here are all the more dramatically significant because (a point I shall return to) her actual responses to Iago throughout the foregoing scenes are so notably *un*vindictive. It anything puzzles us about Emilia's relations with her husband in Acts II–IV, it is her sad (if also resentful) forbearance. She shows far more 'grace' and tolerance than she ever shows 'revenge'. In deed (if not always in thought or word) she has far less in common with the ever-vindictive Iago, who has no 'grace' at all, than with Desdemona, whose practice as well as philosophy is expressed in her reply to Emilia here: 'God me such uses send,/ Not to pick bad from bad, but by bad mend!'

These words reflect a view of marriage that both Desdemona and Emilia characteristically live by, though neither is given to pious self-congratulation about it. Desdemona's point is less simple than it may seem. Within a marriage, she claims, to try to remedy a hurt by inflicting hurt would be in every way injurious; to suffer 'ill' and *not* to repay it – that is, to abnegate one's 'right' to revenge – is paradoxically a form of self-charity as well as charity to the person one loves. The sort of moral calculus Emilia has described is, for Desdemona, necessarily felt and proved false by a heart that loves another and gives itself to another. In other words, her reply shows more than her inability to act out of the sort of crude self-interest characteristic of Iago, for example, for whom a man's sole and most important need is to 'know how to love himself'. It shows why, loving Othello as she does, Desdemona cannot separate or even distinguish her real self-interests from his. For her, to endure pain is less painful than choosing to inflict it. It is not that she is too idealistic, romantic or feeble to know how to love herself; it is rather that her commitment to Othello makes it impossible to conceive *any* injury to him as a benefit to her.

Desdemona's sense of her bond with Othello, and her accompanying sense of herself, become very sharply evident in her lack of any urge or capacity to lash back in angry self-defence against him. We cannot attribute her behaviour simply to a forgiving and non-retaliatory nature. She is, it is true, a 'moth of peace' (as she puts it in I, iii), and so she is naturally helpless when caught in the webs of fantasy spun about her by the self-styled 'spider' Iago and by Othello. Her pacific responses to suffering are clearly contrasted with Othello's and Iago's and with the violent indignation Emilia shows in Acts IV and V, which (significantly) is unleashed not on her own behalf but on Desdemona's:

EMILIA I will be hanged if some eternal villain,
        Some busy and insinuating rogue,
        Some cogging, cozening slave, to get some office,

239

Have not devised this slander . . .
. . .

DESDEMONA If any such there be, heaven pardon him.
EMILIA   A halter pardon him and hell gnaw his bones!
           Why should he call her whore? Who keeps her
              company?
           What place, what time, what form, what likelihood?

                                           (IV, ii, 129–37)

Desdemona is indeed without Emilia's sort of fierceness
and rage against injustice. But that does not necessarily
mean she is a poor wet rag.

   The difference between the two women's moral and
emotional styles here is important – and partly because it is
not entirely in Desdemona's favour. I think we find it
more natural to respond hot-bloodedly, as Emilia does,
towards such a 'cogging, cozening slave' (who we know
exists in the person of Iago), and therefore find Desdemona's charitableness here so extreme as to border on a
sort of limply pious self-surrender. I also find it rather
hard to take her faintly prim puns on the word 'whore' ('I
cannot say "whore":/ It does abhor me now I speak the
word'). Indeed, the play does seem to suggest that Desdemona's submissiveness goes hand in hand with her lack
of 'seaminess'; her utterly despairing yet forgiving speech
here about Othello's having bewhored her falsely is
immediately juxtaposed with Iago's and Roderigo's
conversation in which Roderigo for once does manage to
be recalcitrant: 'I will indeed no longer endure it. Nor am
I yet persuaded to put up in peace what already I have
foolishly suffered' (IV, ii, 178–80). The dramatic effect of
this juxtaposition, and of Emilia's outburst ('A halter
pardon him and hell gnaw his bones'), is partly to make us
reckon with our own difficulty in simply and wholly sharing
Desdemona's generous forgiveness and pacificism. Her
extreme patient tolerance here makes us slightly *im*patient,
rather as does that of Fanny Price in Jane Austen's *Mans-*

field Park, for example.[1] We cannot help wishing Desdemona had a touch of Emilia's full-blooded self-assertiveness
here. However, the two women's unlikeness in this respect
is most telling in the final scene of the play, and is perhaps
best discussed in that context. Here, it is clear enough, I
think, that even though we find it impossible fully to share
Desdemona's forgivingness it nevertheless derives from
something we love her for – her capacity to love. 'Bereft'
of Othello's love, she repeals not a jot of her own for him.
Nothing short of gaining his love could fill the 'heavy
interim' in her life caused by his 'dear absence' (to use her
own unwittingly prophetic terms from the Senate-scene
in Act I). Any remedy of her pain that could not restore his
love would only seem to her a further loss, a further hurt.

It is this attitude, I think, that determines her responses
to Othello all through the play, and makes her so passive
and withdrawn in the last two acts. As we see her from Act
IV onwards, it becomes easier to understand what her
crisis consists in, and why she has needed not to see it
mounting up as she mounted her arguments for Cassio.
For her, to be doubted proves as shattering as it is for
Othello to doubt. It overturns everything she had assumed
to be established and shared between them. For Othello,
to suspect her is to fear, and then to believe, that he has
been 'cashiered', 'denied', 'discarded' from the heart where
he had garnered up his own. For her, to *be* suspected is to
fear, and then to feel, that she has been discarded, rejected
utterly, 'bereft' of the love he has suddenly and unaccount-
ably 'repealed'. Or, to put this another way (as I think the
play itself does), what Desdemona experiences when the
reality of Othello's jealousy strikes her in Act IV is another
and more total version of what the other women in the play
experience in their relationships with the men they love.

---

[1]The difficulty of reconciling a generous impulse of self-denial and one of
sensible self-interest or self-charity is of course an explicit and persisten
issue all through Jane Austen's novels.

As these are presented, Desdemona's responses are shown to be very like each of theirs, though more extreme. And theirs of course dramatically reflect and comment on hers.

Thus – to take the simplest case first – Bianca is even more suggestively relevant than she may at first seem. When in v, i Iago falsely accuses her of being party to Cassio's murder, and Emilia (who is greatly distressed for Cassio) abuses her – 'O, fie upon thee, strumpet!' – Bianca's reply rings with simple dignity as well as indignation: 'I am no strumpet, but of life as honest/ As you that thus abuse me.' Although Bianca is generally played as a (rather sluttish) whore, there is actually no decisive reason in the text why she should be. Where others call her a 'strumpet' their personal reasons for doing so are made clear enough for us to question their disinterestedness; and what little we see of her in person certainly supports her claim to honest and strong feeling for Cassio. When Iago describes her as 'a creature/ That dotes on Cassio – as 'tis the strumpet's plague/ To beguile many and be beguiled by one', we need not accept *his* pejorative meaning. In that Bianca's heart is truly 'beguiled by' and given to Cassio, and only to him (despite the fact that he treats her so off-handedly and refers to her behind her back as a prostitute), she is *emotionally* no more a 'strumpet' than Emilia (whom Iago accuses of promiscuity) or for that matter Desdemona, who has also beguiled many men in her time, including Roderigo, and who is beguiled by only one, a man who in turn calls her a 'strumpet'. To suppose that Bianca is merely a foil for Desdemona is to distort and simplify what the play shows. She is plainly like, not unlike, the play's other women in that, feeling inwardly 'bound' to the man she loves, she is open to feeling (and being) abandoned, negated, rejected by him. Precisely because Bianca loves him with more than a harlot's love she thereby gives Cassio the power to hurt her by exiling her – banishing her from the centre of his

life.[1] Her need of him and her consequent vulnerability
are pointedly emphasized at the close of Act III, in the
context of Othello's feeling that Desdemona has rejected
him, and Desdemona's incipient fear that he is mistrusting
and rejecting *her*. The similarities between the women are
chiefly highlighted by the immediate juxtaposition of their
speeches in this scene, though we also notice the obvious
parallel between Bianca's lament here about the tedium
of 'lovers' absent hours' and Desdemona's speech in Act I
about the 'heavy interim' she would suffer in Othello's
'dear absence' if he went off to Cyprus without her. More
significantly, Cassio here demands that Bianca 'leave me
for this time' – a request, or rather an order, also given to
Desdemona and Emilia by their husbands – because (as
Cassio insultingly puts it) 'I . . . think it no addition, nor
my wish,/ To have [Othello] see me womaned.'

BIANCA Why, pray you?
CASSIO Not that I love you not.
BIANCA But that you do not love me.   (III, iv, 191–2)

It is the familiar cashiering 'But . . .', even though it is
Bianca who actually voices what she feels is in Cassio's
mind. 'But that you do not love me' is of course just what
Othello feels has come of his relation to Desdemona and is
fatally *un*able to say directly. It is a simple paradigm of
what is much more fully shown in Desdemona's and Emilia's marriages. This is why Bianca's parting remark as she
obeys and leaves him here is at once so touching and so
revealing. Quietly, half to herself, she acknowledges her
need to be loved: 'I must be circumstanced.'

Bianca's phrase is revealing, I think, in that it sums up
explicitly what we have seen to be the chief emotional

---

[1] The obvious comparison is with Portia's hurt query to Brutus in *Julius
Caesar*, II, i, 285ff.: 'Dwell I but in the suburbs/ Of your good pleasure? If
it be no more,/ Portia is Brutus' harlot, not his wife.'

problem everyone in the play experiences: having to try
to adjust to or put up with circumstances (or supposed
circumstances) that one cannot really change. In one sense,
her phrase is not unlike Othello's in I, iii, 297: 'We must
obey the time.' But given all the events *we* have witnessed
in the first three acts, we have come to realize that 'being
circumstanced' or 'obeying the time' is not always such a
simple and straightforward matter as it had seemed to
Othello then in Act I, when he declared his readiness to
'obey' the military dictates of the time.[1] Even at that point
we had seen how hard it proved for Brabantio to have to
submit to the fact of Desdemona's elopement; and, since
then, we have seen how galling it is for Roderigo to have to
'be circumstanced' and await the fulfilment of Iago's
promises; how depressing it is for Cassio to submit to the
circumstance of demotion; how hard for Desdemona; and
how impossible Othello finds it to accept calmly what he
takes as the fact of her betrayal. Bianca's case is probably
the simplest of all these, yet for that reason it serves as a
miniature example of what it is to be 'cashiered' and yet
have to 'be circumstanced'. Given the way she loves him,
she has no real option but to accept Cassio's terms. Whatever self-comfort there might be in hitting back at him, in
the long run it would only prove counter-productive, a
kind of self-punishment. To forego her 'right' to demand
'justice' is in the long run a form of kindness to herself – a
form of self-charity. Her visible need of Cassio's love and
the periodic outbursts that show what it costs her to 'obey
the time' make her predicament a mirror of each of the
other characters', especially Emilia's and Desdemona's.

*

[1] Cf. Antony, 'The strong necessity of time commands/ Our services awhile
(*Antony and Cleopatra*, I, iii, 42–3). With each of the tragedies from *Hamlet*
onwards Shakespeare seems to become more explicitly interested in the
ways people experience or react to this need to 'obey' the time: how they
feel it as real, the ways they evade it, or exploit it, and so on.

Emilia's case is more interesting than Bianca's, of course, largely because we are given more of it. Bradley said he could find no sign that her marriage was an especially unhappy one;[1] on the other hand, however carefully we look, it is hard to find any sign that there is much joy left in it for her to find or make. Like Bianca, Emilia knows what it is to be spurned in love, though knowing it evidently makes the rejection no easier to bear. Iago treats her just as he treats everyone else – he tolerates her when she is useful and 'cashiers' her when she is not. As Cassio does with Bianca, Iago banishes Emilia to the periphery of his life. His tone towards her right through the play – sarcastic and unyielding – denies and negates her. If her own language often reflects his (as of course Othello's own comes to do), it also – in ways that suggest she speaks from extensive personal experience – prompts her to generalize bitterly about men's treatment of women (compare, for instance, the terms of her speech to Desdemona in III, iv, 99ff., about men who 'eat us hungerly, and when they are full,/ They belch us', with Iago's speech to Roderigo in II, i, 215ff., about Desdemona's 'appetite' ([she will] 'heave the gorge' etc.). Presumably because Emilia's language is sometimes as coarse as Iago's, she has been as much maligned by critics and directors as she is by her husband. We can hardly accept at face value *Iago's* allegations of her promiscuity when Emilia publicly implies (IV, ii, 144–6) that his suspicions are the fruit merely of an absurd and jealous credulity comparable with Othello's about Desdemona ('Some such squire he was/ That turned your wit the seamy side without/ And made you to suspect me with the Moor'). It is not hard to detect her pain and resentment at his aspersions in her scornful rejections of them. No more than Bianca is she merely a foil to Desdemona's virtue. Part of what makes Emilia an interesting

[1]*Shakespearean Tragedy*, p. 176.

(and attractive) figure is the range of attitudes and feelings she is capable of – a range that spans both Iago's 'seaminess' and Desdemona's gentleness and generosity.

The tenor of Emilia and Iago's relationship is forcefully suggested in the first scene in which she speaks (II, i) – the one by the Cypriot shore – where Iago casually and publicly insults her. What we see of her here is repeatedly confirmed in later scenes: unhappy as Iago's rejections make her, she cannot or does not rebuff him. She seems to have neither the capacity nor even the will to grace her cause in speaking for herself. Desdemona's remark is telling: 'Alas, she has no speech' (II, i, 103). The most Emilia manages to do here in self-defence is (like Desdemona at the end of the play) assert that her husband's charges are unjust: 'You have little cause to say so.' After that, she withdraws.

I think we sense Emilia's unhappiness, the 'causes' of it, and her sad passivity in response to it, most clearly in the scene where she filches Desdemona's handkerchief (III, iii, 287ff.). She does so, it emerges, because she knows her only hope of happiness with Iago lies in gaining his 'approval' and 'rich opinion'. When, pleased to please him, she offers him the handkerchief, Iago sneers at her, snatches it, and gives her in return not thanks or kindness, but only

> Be not acknown on't: I have use for it.
> Go, leave me. (III, iii, 316–17)

Emilia's soliloquy just before this has already made it plain that Iago never confides in her and that she has no idea of what mysterious business he is about.[1] Even as it reveals this, however, her soliloquy also makes it plain why she puts up with a man who so mistrusts, chides and abuses her. Simply and sadly, her words express her half-hidden but still genuine love for the man she leniently describes to herself as 'my wayward husband'. The closing words of her

[1] This is yet another of Shakespeare's highly significant alterations of Cinthio's tale.

soliloquy here are surely among the most poignant and suggestive in the play:

> What he will do with it, heaven knows, not I:
> I nothing, but to please his fantasy.   (III, iii, 295–6)

There is nothing self-pitying or martyrish about her tone in saying this. Clearly, Emilia finds it hard and lonely to 'be circumstanced', but, needing Iago's love, she submits to his will. It is as if she knows (by instinct or – more likely – from experience) that it is less painful to suffer his scornful abuse than to challenge or try to change him.

'I nothing, but to please his fantasy.' It is to the bleak realization of *this* and what it means that Desdemona too is driven during the course of the play. And as we watch the process by which she comes to realize it, we come to understand how, given both the nature of Othello's 'fantasy' and her own love for him, her apparent self-abnegation, her 'obedience' and her charity towards him in the last two acts become (as for Bianca and Emilia) truly the only forms of 'self-charity' that remain open to her.

The similarities between Emilia's case and Desdemona's are underlined quite specifically. Emilia's closing words in that soliloquy just quoted, for example, strike a painfully ironic echo from Desdemona's words to Othello (in Emilia's hearing) earlier in the same scene, when Othello asks her to 'leave me but a little to myself';

DESDEMONA   Be as your fancies teach you.
            Whate'er you be, I am obedient.   (III, iii, 88–9)

Desdemona's 'obedience' here is still a surreptitious challenge to him. By the last two acts, however, her compliance – 'I will not stay to offend you' – is real submission. As Lodovico remarks: 'Truly, an obedient lady'. Yet to

Othello, taught by his fancies, it seems merely a false façade, a threat, a source of his bitter anguish: 'And she's obedient; as you say, obedient,/ Very obedient – proceed you in your tears.' In Act IV, as Othello's spirit (to use an earlier phrase of his own from III, iv, about the handkerchief's alleged power over his father) begins to 'hunt after new fancies', her perplexity grows until she cannot help asking directly, 'What horrible fancy's this?' Yet 'whate'er' he is, she yields to him, knowing she 'must obey the time'. She seems now fully to feel how hard – how well-nigh impossible – it is to 'please' herself by pleasing him. The most she can hope to do is manage not to '*dis*please' him further. Yet she also seems to find in herself the resources to face and accept this loss of freedom and autonomy that her bond with him now implies: 'I nothing, but to please his fantasy'. And her experience of this makes us see more sharply its double force. She feels she is 'nothing', no one, except in relation to him, that – as Cassio puts it elsewhere – she doesn't 'exist' except in being 'a member of his love'. At the same time, she sees that her actual reality no longer impinges on him, much less withstands his horrible fantasy-sense of her. When, in Act II, Iago had labelled fair things 'foul' and foul things 'fair', these moral inversions had struck Desdemona simply as 'old fond paradoxes to make fools laugh i'th'ale house'. But now she finds herself the object of Othello's terribly specious labels, and they can only make her weep:

> How have I been behaved, that he might stick
> The smallest opinion on my least misuse?
>
> (IV, ii, 107–8)

By IV, iii even her impulse to protest against Othello's injustice seems to have ebbed away. Yet her grief is deeply subdued, un-self-pitying and unchiding. Set beside Emilia's wonderfully tactful sympathy and gentleness here, it makes their conversation at the start of the willow scene another of the most moving exchanges in the play:

EMILIA   How goes it now? He looks gentler than he did.
DESDEMONA He says he will return incontinent.
           He hath commanded me to go to bed,
           And bade me to dismiss you.
EMILIA   Dismiss me?
DESDEMONA It was his bidding: therefore, good Emilia,
           Give me my nightly wearing, and adieu.
           We must not now displease him.   (IV, iii, 10–16)

'We must not now displease him'; 'I nothing, but to
please his fantasy'. As the play presents it, Desdemona's
experience at the end of the play is what brings most fully
home to us the fallacy of Iago's belief in the power of the
will to make or unmake feelings. It is not in Desdemona's
'virtue' (as Roderigo put it) to 'amend' her heart by any
act of will, and she knows enough to realize this. Nor does
she now imagine (as she did earlier in the play) that her
will can effect a change in Othello's. Since his fancy so
grossly 'mis-gives' her to him, she can no longer 'please'
him, she can only seek not to 'displease him' – she can only
be circumstanced. Loving and needing his love as she does
her will to resist his will slackens and dies, inevitably. For
her it is far more true than for Cassio that, as he put it, the
'want' or loss of Othello's love 'e'en kills me'. Her experience – like Emilia's, and Othello's too of course – makes the
Duke's sententious advice to Brabantio in I, iii seem an
even crasser superficiality than it was then. 'Griefs' are
not 'ended' when 'remedies are past'. On the contrary, her
grief at losing Othello's love (like Brabantio's upon losing
hers) is – as Brabantio had said – of such 'flood-gate and
o'erbearing nature' that it 'engluts and swallows other
sorrows/ And yet is still itself'. The closing scenes of the
play dramatize very starkly the truth of Brabantio's retort
to the Duke:

He bears the sentence well that nothing bears
But the free comfort which from thence he hears;

But he bears both the sentence and the sorrow
That to pay grief must of poor patience borrow.

(I, iii, 210–13)

*

'Patience', as so often in Shakespeare, is a key word. It is as a form of patience, not mere passivity, that we are brought to see Desdemona's responses to her situation in the last scenes of the play. Indeed, the nature, the various forms, the cost, and the moral implications of patience are as continuous a preoccupation in *Othello* as in the other great tragedies. The words 'patient' and 'patience' come up again and again. They are spoken by Roderigo, Othello, the Duke and Brabantio in Act I, for example; by Cassio (II, i, 97: 'Let it not gall your patience, good Iago'); frequently by the ever-impatient Iago (for instance, II, iii, 239–40: 'indignity/ Which patience could not pass'; II, iii, 359: 'How poor are they that have not patience!'; III, iii, 449: 'Patience, I say . . .'; IV, i, 75, 87: 'Confine yourself but in a patient list . . . Marry, patience!'; V, i, 87: 'Patience a while, good Cassio'); by Desdemona (III, iv, 125: 'You must awhile be patient'); and even Othello, who shows himself so grievously unable to 'confine' himself in *any* 'patient list', speaks several times of patience (as at IV, i, 90: 'I will be found most cunning in my patience'). Every one of the characters struggles to find some sort of patience within himself, but Desdemona is the only one who really manages to – and with her, patience is hardly distinguishable from despair.

It is because of this – the desolateness of Desdemona's patience – that we are never led to suppose it either costs her less or benefits her more than, in particular, Othello's desperate struggles *not* to have to bear or even recognize his misery. The differences between them actually underline the essential similarities between their predicaments. In IV, ii, for example, Desdemona makes one of her rare

protests against Othello's treatment of her, to Iago and
Emilia:

> . . . those that do teach young babes
> Do it with gentle means and easy tasks:
> He might have chid me so, for, in good faith,
> I am a child to chiding.   (IV, ii, 110–13)

Her despairing patience here strikes a subdued but poignant
echo of Othello's equally despairing, though much more
rhetorical, speech to her very shortly before. In both, there
is the same need of love, and the same desperate sense that
it has been inexplicably and totally denied.

OTHELLO   Had it pleased heaven
> To try me with affliction . . .
> . . .
> I should have found in some place of my soul
> A drop of patience.
> . . .
> But there where I have garnered up my heart
> . . .
> . . . to be discarded thence
> Or keep it as a cistern for foul toads
> To knot and gender in! Turn thy complexion there,
> Patience, thou young and rose-lipped cherubin,
> Ay, there look grim as hell!   (IV, ii, 46ff.)

In the twisted syntax of the last few lines his struggle to
find some patience and his sense of its unendurable cost
strain against each other. Twice over, it leads him to cry
out. Like Desdemona's speech, this one catches his mounting realization that there is no real choice for him but to
'be circumstanced', even though 'obeying the time' is – as
it is for her too – to submit to finding what it means actually
'to be discarded thence', where 'either I must live, or bear
no life'.

It is characteristic of Shakespeare's all-pervasive imagination that he should give to Cassio – the man whose

impatient wish to be reconciled with Othello so ironically
occasions the fatal rift between the two people he most
reveres – the speech that most sharply alerts us to the
underlying likeness between such forbearance as Desdemona's in the closing scenes and the overwhelming need
for revenge in Othello. I have touched on this speech
several times already; yet since it is not often noticed, it is
especially worth while to consider it as a whole, and its
bearing on others' lives as well as Cassio's own:

> Madam, my former suit. I do beseech you
> That by your virtuous means I may again
> Exist and be a member of his love,
> Whom I, with all the office of my heart,
> Entirely honour. I would not be delayed.
> If my offence be of such mortal kind
> That nor my service past, nor present sorrow,
> Nor purposed merit in futurity,
> Can ransom me into his love again,
> But to know so must be my benefit:
> So shall I clothe me in a forced content,
> And shut myself up in some other course
> To Fortune's alms.   (III, iv, 106–18)

When Othello strikes Desdemona she has no more comfort than the bleak knowledge that nothing past, present
or future can ransom her into his love again. Her only
benefit now is 'but to know so' – a 'benefit' at least in the
sense that it might enable 'if not a present remedy, at least
a patient sufferance' (to use Conrade's phrases in *Much
Ado*, I, iii, 7); and the closing scenes of the play reveal not
just the desperation and the cost involved in her attempt to
'clothe' herself 'in a forced content' but the deeply 'equivocal' nature of this remedy. ('Equivocal' was Brabantio's
word for the Duke's proffered remedy in I, i: 'These
sentences, to sugar or to gall/ Being strong on both sides,
are equivocal.') Her effort to confine herself in a patient
'list' – to 'shut [herself] up in some other course/ To

Fortune's alms' – is her only means of 'bearing life': but it entails a full recognition of the grim paucity of Fortune's alms. The play forces on us the point of Iago's exclamation, 'How poor are they that have not patience!' Yet it also makes us realize that those who manage (like Desdemona) to find in some place of their soul a drop of patience are no more cheered up by it than those who (like Othello) cannot.

This is why it seems to me inadequate to call *Othello* 'a tragedy of incomprehension' in the sense John Bayley does: 'No one in *Othello* comes to understand himself or anyone else. None of them realize their situation.'[1] One can see why this is true, up to a point. But, as I have been arguing, the continuous thrust of the play's action both forces us to realize why the characters so actively misunderstand themselves and others, why they *need* to, and also forces the characters to the point where those self-preserving misunderstandings crumble. Indeed, the end of the play is so painful and so terrifying precisely because each of the main characters (with the one significant exception of Iago) does come to 'realize his situation' only too well – just at the point where there is now nothing he can do to remedy it. It would be a different kind of tragedy, and our response to it would be less disturbed, if the main characters did retain to the end their comforts of ignorance and self-delusion, instead of being stripped of them. 'Incomprehension' is certainly an important factor in the development of the tragedy; but the last twist of the play is the absolutely desolate awareness to which it brings both Othello and Desdemona.

In IV, i, when Desdemona kneels to heaven (a gesture sharply set against Iago and Othello's impious kneeling in the previous act), she pledges herself –

[1] *The Characters of Love*, p. 146.

[If] that I do not yet, and ever did,
And ever will – though he do shake me off
To beggarly divorcement – love him dearly,
Comfort forswear me! Unkindness may do much,
And his unkindness may defeat my life,
But never taint my love.   (IV, ii, 155–60)

The subsequent scenes reveal both the truth of this vow
and also why, being the woman she is, Desdemona *must*
respond to Othello as she does. For her, 'there is no other
way'. The facts become heavier to bear and more dire than
they had seemed in III, iv, when she remarked to Cassio,
'My lord is not my lord.' Eventually, she can reply to
Emilia's reference to 'thy Lord' only with desolate patience:
'I have none.' (It is a truth that is to take Othello unawares
in the final scene: 'My wife! What wife? I have no wife.')
In Act IV, her love prevents any urge to defend herself,
just as it also prohibits any urge to repudiate him. On the
contrary, the wish not to 'indict' him, which appeared as
early as III, iv, only grows stronger as her 'cause' to do so
deepens. Her non-resistance is everywhere accompanied
now by a tender charity towards Othello, and it is this that
makes her response something other than mere resignation:
she does act, in the only way she can – by choosing not to
blame.

   In the willow-scene – which stands in complex dramatic
relationship with the crisis-scene (III, iii) in which the bond
between Othello and Iago is welded – Desdemona and
Emilia's friendship is touchingly sealed in their carefully
generalized remarks about 'men' and in the silences they
share. There is no clearer index of the change that has
come in Desdemona's life than the difference between the
buoyant confidence of her speeches in the early acts and the
uneasy, pensive, overladen movement of her speeches from
now until the end. Yet even in her intuitive sense that her
death is imminent, when she seems almost to acquiesce in
it –

Good faith, how foolish are our minds!
If I do die before thee, prithee shroud me
In one of those same sheets –

her voice has a numb sorrow that makes it perfectly clear
that her acceptance (if such it is) springs from no escapism
like Roderigo's in Act I. Her attitude is worlds apart from
his assertion, in response to his unhappiness, that 'It is
silliness to live, when to live is torment: and then we have
a prescription to die, when death is our physician.' There
is no suggestion in her voice that death is welcome as a
healing or soothing 'balm', nor that (as Othello puts it in
v, ii) 'in my sense 'tis happiness to die'. Rather, not unlike
Henryson's Cresseid, she is in a state emotionally 'destitute/
Of all comfort and consolatioun', where death seems not a
looked-for escape, but the silently dreaded yet unavoidable
culmination of her misery.[1] The strange calmness of her
words, 'If I do die before thee', seems to issue from a
patience that is identical with an unwithdrawing recognition
of her marriage as both real and irremediably lost – a
recognition that (as Iago significantly put it in another
context in the very first scene of the play), 'There's no
remedy. 'Tis the curse of service.' She feels utterly 'for-
saken'. Having somehow ('I know not how . . .') lost
Othello's love, it is as if for her all present and future life
seem lost as well. This, I think, is why she muses on the
pre-Othello days of her childhood, as her mind turns to a
remembered image of someone else's plight – an image
whose very simplicity expresses her sense of her own
'fortune' and the end that will complete it. For a moment
she stands mentally outside her fate, outside her own life-
story, glimpsing its total shape in a sort of reflected image,
even while she is in the process of living it.

[1] *The Testament of Cresseid* seems to me to have very suggestive affinities
with both *Othello* and *King Lear*, though of a kind not brought out by the
usual view of Henryson. For my own view of the poem see 'Henryson's
Testament of Cresseid: "Fyre" and "Cauld"', *The Critical Review*, 18
(1976), pp. 39–60.

My mother had a maid called Barbary:
She was in love: and he she loved proved mad
And did forsake her. She had a song of willow;
An old thing 'twas; but it expressed her fortune,
And she died singing it. That song tonight
Will not go from my mind: I have much to do
But to go hang my head all at one side,
And sing it like poor Barbary – prithee, dispatch.

(IV, iii, 25–32)

Singing Barbary's song, Desdemona's heart is so full of
Othello – or rather, so full of her need of his love – that she
makes a poignantly self-revealing mistake about the order
of the lines; and so expectant is she of his coming, so much
does she silently fear it, that she imagines a knock at the
door – yet another instance of how apprehensiveness causes
people to 'apprehend' what they fear.

> [*She sings*]
> Sing willow, willow, willow –
> [*She speaks*]
> Prithee hie thee; he'll come anon.
> [*She sings*]
> Sing all a green willow must be my garland.
> Let nobody blame him; his scorn I approve –
> [*She speaks*]
> Nay, that's not next. Hark, who is't that knocks?
> EMILIA It's the wind. (IV, iii, 46–51)

*

'Let nobody blame him': Bradley and pro-Othello readers
have obeyed Desdemona's wish, while Leavis and anti-
Othello critics have disregarded it. But if we are to do
justice to the play we need to realize everything it presents:
Othello's culpability, Desdemona's wish to exonerate him,
and the feelings that prompt both. The difficulty of not
denying the reality either of Othello's heart or of Desdemona's is what makes the ending so easy to misrepresent
and so very hard to stand. Nevertheless, if we recognize
that the play's power lies precisely in the demands it makes

on *our* patience, our capacity to 'be circumstanced' and submit to the reality of all it presents, we clearly cannot allow ourselves the luxury of being 'partially affined'. We have to respond fully and honestly to both the lovers, if we are to understand the significance of their bond and so of their tragedy.

Even though she shrinks from what she sees in Othello's eyes, Desdemona in these closing scenes obeys him quietly. When Othello finally enters the room where she lies alone in their wedding-bed, in her shroud-sheets, she seems to be asleep. Here, what we find hardest to bear is again the terrible silence that surrounds Othello's speech. The silence seems all the deeper and all the more oppressive by contrast with the clamorous murder-scene Shakespeare placed immediately before this one. In that scene (v, i), Roderigo and Cassio, the victims marked down by Iago, 'cry so grievously', call aloud again and again for 'help, ho! . . . help! . . . Murder, murder! . . . for heaven's sake help me! . . . give me some help . . . O, help me here!' Each violently denounces his assailant: 'O, wretched villain!'; 'I am undone by villains!'; 'O damned Iago! O inhuman dog!' As it subsequently emerges, both these noisy 'murders' actually miscarry (despite Othello's wishful thought that Cassio is slain and Iago's that at least he has got rid of Roderigo). In spite of *our* wishful thoughts, however, the murder of Desdemona does happen. She has no strength or will to resist it or even to cry out for help. In this final scene, the only denunciations of her assailant come not from her own lips but from Emilia's (and later from Othello's own). Emilia performs her friendship to the last article, crying out with courage and loyalty. It is her voice that breaks the awful silence into which not only Othello's words but even Desdemona's seem to disappear:

> O gull! O dolt!
> As ignorant as dirt! Thou hast done a deed –

I care not for thy sword – I'll make thee known,
Though I lost twenty lives. Help! . . . Murder!

(v, ii, 162–5)

Desdemona herself, far from threatening to make Othello
'known', continues to obey him even to the very end, even
when he has told her he has come to kill:

OTHELLO   Peace, and be still!
DESDEMONA I will – so. What's the matter?   (v, ii, 46–7)

Shakespeare could hardly have indicated more sharply
the difference between Desdemona's responses to the
husband who has (in his own word later on) 'traduced' her,
and Emilia's responses to Iago when at last she learns his
part:

EMILIA You told a lie, an odious, damnèd lie . . .
             . . .
IAGO   Go to, charm your tongue.
EMILIA I will not charm my tongue; I am bound to speak . . .
             . . .
IAGO   Zounds, hold your peace!
EMILIA   'Twill out, 'twill out. I peace?
            No, I will speak as liberal as the north . . .
             . . .
IAGO   Be wise, and get you home.
EMILIA   I will not.   (v, ii, 179ff.)

Our feelings rush out against Iago with Emilia's. We long
for her to disobey Iago here, just as we wanted Desdemona
not to obey Othello, not to 'be still'. (And of course on this
issue of marital obedience this scene is related in deeply
ironic ways to earlier moments – Othello hysterically
reacting to Lodovico's praise of Desdemona as 'truly an
obedient lady', for instance, or Emilia submitting to Iago's
'will', 'fancy', 'bidding'.)

Tangled up though it is with other more momentous

258

events in this scene, Emilia's own private crisis here is
dramatically important in itself, and (as always) the ways
she reacts to it are both distinctive and reminiscent of
others' behaviour elsewhere. At first she simply cannot believe what Othello tells her about Iago; but she cannot not
believe it either, and she slides inevitably to 'if': 'If he say
so . . . he lies to th'heart'. So her explosive outburst at
Othello ('O gull! O dolt!/ As ignorant as dirt!') also carries
a violent charge of deflected self-condemnation as she now
begins to grasp how she has been duped and ignorantly
incriminated. Her chill, dry greeting when Iago enters
clearly betrays her underlying conviction of his guilt; but
she longs for it not to be true – her whole life hangs on the
resolution – and her hopes rush up in an appeal whose
very urgency and repetitious insistence only betray her near-
desperation:

> Disprove this villain, if thou be'st a man:
> He says thou told'st him that his wife was false.
> I know thou didst not: thou'rt not such a villain.

> (v, ii, 171–3)

'Disprove this villain': that was what Othello could never
say to Desdemona. Yet the ironic reminder here of his cry
to Iago – 'Villain, be sure thou prove my love a whore;/
Be sure of it: give me the ocular proof' (iii, iii, 356–7) –
reinforces our sense that Emilia too shares this passionate
need to *know*, not to have merely to fear and suspect the
truth that for her spells absolute loss of everything she lives
for. Her words 'I know thou dids't not' tremble with her
fear of the opposite, for of course she does not 'know' at all.
And only when she at last has the admission from Iago's
own mouth does she round on him, forcing him (as Othello
had threatened in that same speech in iii, iii) to 'answer
my waked wrath'. All her rage and misery and remorse
fly out now, as she learns that not only is her mistress
murdered, but that she herself has been used as an unwit-

ting accomplice in setting on the crime, by a husband who is irredeemably loathsome, 'odious'. It is bitter indeed. And the play gives full weight to her acute unhappiness – 'Speak, for my heart is full' – as well as bringing us to admire and respect the dignity both of her passionate rage and her no less expressive reserve:

> Good gentlemen, let me have leave to speak.
> 'Tis proper I obey him, but not now.
> Perchance, Iago, I will ne'er go home.
>
> (V, ii, 194–6)

Bradley was right to claim that Emilia's outbursts are important in this scene; they do release and express some of our own pent-up violence. But it is a mark of the drama's complexity that our responses cannot move simply and wholly with Emilia's. Clearly, we feel the need to let our moral outrage loose against Iago; but our feelings towards Othello are much less straightforward than hers. She, we may notice, is the only one who pushes Othello to call his deed 'murder' and to recognize his atrocious moral stupidity and cruelty: 'The more angel she, and you the blacker devil!'; 'Thou dost belie her, and thou art a devil.' Yet we have other feelings too. Knowing Desdemona, we know how fully warranted Emilia's outrage is. Knowing Othello, however, we also know – as Desdemona did – what Emilia cannot. Emilia's scorching reaction to what has been done to her mistress forces on us a crucial recognition about our own reactions to the play. To the very extent that we *do* share her impulse to lash out against Iago and to expose Othello's guilt we also share the same need for punitive 'justice' as drove Othello to kill Desdemona. Our lust for moral certainties and justice involves the same emotional mechanism that led to Desdemona's murder, and soon leads to Emilia's.

In many ways (as criticism of the play has so amply if unwittingly demonstrated) we share with Emilia and

Othello and the play's other characters a positive need to
view things in terms of black and white, angels and devils.
'I'll make thee known . . .!': Emilia's cry answeres a natural
enough impulse to expose a Iago or to make an Othello
recognize what he has done and what that shows him to be.
What we do not realize until it is too late is that it is dangerous to corner a man like Iago: as the clown had said in
III, iv, 'To say a soldier lies is stabbing'; and Emilia's fury
over Desdemona's murder indeed proves suicidal. By
sharing her need to expose Iago we are also implicated in
her death. Furthermore, we do not realize until too late
that it is too much for a man like Othello to have to confront
himself. The recognition of what he is, hastened by Emilia's
urge to 'make thee known', ultimately and inevitably results
in his self-murder. If, like Emilia, we feel the need to rid
or deprive others of their delusions and strip away what
conceals their guilt, there is no doubt always a touch both
of self-consolation and cruelty in our moralistic judgments;
and I think the presence in this final scene of Desdemona
as well as Emilia, and of Othello as well as Iago, strongly
presses us to recognize it here. More than anything else, it
is Desdemona's last action that prompts us to see it.

Ever since Act IV Desdemona's whole impulse has been
to love yet not to blame. Here, when Othello literally kills
her with blame for having 'discarded' him, and discards his
love for her in what he feels is the only way he can – by
tearing it from him with his hands – her dying words
unequivocally re-affirm the existence, the bounteousness
and the strong purity of her love for him:

DESDEMONA A guiltless death I die.
EMILIA   O, who hath done this deed?
DESDEMONA Nobody – I myself – farewell.
            Commend me to my kind lord – O, farewell!
                  [*She dies*]   (v, ii, 123–6)

Desdemona tries *not* to make Othello 'known' – to himself,

or to anyone else. As if instinctively, she lets him keep the self-delusion that can alone now prevent him turning his 'bloody passion' on himself. Significantly, she does not say she 'forgives' him: it is as if she knows that forgiveness always implies culpability and that Othello could never forgive himself if he came to 'know' what he has done. She does more than seek to free him from blame and the need for self-blame, however. As Muriel Bradbrook puts it, 'she takes Othello's mistakes and guilt on herself'.[1] Cryptically, Desdemona asserts that the deed was done by 'nobody' – a deed not only without a name, but one without an author – and yet that it had an author, 'I myself', and thus an unspoken name. Implicitly, that is, she claims that her death is not a murder, but a kind of (innocent) suicide, committed out of guiltlessness.

Desdemona innocent *and* Othello not guilty? Of course, it is only in her heart that both these things can be true. So shaken as we are by the fact that Othello has killed her – an objective fact that we cannot deny, evade or euphemize – our natural first response to her dying claim is to reject it as a 'white lie', a supremely generous and selfless, perhaps even over-indulgent, gesture to free Othello from guilt and blame. But for her, we then realize, it is not a 'lie' or an indulgence. Her love fully 'credits' it – makes it a truth. And voiced so undemonstratively, so unprotestingly as this, *her* sense of what has happened surely matters too much for us to brush it aside as false or merely sentimental. Really to attend to it is to see that it represents precisely the kind of patient, out-going and uncensorious love we have watched Othello defile in himself. We have to respond with more than the admiration and respect we give Emilia, to Desdemona's capacity to love him even now; and that very capacity in her testifies not just to the depth and wholeness of her commitment to him but also to the fullnes

[1]'Shakespeare the Jacobean Dramatist', in *A New Companion to Shakespeare Studies*, ed. Kenneth Muir and S. Schoenbaum (Cambridge, 1971), p. 147.

– as she has felt and responded to it – of his commitment to her: each 'had eyes', and chose the other. In fact, I think it is only to the extent that we can understand the emotional truth of her last words and the moral force of her wish to exonerate him – even while we have to realize their literal untruth – that we can fully grasp the implications of this last scene. Desdemona 'suffers' her death in both senses of the word. She is Othello's victim, and yet, by loving him not 'wisely', perhaps, but too well to blame or evade or fight against the loss of his love, she has in her desolation *allowed* herself to become his victim. He himself and his love for her have grown more crucial to her than her life; and in recognizing that she cannot exist without his love, accepting her death is the only way she has of being circumstanced, shutting herself up to Fortune's alms, by a kind of suicide. For Othello to recognize this about his abiding existence in her love is to recognize not only that he has murdered her, but also that in that very deed, by which he had tried to kill his love and remedy his pain, he has in effect killed himself as well.

8

The 'power to hurt' and 'be hurt', 'past all surgery': the final scene

EMILIA Thou hast not half that power to do me harm
As I have to be hurt.   (v, ii, 161–2)

OTHELLO I kissed thee, ere I killed thee: no way but this,
Killing myself, to die upon a kiss.   (v, ii, 354–5)

Dreadful as we feel them to be, the events of the last scene (v, ii) come as the inevitable end of Othello's 'journey': his ultimate attempts to remedy the ultimately irremediable. At least, that is how they appear to *us*. To the characters, even to Othello himself (or, rather, especially to Othello himself), they appear very differently. Indeed, in this final scene the difference between his view, his feelings, his sense of himself, and ours, becomes larger than ever before. It also becomes more acute, more painful, which is why it is so easy, and yet too easy, for us to remedy the painfulness either by morally 'cashiering' him or by dissolving everything we feel into pure and simple pity.

As the scene opens, Othello's desperation is thinly concealed from us and heavily disguised from himself. Given our vivid sense of Desdemona's chastity and love, and the solicitude for her that has grown in us throughout the preceding scenes, our view here of what is happening both includes and (as it has ever since Act III) also conflicts with his. Our judgments and feelings themselves conflict,

264

making it equally impossible for us to 'identify' with him or to remain wholly detached from him. The current of our sympathies pulls with and against him at the same time. We must judge, yet we cannot merely condemn. After his virulent outbursts earlier, he now seems strangely calm. For the moment at least, he seems to have 'fixed most firm' his 'resolution' – to have reached some ground for tranquillity, a satisfactory 'cause' why 'she must die'. We, on the contrary, are taut, resistant, dreading what is to come:

> [*Enter Othello, with a light,*
> *Desdemona in her bed*]
> OTHELLO It is the cause, it is the cause, my soul:
> Let me not name it to you, you chaste stars!
> It is the cause. Yet I'll not shed her blood,
> Nor scar that whiter skin of hers than snow,
> And smooth as monumental alabaster:
> Yet she must die, else she'll betray more men.
> Put out the light, and then put out the light:
> If I quench thee, thou flaming minister,
> I can again thy former light restore,
> Should I repent me; but once put out thy light,
> Thou cunning'st pattern of excelling nature,
> I know not where is that Promethean heat
> That can thy light relume. When I have plucked thy
>   rose,
> I cannot give it vital growth again,
> It needs must wither. I'll smell it on the tree.
> [*He kisses her*]   (v, ii, 1–15)

For him, Desdemona is now 'she', an object, a 'pattern of nature', and her vitality simply a 'light' to extinguish, a 'rose', an 'it', to pluck from the tree. He seems able to call her 'thou' only because she is unconscious of it and unable either to hear or reply. Her sleeping body seems to him not merely the image of her death, but inanimate already. Her death is for him so imminent that he speaks almost as if she is dead even now, a motionless statue or monument,

her skin pure and cold as snow, smooth and lifeless as
'monumental alabaster'. For us, partly *because* of his
frighteningly different sense of her, Desdemona is intensely
alive and present, lying there in her marriage-bed, acutely
vulnerable.

> O balmy breath, that dost almost persuade
> Justice to break her sword! One more, one more.
> Be thus when thou art dead and I will kill thee,
> And love thee after. One more, and this the last.
> So sweet was ne'er so fatal. I must weep.
> But they are cruel tears: this sorrow's heavenly –
> It strikes where it doth love. She wakes.
>
> (v, ii, 16–22)

Not only is Othello's sense of Desdemona so different
from ours; his awareness of himself and of what he is doing
is correspondingly different as well. Although he says,
'when I have killed thee', he speaks as though her death
were not something *he* has chosen or resolved on, but
rather as something that has somehow been decreed in the
nature of things – from beyond the realm and power of his
personal choice and hence beyond his responsibility. To
himself, suppressing the possibility that he might be wrong,
might come to 'repent' his deed, he insists he is not even
the voluntary perpetrator of the deed, but the mere instrument of an impersonal power, Justice, which is 'out there',
fixed, distant, unchangeable, cold, like the 'chaste stars' he
invokes to sanction what he is instrumentally going to do.
Consequently her death seems to have for him no specific
or unique actuality: 'pluck thy rose', 'put out the light',
'kill thee': as he mentally rehearses the task, it seems simple,
natural, clear. Conceived in such pure, aesthetic images as
these, the murder he intends seems to him not a 'contrived
murder' at all, but a kind of bloodless sacrifice.[1]

[1] Cf. Othello's language in this speech with Brutus's in the forum speeches
in Act III of *Julius Caesar*, which Maynard Mack has well described as
prose in which 'the actuality of the assassination is intellectualized and held

This 'intellectualizing' is plainly why no shrinking from the deed troubles the quietly eloquent surface of his speech. No anguish retards or clogs its rhythms. His claim that Desdemona's 'balmy breath doth almost persuade/ Justice to break her sword' expresses no personal misgiving, but precisely the opposite – a balming, reassuring sense that Justice will *not* break her sword or be unprovided, no matter how strong the persuasions may be. He mentions 'cruel tears' and 'love': 'I must weep'; but, like the sorrow that describes itself as 'heavenly', these feelings are somehow disembodied – externally imaged, not subjectively experienced – somehow not his own. Since he sees Desdemona's death as the inevitable, necessary effect that must follow – somehow automatically – from 'the cause', there is no space for any perplexing 'if' or 'perhaps' relating to her fate. The even, steady movement of his voice reflects his sense of being at last unhampered. The possibility of repentance is allowed to slide by, unrealized; it is now simply 'she must die'; 'once put out thy light'; 'When I have plucked thy rose'; 'when I have killed thee'. Indeed, far from resisting the deed he seems calmly to embrace the fact of its now (to him) unquestionable necessity. Far from seeming daunted by its irreversibility, he dwells on this, as if to confirm it. He lingers, in short, as if the very fact of its finality were a source not of anxiety, but of relief.

But to notice this last – the apparent comfort (rather than pain) Othello seems to draw from the idea that her death is absolutely final – is of course to notice one of the fundamental differences between his awareness of himself and

---

at bay by the strict patterns of an obtrusively formal rhetoric, almost as though corporeal death were transubstantiated to a "ballet of bloodless categories" '. See 'The Jacobean Shakespeare', in *Jacobean Theatre*, ed. John Russell Brown and Bernard Harris (London, 1960), p. 16. Brutus's 'Let's be sacrificers, but not butchers' (*Julius Caesar*, II, i, 166) is like a cruder version of Othello's rationalization, 'but I'll not shed her blood . . .'

ours. To us, his voice seems strangely hushed, possessed, as though absorbed and abstracted in the performance of some ritual. 'It is the cause, it is the cause, my soul . . .' This first line seems to us, as John Money remarks, 'ambiguous as well as ironical' – ironical because the alleged cause is not a real cause, and ambiguous because 'in Othello's appeal to his own soul to justify "the cause" . . . there is a sense in which his soul *is* "the cause", and this sense is pointed to by the final placing of the words in the line'.[1] As Othello speaks, at first we are perhaps most perturbed by the way his conception of what is about to happen so carefully filters out all those aspects that would otherwise most perturb him and so make him falter. But our awareness of this shifts, I think, during the course of his speech, as we begin to see how flimsy – and yet how necessary to him – that filter is. At every point his turns of phrase seem unconsciously to belie his calm detachment, to betray other, unacknowledged feelings that lie beneath and necessitate it. 'Yet I'll not shed her blood, nor scar . . .'; 'Yet she must die': these 'yets' serve to arrest the drift of his mind towards other very different possibilities from those he tries to entertain. The very need to adduce reasons why 'she must die' itself seems to spring from a hidden need to confirm the unshakable rightness of what he is about to do; and lurking beneath that need is the terror of having otherwise to face another 'if' – what if she were to live? *That*, we realize, would make life impossible for him. The strain of facing any fresh doubts or questions is now simply more than he can stand.

Hence the absurdly transparent self-deceptive thinness of the 'reason' he gives himself to explain why she must die – 'else she'll betray more men'. We can have no such delusions about his altruism. What we see is rather self-charity: his acutest need is clearly to save, not others, but

[1] 'Othello's "It is the Cause . . .": An Analysis', *Shakespeare Survey*, 6 (1953), pp. 94–105.

himself from present and future pain. The very fact that he resorts to a plural 'more men', and so externalizes his own anguish at being betrayed (and also reinforces his case why she must die), is precisely what betrays that anguish to us most clearly. Despite the claims of various critics who have followed Othello's own claim, Desdemona 'must die' not because Othello is an honourable man who cannot stomach dishonour and whose fastidious sense of propriety is outraged. He is not to be confused with, say, Hardy's Angel Clare. The real reason for Othello's intent, the real 'cause', is one he cannot 'name' or articulate because he cannot acknowledge it: it is the one he had fleetingly admitted in IV, ii – that without Desdemona's love he can 'bear' no life at all. To fix his will he has (Iago-like) to distract his mind with 'causes' whose very inadequacy is revealing in itself – the dictate of Justice, the presumed vulnerability of other 'men'. Hence the strange incantatory repetitions: 'it is the cause'; 'put out the light', 'one more': each phrase comes to his lips three times as his mind seeks rest in the double thought of the necessity and the irreversibility of her death. But as we listen, the repetitions force upon *us* the question Othello himself later puts to Emilia as she gasps, 'My husband?' again and again in shocked incredulity: *'What needs this iterance?'* Were Othello indeed as calm and assured as he thinks, why would he need to reiterate these phrases, why need to dwell on what will *not* be the case? 'I'll not . . . nor'; 'I know not . . .'; 'I cannot . . .' What needs this prevalence of negatives? But of course, as we have seen so often earlier in the play, Othello characteristically overstates his case and resorts to denials and multiple negatives whenever his deepest feelings are in fact least quiet and assured. Here, he simply cannot consciously entertain the possibility of 'restoring' Desdemona's life or 'regretting' his deed, yet his mind nevertheless flickers over such possibilities, treating them as merely hypothetical, and transferring them to the light in her chamber – 'If I quench thee, thou flaming minister,/ I can again thy former light restore,/ Should I repent me' – before moving on to repeat the impossibility of reluming Desdemona's light once it is 'put out', or of restoring vitality to a plucked rose: 'it needs must wither'.

To us, therefore, Othello's self-soothing rhetoric, his impulse to reach for mollifying metaphors and analogues, his terrible, sensuous (yet paradoxically abstracted) loitering and iterance, all suggest that the surface calm of his speech stretches over an abyss of quite other feelings – feelings that keep sliding out in the unwitting drift of his syntax, and so keep threatening to rise into consciousness. To us it becomes clearer and clearer that he has to see things in these terms, however difficult it may be, because he could not bear to see himself or his actions or Desdemona in any other way. His deepest feelings can only be suppressed or transmuted; he can cope with them only by holding to a fixed image of himself and a fixed image of her. There is no way but this to 'satisfy' his desperate need for rest, assurance, stability, a condition free of all 'ifs' and 'buts'. What we see, however, especially in the language that betrays his subconscious terror, is that neither his full being nor Desdemona's can be fixed for ever: fluidity, change-ableness, is the very condition of loving and living. Already we are being forced to recognize what Othello cannot: that his need of absolute surety can be 'satisfied' only if he kills himself as well as her. In this speech – 'It is the cause, it is the cause . . .' – Othello is a very long way from any such recognition. His metaphors of roses and lights are nothing more nor less than essential, self-protective euphe-misms; such steadiness as they afford him is – as we see it – superficial and precarious.

Nor is the willed self-alienation as complete as it seems. 'I', 'thou', the appalling actuality of murder – all the realities, in short, that the speech strives to deny – threaten to well up into Othello's consciousness. His need – to confirm the inevitability of the killing and to eschew both his own personal agency and responsibility by projecting both onto an 'objective' Justice – is the need not merely to find a comforting rationale for his will, but, more crucially, to provide it with the impetus to go through with the deed. As we see it, he stands to gain nothing, but rather to lose everything, by murdering Desdemona. As *he* sees it (though he cannot put it this way as Iago calmly could and did about himself in the previous scene) he stands only to benefit from it: her death 'makes me' and her survival 'foredoes me quite'. Her survival therefore is something he cannot even contemplate; but increasingly, as the speech proceeds, it grows clear to us that all his apparent calm and control depend on his realizing *nothing* in his mind or heart.

Just how precarious and fragile is this steadiness grows even clearer to us (and indeed partly clear to him) as soon as Desdemona wakes and starts to speak with him. We see at once that he was quite right, in Act IV, when he implicitly admitted his fear of her power to unnerve him, to sing the savageness out of his heart. As soon as he starts to 'expostulate with her', her body, her beauty, and (far more than either of those) her love instantly 'unprovide' his mind again. She disrupts all his hard-won 'resolution', simply by being the person she is and by speaking out of their old relationship. Just by being alive and speaking she can no longer be kept still in any fixed notion of her. She naturally assumes, and so grants to him, his rights and power and his responsibilities as her husband. Calling him 'My lord' at every point – 'Will you come to bed, my lord?' – the very gentleness of her tone confirms her truth and innocence and so implicitly calls in question the justice, truth, soundness and even the common sense of his notion of her. Unbeknownst to herself, her very demeanour challenges 'the simple rigidity of [his] resolve'.[1] When she wakes he can at first trust himself enough to call her by name, 'Ay, Desdemon'. But his stern control rapidly dissipates. It collapses into shrill commands that make him sound, as he needs to feel, like someone controlling a dog (or trying to): 'Out, strumpet!', 'Down, strumpet!' Yet to us the growing fury clearly discloses the growing panic behind it. The threats and denunciations all betray how profoundly threatened he feels. Everything she says further un-prepares his spirit, further erodes his self-government, *un*-reconciles him to the 'sacrificial' act that now threatens to look, even to him, like a crime. Hence the need to twist and project his own feelings onto her: 'If you bethink yourself of any crime/ Unreconciled as yet to heaven . . .'; 'I would not kill thy unprepared spirit.'

The frightful vulnerability of each to the other increases at every turn. Whatever Desdemona says seems not to diminish but unavoidably to augment and accelerate the current of feelings sweeping them both towards her death. She speaks more truly than she knows – 'some bloody passion shakes your very frame' – for he is shaken indeed, but less by a decisive murderous passion than by a passion of growing dismay that resembles as well as causes her own. Her recessive cries – 'Alas', 'alack', 'Lord have mercy on me' – only further excite the fury that cannot now disguise his own nightmare sense of helplessness. Terrified, shrinking and meek though she is, Desdemona expressly refuses to fit his fixed image of her as a whore. Persistently now, she disclaims all guilt, and claims her right, as his wife, to justice or at least to mercy – refusing to 'confess' *any* 'sin' except the 'loves I bear to you'.

---

[1]The phrase is George Eliot's, from *Middlemarch*, Ch. 64. (Her detailed description there of Lydgate, 'paralysed by opposing impulses', is very apposite to Othello's much more extreme state throughout Acts III–V – not that Rosamund is another Desdemona, of course, and indeed one sometimes wishes Lydgate *would* let his rage loose on her.)

But so desperately now does he need her confession of guilt to ratify his sense of the unquestionable justice of what he is doing, that he resorts once more to violent, bullying denials, threatening what will *not* happen even if she goes on refusing to obey his demand:

> Therefore confess thee freely of thy sin;
> For to deny each article with oath
> Cannot remove nor choke the strong conception
> That I do groan withal. Thou art to die.
>
> (v, ii, 53–6)

Here as always the negative only reveals the power of what it disclaims. Her refusal to confess torments him: it *does* keep threatening to 'remove or choke' the fixed conception of things he is struggling to give birth to and keep alive. The image of violent labour-pains – 'I do groan withal' – vividly betrays just how frail his conception of things actually is, and the anguished effort it costs him, in the face of her insistent protestations of innocence and purity, either to hold it or to bring it out naked, to be seen and faced and examined. Suddenly, the tables have turned. It evidently feels to him now as though *she* is the murderess, he the victim whose soul she will kill. And indeed this feeling becomes so potent that he is reduced almost to pleading for mercy against her power to deny and negate him:

> By heaven, I saw my handkerchief in's hand!
> O perjured woman! Thou dost stone my heart,
> And mak'st me call what I intend to do
> A murder, which I thought a sacrifice.
> I saw the handkerchief.   (v, ii, 62–6)

All his efforts to eradicate his feelings and to turn his heart to stone have come to nothing. Far from being flinty, unyielding, his heart is only too rawly exposed to the wounds she seems to be inflicting – 'stoning' and torment-ing him by refusing to yield and 'confess', and so forcing him to see himself not just as her victim but also as nothing short of a murderer, and one without even a 'cause'. For Desdemona herself, of course, the reverse is agonizingly true. Her tears and all her pleas for mercy meet only what is, for her, the unyielding stoniness of his heart. If we recall the haunting lines from her willow song, 'Her salt tears fell from her and softened the stones', Desdemona's plight here seems only to prove such 'softening' a hopeless impossibility. Yet as we realize what Othello's cry that she is 'stoning' his heart reveals of *his* state, that line from the song seems in another way truly prophetic indeed: Desdemona's tears not only begin to soften and agonizingly erode the willed stoniness of his heart but seem to him, for that very reason, to be more like pain-inflicting stones than liquid tears. The result is to make him feel such a frantic 'necessity' in her death that he is 'bound to put it on her' precisely because of her irresistibly mollifying effect on his hardened heart and will. Only by increasingly hysterical assertions of her guilt – 'I saw the handkerchief' – can he cling to the notion of himself as performing an appropriate and decorous sacrifice on the altar of Justice. Her awful intransigence (as it seems to him), her insistence that 'guiltiness I know not', threatens to deny him the only role in which he might immure himself, anaesthetize his heart, and free himself of all responsibility for her death.

When Desdemona calls for Cassio's testimony of her innocence (just as in Act I Othello had called for her testimony to rebut Brabantio's false charges), he at first parries her move with threats: 'Take heed of perjury: thou art on thy death-bed.' But when, appealing again for Cassio's evidence, she fatally picks up Othello's word 'confess' – 'Send for him hither./ Let him confess a truth' – Othello leaps with prompt alacrity upon what he supposes to be a suggestion of guilt in 'confess'; and their exchanges from here rush headlong, with sickening speed, to the end. For what Desdemona does – and what else could she possibly do? – is in effect to force his attention to *other* possible realities than those he clings to. She forces him to expose his heart again to another possible 'perhaps' – perhaps she is true, and always has been – and to submit once more to the possibility of loving her and *being* loved. But for him, submitting to that possibility is now impossible, since it would entail submission to yet another, the inevitable risk of perhaps, one day, being totally negated by her. No way is now left for him to seal himself off from the agony of doubt and irresolution but to act resolutely, once and for all. And just as in Act III Iago's appeals to Othello to 'leave it to time' – 'your mind perhaps may change' – had tortured him to the point of crying 'Never', so here Desdemona's desperate appeals for time – 'let me live tonight!'; 'but half an hour!' – actually precipitate his frantic drive to finalize, to do away with feelings for ever: 'Being done, there is no pause . . .' 'It is too late.'

Desdemona *is* his heart. The destructive act of smothering her is his attempt to stifle his own feelings. It is a way of trying to conserve his self, or rather to conserve the only idea of himself he can live with (or thinks he can live with): as a man forever and entirely devoid of feelings. For a time it succeeds. Yet the question he immediately asks of her equally applies – as *we* realize – to his own anguish: 'Not dead? Not yet quite dead?' For us it is clear that in one way he has killed the quick of himself in killing her – the murder is suicidal; in another way, however, we also realize that although she is almost dead, what she means to him is still alive within him, and his own feelings for her can never be arrested or finally stifled except in his own physical death. But for a moment he can now feel quite calm in relation to her. Her death can be quietly, painlessly finalized – 'So, so'. Straight away he reverts to his previous idea of himself as the clement agent of stern justice: 'I, that am cruel, am yet merciful:/ I would not have thee linger in thy pain.'[1] The preposterous touch of self-congratulation underlines for us what he can least afford to recognize – that it is really himself that he could not (rather than 'would not') bear to have 'linger in pain' one moment more. The 'pain' he speaks of – hers – seems in the very *way* he speaks of it somehow fictional, hypothetical, having no present actuality. There is no sense of shock at what he has done. He seems mentally distant, out of touch with its reality, and his heart now seems for the time mercifully dulled, even lifeless, like her – 'no more moving?/ Still as the grave . . ./ I think she stirs again. No.'

But of course his own feelings are bound to stir again; and it is Emilia now who ensures this, by pressing on him the facts of Desdemona's love and innocence and so forcing him to face himself and his own guilt. At the very instant when he smothers Desdemona, Emilia's voice cries from outside the room with a pathetic echo of the (by her, unheard) words of her mistress:[2]

DESDEMONA O Lord, Lord, Lord!
           [*He smothers her*]
EMILIA   My lord, my lord! What, ho! My lord, my lord!

The echo is muffled just as Desdemona's own cry was muffled, but it refuses to be stilled or silenced. It dramatically establishes Emilia as Desdemona's vital spokesman now. For a moment Othello does not unlock the door of the room or even of his own consciousness. Emilia's cries and knocking – as if at the door of his soul – prompt him to blank abstracted questions, as his mind tries to orient itself between the realities of Desdemona's silence and Emilia's urgent calls:

Yes, 'tis Emilia. – By and by. – She's dead.
'Tis like she comes to speak of Cassio's death:

---

[1]Cf. 'O, that the slave had forty thousand lives!' (III, iii, 439); 'I would have him nine years a-killing!' (IV, i, 177).
[2]Desdemona's cry is omitted in the Folio text.

> The noise was high. Ha! No more moving?
> Still as the grave. Shall she come in? Were't good?
> I think she stirs again. No. What's best to do?
>
> (v, ii, 92–6)

Emilia's loud knocking, in short (like Macduff's knocking
in *Macbeth*), refuses him the silence in which he might rest,
even momentarily, in relief and a sense of freedom at having
performed the 'sacrifice'. Her insistence turns him round
to face the new facts of the situation:

> If she come in, she'll sure speak to my wife –
> My wife! My wife! What wife? I have no wife.
> O, insupportable! O heavy hour!
> Methinks it should be now a huge eclipse
> Of sun and moon, and that th'affrighted globe
> Should yawn at alteration.   (v, ii, 97–102)

Yet if he now has to recognize that he has no wife, he
does so with a conveniently blurring, muffling rhetoric.
The gleams of actuality glimmering within and behind this
speech are so faint and distant as to be virtually imper-
ceptible – to him at least. Once again his speech projects
and claims to realize what is in fact a mere *notion* of feelings:
he projects the idea of 'insupportable' loss, but of course no
one actually experiencing the 'insupportable' can yet be
conscious that it is so. In his weirdly self-alienated state
he is almost totally anaesthetized to the emotional actuali-
ties of 'eclipse' and 'alteration', even though his language
nevertheless reveals what 'in some place of [his] soul' he
knows he must feel were he ever fully to realize that Desdemona is dead. Clearly, the cosmic imagery here links with
that in other speeches ('Chaos is come again . . .'; 'Heaven
mocks itself . . .', etc.) which likewise suggest how she has
become the whole world to him. As he has always done
when his deepest feelings threaten to rise and overwhelm
him, he projects an external image of them on which to
concentrate his attention – here, a safely distant image of

how the cosmos 'should' respond to and mirror the magnitude of such a loss with an appropriate 'huge eclipse'. And it is significant that this distancing effect is especially strong at this moment (the most revealing comparison is with his earlier outburst at Desdemona in IV, ii, 76ff. about her alleged adultery, saying how 'heaven stops the nose at it, and the moon winks' – a speech whose tormented sensuousness conveys his revulsion, shock and tenderness far more immediately than does this later speech about 'eclipses'). It is as if his mind can see what he ought to be feeling and must ultimately come to feel; but only by seeing it as a cosmic, not a personal 'alteration', can he avert his attention from the real catastrophe which his heart cannot yet begin properly to register, let alone support. As always, his rhetoric betrays to us what it manages to conceal from him: why, for example, should the word 'affrighted' creep into the analogue? It suggests to us very clearly his incipient sense of the fear, chaos, measureless depths of misery and horror lurking beneath the expressed but unrealized notions of 'eclipse'. It is into *this* abyss that Othello must at last plunge, if ever his heart is pushed or 'affrighted' into full consciousness of the actual huge 'alteration' Desdemona's death represents: if he cannot avert that recognition he will suffer a total 'eclipse'. In short, if he were now fully to grasp the meaning of Desdemona's murder, the realization would annihilate him. Her 'loss' is such that his self would shatter to pieces if he recognized it.

In uttering the speech Othello's imagination dimly figures that truth and its attendant feelings; but it also manages, for the moment at least, to pre-empt them. For a time he can prevent himself from grasping what it means to 'have no wife', by reverting to his earlier delusory sense of himself and her and his deed. When Emilia enters, flustered and dismayed, to announce the supposed death of Roderigo: 'O, my good lord, yonder's foul murder done', he at first cannot get clear what 'murder' she is referring to; but then he mumbles distractedly about 'the very error of the moon . . . [that] makes men mad', as though murderers do not act by personal volition upon their victims, but are rather acted upon by external circumstances, as themselves the mere instruments and victims of nature's inscrutable design.[1] Emilia's announcement, 'No, Cassio is not killed', again disrupts his calm. 'Not Cassio killed!' What had seemed 'sweet revenge' grows 'harsh' again – 'Then murder's out of tune.' (The irony of the metaphor clangs in our ears.) And suddenly, as if come back from death to utter and so force upon him the censored motion of his own heart, Desdemona 'stirs again'. Neither she nor his feelings are 'yet quite dead': 'O, falsely, falsely murdered!'

Like Emilia's, though to more potent effect, these words of Desdemona's shatter the silence within Othello that so far has allowed him not to be insupportably shaken by her death by refusing fully to realize what it is. She articulates exactly what he is trying to suppress in himself. Supposed to be unchangeably dead, she stirs for the last time to repeat the very assertion that had driven him to kill her because it leaves him no self he can bear to be: 'A guiltless death I die'; 'falsely, falsely murdered!' Once more attesting her innocence and naming her death a crime, she inevitably implies his guilt. But she does not name him; on the contrary, she instantly counters even the implication of his guilt by naming herself the author as well as the innocent victim of her death: 'Nobody. I myself [have done this deed]'. Significantly her words now are addressed to Emilia. She talks of, but no longer to, Othello – not, I think, because she has already said everything she can to him (though what else *could* she say?), but rather as a final attestation of the love she still bears him, her still unbroken impulse to shield him from reproach and guilt and mortal self-laceration. But of course she cannot – nobody could – finally shield Othello from himself, despite

[1]Cf. Edmund's speech in *King Lear*, I, ii, about this sort of 'evasion'.

the fact that, loving him as she does, she can truly claim that she does not judge or 'indict' him.

As we see it, the fatal irony of the situation is that, simply by being what she is, Desdemona confirms his guilt. And since only his own false view of her can save him from recognizing it, Othello must sooner or later inevitably be driven or drive himself to realize the truth of what she had said just before he killed her – 'guiltiness I know not'. For us watching the play, it is equally clear too that what Iago had said of the innocent Bianca in the previous scene applies only too well to the guilty Othello: 'Nay, guiltiness will speak/ Though tongues were out of use.' From the moment of Desdemona's death up until Othello's own what we have to witness is his increasingly desperate effort to fend off both these realizations, realizations which the drama has shown him having to try to avoid, 'for necessity of present life', ever since Act III.

This is why Othello is caught so off balance in the following exchanges with Emilia. Although Desdemona has not even mentioned him in direct relation to her murder, Othello's guilty mind translates 'nobody' into himself and declares she has declared he did not commit the crime. But, unprepared, his lines of self-exculpation get confused. Seizing on her evidence, he at first claims its truth and then does a complete volte-face:

OTHELLO You heard her say herself it was not I.
EMILIA She said so: I must needs report the truth.
OTHELLO She's like a liar gone to burning hell:
'Twas I that killed her. (v, ii, 128–31)

He claims his crime because he must justify it, both to himself and the world: he must prove that he is a fair and honourable man, a victim of others' perfidy and cruelty.

The only thing that can shelter him now from knowing the extremity of his injustice is his argument that 'I did proceed upon just grounds/ To this extremity'; and from here on he clings to it blindly, appealing to Iago's corroboration as a man who 'hates the slime that sticks on filthy deeds':

> Nay, had she been true,
> If heaven would make me such another world
> Of one entire and perfect chrysolite,
> I'd not have sold her for it.   (v, ii, 142–5)

But Desdemona's guiltlessness 'will speak' despite her tongue being 'out of use'. For, like her, only much more fierily, Emilia refuses to let Othello hold to his false conception either of himself or of Desdemona. She picks up his own ugly metaphor of buying and selling, his own phrase 'filthy deeds', and flings them back in his face: 'She was too fond of her most filthy bargain.' Her sheer scorching contempt and daring make her testimony now far more formidable than her previous assertions of Desdemona's chastity in Act IV, for when she challenges him to 'Do thy worst', the challenge itself sanctions and buttresses the authority of her claims. Not only does she now endorse Desdemona's avowal that 'I never did/ Offend you in my life'; she defies Othello to say otherwise, and refuses to be silenced or overruled. Where Desdemona's love had transformed and defused any charge against Othello, Emilia forcibly thrusts his guilt at him as an incontrovertible fact.

The tensions grow more acute at every turn, as more tenaciously than ever Othello clutches at the saving claim that he has acted justly: *Iago's* reports 'set the murder on'; 'O, she was foul!'; 'I know this act shows horrible and grim . . . but yet Iago knows/ That she with Cassio hath the act of shame/ A thousand times committed'. 'A thousand times' leaps from an imagination so inflamed that it has lost all touch with possible realities in its own need to feel justified a thousand times over – a need that clearly springs from a violent turmoil of contradictory feelings. Inevitably, therefore, Emilia's announcement that 'Iago begged of me to steal [the handkerchief]' is shattering for Othello and (in a different way) dismaying for us. For it tears from him his sole objective 'proof', and doing so it strips him of all but the very flimsiest of self-deluding props. Only Emilia's death and forced silence will allow him – as Desdemona's had done – inwardly to evade the implications of her claims, temporarily at least.

Yet Emilia's dying speech eventually cuts even deeper through Othello's evasions by its very truth, simplicity and quiet. When this speech comes, Othello is so enmeshed in guilt and self-contempt that he seems hardly to notice it; perhaps, indeed, he doesn't. Nevertheless, his final, passionate desperation answers to what her words so powerfully disclose:

> EMILIA   What did thy song bode, lady?
> Hark, canst thou hear me? I will play the swan
> And die in music. [*Singing*] Willow, willow, willow.
> Moor, she was chaste; she loved thee, cruel Moor,
> So come my soul to bliss, as I speak true;
> So speaking as I think, I die, I die.   (v, ii, 244–9)

Vividly evoking and invoking Desdemona's presence, this represents what Othello finally cannot help realizing, and yet cannot bear to. Not only has Desdemona never rejected him, not even when he killed her, but his rejection of her love – the self-mistrust that led him to mistrust, traduce and kill her – has *proved* indeed, with shattering finality, what he had always secretly feared: his unworthiness to be loved by her at all. The noxious, corrosive truth within his own heart, which now (as Iago had predicted in III, iii) indeed begins to 'burn like the mines of sulphur', is one from which nothing can 'medicine' or 'cure' him. Both Desdemona's refusal ever to acknowledge it or let him feel it, and Emilia's attestation of it, drive him towards the recognition of what must destroy him if he cannot evade it:

Do thy worst:
This deed of thine is no more worthy heaven
Than thou wast worthy her.   (v, ii, 158–60)

*

Dr Johnson wrote that 'no disease of the imagination . . . is
so difficult of cure, as that which is complicated with the
dread of guilt: fancy and conscience then act interchangeably upon us, and so often shift their places, that the illusions of one are not distinguished from the dictates of the
other'.[1] Othello's every turn of speech and everything
he does, from Act III and especially from Desdemona's
death until the moment of his suicide, bear out that
truth about the subterfuges of dread. After Emilia's blazing
accusations and her consequent sudden murder, the frightful strains within Othello appear to us once more in the
terrible resounding silences behind and between his public
words. Caught now where nothing supports him, desperate
yet still inarticulable feelings begin to press further towards
consciousness and expression. We see his self-protective
moves become more compulsive, more sporadic, and more
and more distraught. Now he falls back on self-justifications;
now he releases feelings in the only direction possible –
outwards, at Iago: 'Are there no stones in heaven/ But what
serve for the thunder? Precious villain!' Montano – in an
action that is both politic and symbolic – disarms him.

Neither we nor Othello can miss the significance of this
disarmament. In stripping him of the weapons by which
he might attack others, Montano also strips him of his
power to defend himself: the physical disarming mirrors
a psychological one, as Othello's next speech makes plain.
Montano's act is in effect the physical equivalent of Emilia's
announcement that she stole the handkerchief for Iago –
the fact which removes his most potent defence. Thus, left
virtually by himself while Montano pursues Iago, Othello's

[1] Imlac in Ch. XLVI of *Rasselas*.

mounting sense of impotence hardens into sneering self-contempt: he sees his own puniness, the fact that he is now neither honest nor even honourable to himself:

> I am not valiant neither,
> But every puny whipster gets my sword.
> But why should honour outlive honesty?
> Let it go all. (v, ii, 241–4)

It is significant that this is virtually a soliloquy (only the dying Emilia is present), for only alone, and then only briefly, can Othello even begin to face what he is and what he now is not. 'I am not valiant neither': the recognition marks the huge gap between the desolate now and that time when that epithet always seemed so naturally and truly his own – 'Valiant Othello, we must straight employ you.' Moreover, it is important that Emilia's dying speech immediately breaks across the silence after Othello's words here, for the implications of what she says strongly reinforce what he is beginning to see, but in a way which is yet unfaceable, forcing him to resort and cling to the one remaining means with which he might protect himself from that full self-recognition. Physically, his ultimate weapon is 'a sword of Spain, the ice-brook's temper', one he has always relied on to command reality; psychologically, his ultimate weapon is the weapon of his own eloquence – the power of speech with which he has always managed to 'temper', dissolve, re-create, and so command reality.

In the early acts, we recall, Othello's mastery of speech was the manifest sign, and sometimes the very means, of his mastery in and over his world. It not only sounded authoritative and conscious of its power, but was actually forceful enough to disarm Brabantio and others:

> Keep up your bright swords, for the dew will rust them.
> Good signor, you shall more command with years
> Than with your weapons. (i, ii, 59–61)

The commanding eloquence of that was no mere trick of language, but sprang from and bespoke the real authority of Othello's self. As so often in the first half of the play, his speech realized his earned warrant to think of himself as a man whose proven 'worth' and 'valour' had won him the right, reflected and assumed in his language, to be respected, admired and obeyed. More than that, however, as I have argued (in Chapters 4-6), his gift of speech had also constantly empowered him – either in fact or in his own 'fancy' – to master reality, including that of his inner experience, by restructuring it, re-creating it, by projecting images of it (or of himself) which were figured, and therefore disposable, in accordance with obscure pressures and needs in himself. Early on – as in his reported wooing-speeches – he deployed language to represent and so to confirm the reality both of himself and his world by touching up, but not fundamentally altering, the truth of both. But ever since III, iii, his power to 'master' and control experience in this way has become ever more distorting and ever more urgently necessary to him as reality has threatened increasingly to master *him*. By v, ii, after the deaths of Desdemona and Emilia, he is – and seems half-aware that he is – almost 'naked', almost helpless now to hold it at bay. Having been 'disarmed' in various ways by Montano's action, by Emilia's words, and worst of all by Desdemona's love and charity, he can use only the most tried and trusted weapon, the blade of speech, the 'ice-brook's temper', to temper and disarm reality now.

Yet for that instinctive weapon of self-dramatization to work at all, he needs an audience, consolation, not isolation. Clearly he dreads to be alone, dreads the moment when solitude should deliver him to the tyranny of self-reflection.

OTHELLO   I have another weapon in this chamber.
. . .

   [*To Gratiano*]   Uncle, I must come forth.

GRATIANO [*within*] If thou attempt it, it will cost thee dear;
          Thou hast no weapon, and perforce must suffer.
OTHELLO   Look in upon me then, and speak with me,
          Or naked as I am I will assault thee.

(v, ii, 250–6)

Gratiano's words are far truer and far more ironic than he can possibly know. Despite Othello's secret 'weapon', he is in fact psychically almost stripped bare, and whatever he attempts must necessarily cost him dear; whatever verbally self-protective trappings he tries to wear, he 'perforce must suffer', just because in the end he 'must come forth', naked to his own gaze as well as to that of the world. The heated urgency of his voice makes his command and his threat sound more like a desperate plea – 'Uncle, I must come forth' – and it is this pleading note which most sharply makes us realize the distance he has travelled from the cool composure of his remark in Act I: 'I must be found./ My parts, my title, and my perfect soul/ Shall manifest me rightly.' Here in the final scene, his need to 'come forth' and 'be found' has to overcome his equally urgent need to be weaponed, to fortify himself with eloquent self-images which, if only for a time, can 'manifest' him falsely – *prevent* his real self from being 'found'.

One of the sharpest dramatic ironies of this exchange between him and Gratiano is that it comes so soon after Gratiano's announcement of Brabantio's death. Brabantio too had come a long way since the opening scenes of the play. Then it was he who had tried so desperately to defy and deny reality, who took up arms and summoned weaponed supporters in his 'cause'. But (as at the end, we now see, must inevitably turn out to be the case with Othello as well), all Brabantio's threats and assertions of power, all his efforts to shield himself and to gloss reality (both within and without him) to a more tolerable meaning, were to no avail at all:

GRATIANO Poor Desdemon, I'm glad thy father's dead:
Thy match was mortal to him, and pure grief
Shore his old thread in twain.   (v, ii, 203–5)

Other parallels and differences between those early
scenes and this are painfully obvious too. Then, we remember, Brabantio had ordered the officers to 'lay hold
upon him: if he do resist,/ Subdue him, at his peril',
insisting that Othello be taken 'to prison, till fit time/
Of law . . ./ Call thee to answer.' Now, in this final scene,
faced with a charge of murder (rather than a mere allegation
of witchcraft) Othello cannot just coolly shrug off Montano's command to 'Let him not pass,/ But kill him rather',
nor can he expect or even wish simply to out-tongue his
captors when Lodovico declares that 'you shall close
prisoner rest,/ Till that the nature of your fault be known/
To the Venetian state'. Here, as so often in the play, the
similarities we perceive further underline the vast differences between that earlier time and this. Othello, who then
had all his 'absolute content' before him, his life radiantly
warmed and illumined by Desdemona's love, has now
indeed put out the light of her life and can never relume
it, and has thereby quite literally 'given to captivity me
and my utmost hopes'.

The 'labouring bark' of his life and love has by now
plunged almost 'as low/ As hell's from heaven'. Even yet,
however, he has still not quite reached what he now so
romantically calls 'my butt and very sea-mark of my utmost
sail'. Indeed, his very capacity to define – and so to circumscribe – his experience in these terms is precisely what, and
only what, can prevent him now from realizing its literally
'utmost' extremity and from being shorn in twain by it. His
sole remaining 'weapon' is his instinct for 'how to tell my
story' – his capacity to project a tolerable image of his self
with such eloquence as might seduce his hearers, including
himself, into believing it. But if this power to gloss over
his real state should be denied him by denying him an

audience, or if it should break down, it will leave him with nothing with which he could go on living. Dramatically, therefore, it is both unsurprising and perfectly right that his next speech, the famous one beginning 'Behold, I have a weapon', should be at once so eloquent and so desperately flailing in its rhetoric, its abrupt breaks and about-turns. With terrible clarity, it demonstrates the unwitting truth of the Duke's remark to Brabantio upon *his* crisis and imminent collapse in the play's first act:

> . . . take up this mangled matter at the best:
> Men do their broken weapons rather use
> Than their bare hands. (I, iii, 171–3)

As if to shore himself up against the ruin of his last fragments of consolation, Othello in this speech runs the whole gamut of his characteristic stratagems to fend off reality. One by one he attempts every defensive posture or habit we have witnessed in the play, as if the sheer multiplicity of such guises might somehow compensate for the increasingly evident threadbareness of each. This speech, 'Behold I have a weapon . . .', certainly exhibits what Leavis called Othello's 'rhetorical trick of self-boosting'.

Nevertheless, we cannot simply label and dismiss it any more than we could do so with everyone else's 'self-boostings'. Once we notice how transparent Othello's self-dramatizations are, we also recognize how crucially necessary they are to him: without them, he could not survive. Hence, they prompt us to a much more complex and disturbing judgment than Leavis's frowningly superior comment that Othello exhibits 'an attitude *towards* the emotion expressed – an attitude of a kind we are familiar with in the analysis of sentimentality'.[1] The 'sentimentality' is Othello's own, not Shakespeare's, and what Shakespeare imaginatively grasps and dramatizes and makes us respond

[1] 'Diabolic Intellect and the Noble Hero', p. 143.

to are the vital reasons for, and the vital reality of, this man visibly straining *not* to recognize how idealizing and sentimental – indeed, how false – his extenuating self-images are. What we are dramatically shown is more than Othello's exhibition of 'an attitude towards the emotion expressed'. We are shown a desperate action: specifically, Othello's effort to dull his emotions, even to replace them with 'attitudes', since he can neither express nor bear nor transform them in any other way. As in Acts III and IV, his mind projects and focuses on an 'attitude towards feelings' *instead* of those feelings which would prove insupportable. If this is a form of 'bovarysme', as Eliot claimed, it is a form so acute and so desperate that attaching moralistic labels seems only to betray a blindness or evasiveness in our own feelings about the tragedy.

The same seems to me true of the terms Eliot applied to the end of the play: 'Humility is the most difficult of all virtues to achieve; nothing dies harder than the desire to think well of oneself.'[1] Phrases like 'sentimentality', 'humility', 'virtue', 'desire to think well of oneself' and so on, seem both inadequate and misleading; for what the ending reveals is rather that nothing dies harder than the need not to think so ill of oneself that the self actually disintegrates, being unable any longer to delude itself that it has not been totally and irredeemably a 'fool, fool, fool'.

Othello's rhetoric in this speech (v, ii, 257ff.) flounders with his floundering inner state, and betrays it with dreadful clearness. His powers of speech are reduced to merely the last instrument of his will – the will whose 'power and corrigible authority' lies (as Iago thinks, and as Othello has tried to maintain since III, iii) in re-shaping the self, 'correcting' its needs and feelings. As we have seen, Othello's will to convince himself that he really is what he claims has grown more and more impotent ever since his

[1] 'Shakespeare and the Stoicism of Seneca', p. 130.

crisis began, whilst his need to believe what he claims has grown more and more demanding. His intense efforts (to project a fictional self to believe in and to *be*) cannot much longer stave off his consciousness of failure. Thus, here, we see him struggling to furnish his mind with yet another 'pageant, to keep [him] in false gaze': we are made to see that, as so often since Act III, he is managing to do no more than 'discourse fustian with his own shadow'. He ricochets from histrionic gestures ('Behold, I have a weapon') to indulgent pathos ('this little arm and this good sword') to a 'vain boast' ('I have made my way through more impediments/ Than twenty times your stop'). From that, he lurches to the crude comfort of seeing himself as a predestined tragic victim, as if his own condition were merely the normal, hapless condition of life ('Who can control his fate?'). Seeing his audience bewildered, he projects his own fear and dismay onto Gratiano ('Be not afraid, though you do see me weaponed'; 'Do you go back dismayed? 'Tis a lost fear'). From that in turn he slides to another self-dramatizing image of himself as pathetically impotent ('Man but a rush against Othello's breast,/ And he retires. Where should Othello go?').

At this point, significantly, the speech breaks off for a moment. He 'goes' where it has been taking him – to Desdemona. Yet again his imagery betrays his need to expunge from himself any response to her as the sexual being he had so totally loved and loathed. (One thinks of his inner turmoil in the handkerchief scene, for instance – 'This hand is moist, my lady . . . Hot, hot and moist'; now he can recognize and address her only as an object, not warm but 'cold', a victim of fate ('O ill-starred wench!/ Pale as thy smock! . . . cold, cold . . . Even like thy chastity'). He projects yet another image of his soul ('this look of thine will hurl my soul from heaven/ And fiends will snatch at it'). Next, he turns his feelings outwards, lashing at Iago ('O cursèd, cursèd slave!'), and the image becomes an image of himself – a rhetorical, self-flagellatory vision of damnation: 'Whip me, ye devils,/ From the possession of this heavenly sight!/ Blow me about in winds! Roast me in sulphur!/ Wash me in steep-down gulfs of liquid fire.' The worst physical torments he can envisage would be a merciful distraction from the far worse torture his own heart begins to inflict on itself. And ultimately his speech drives him irresistibly to the very recognition that it has been struggling all along to avert: 'O Desdemon! Dead Desdemon! Dead! O! O!'

Momentary relief or distraction does arrive, not in the form of infernal levies but in the persons of Lodovico, Cassio and others with Iago, now under guard (just as the Iago within Othello has now been arrested by his conscience, exposed and marked out for his condemnation). Their arrival temporarily furnishes Othello with another way of stealing his thoughts away from his present state: in discourse with Lodovico, Othello can stand outside and dissociate himself from his own experience; he can refer to himself not only in the third person, but in the past tense:

LODOVICO Where is this rash and most unfortunate man?
OTHELLO   That's he that was Othello: here I am.

(V, ii, 280–1)

In one way, this is a bitter admission – that Othello the valiant and honourable (if 'rash') man no longer exists. At the same time, Lodovico's very word 'unfortunate' and his expressed view of Iago as the 'viper' and the 'villain' re-open the way for Othello to evade the recognition of his own guilt by casting himself in Lodovico's extenuating terms as the unlucky victim, 'fallen in the practice of a damnèd slave'.

LODOVICO O, thou Othello, that wast once so good
                . . .
            What shall be said to thee?

OTHELLO   Why, anything:
An honourable murderer, if you will:
For naught did I in hate, but all in honour.

(v, ii, 288–92)

The bravado and the self-justification are preposterous.[1]
And yet we can see plainly what it is that both enables and
forces Othello to assert his bold readiness to be judged
('Why, anything') and then calmly to dictate the extenuating terms of that judgment: 'if you will' is an instruction,
not a humble request, and the stress falls not on 'murderer'
but on 'honour', 'honourable'. Clearly, the habitual respect
of Lodovico and others offers an irresistible distraction
from the rising chaos of his heart; once more, he can expend
emotional attention on vindictiveness, blaming Iago rather
than himself: 'O villain! . . . O the pernicious caitiff!' But
by now the condemnation of Iago sounds thin, desperately
empty. The sense of his own perniciousness keeps threatening to engulf him. Hence, to the loyal, generous, gently
reproving Cassio – 'Dear General, I never gave you cause' –
his apology for commissioning the murder-attempt is
notably minimal, as he struggles more and more vainly to
arrest the gathering momentum of self-loathing by focusing
it on Iago:

I do believe it, and I ask your pardon.
Will you, I pray, demand that demi-devil
Why he hath thus ensnared my soul and body?

(v, ii, 297–9)

But of course neither we nor Othello himself can pretend
any longer that the question of Iago's motives is relevant
to or can mitigate the consequences of Othello's own
disastrous self-snaring 'error' and disastrously ungoverned
imaginings.

From here on, it is above all his silences, and the appalled

[1] Cf. I, i, 120–1: BRABANTIO This thou shalt answer. I know thee, Roderigo.
RODERIGO Sir, I will answer anything.

repetition of 'O fool, fool, fool!', that betray to us Othello's growing inner sense of 'mere perdition' and 'chaos'. Even so, he can yet express it only in so self-shielding a word as 'fool'. His last shocked and shocking words to Desdemona as he killed her – 'Being done, there is no pause . . . It is too late' – now rebound upon him.

By the time Lodovico announces that 'your power and your command is taken off', we are fully aware, as is Othello himself, that already he has virtually been stripped of all his power emotionally to command or re-shape or evade what he is and what he has done. There is almost nothing now that can stave off the recognition of his total, unmitigated guilt. He has driven himself to his ultimate *crise de conscience*, his final, devastating confrontation of himself, the confrontation whose potentially shattering force we have long dreaded and foreseen in the very force of his efforts to evade it. Watching him now, we cannot escape the fact that for him there is no escape, except one whose dire extremity matches the direness of his plight. And it scarcely consoles us to realize that (as Casca puts it in *Julius Caesar*, I, iii, 101) 'every bondman in his own hand bears/ The power to cancel his captivity'.

The opening of his famous valedictory speech is clipped, direct, controlled – at least on the surface:

> Soft you; a word or two before you go.
> I have done the state some service and they know't:
> No more of that.

The tone of quiet and courteous authority may recall that of his speeches in the opening acts, but now it barely holds his self together. He is straining to reconstruct – and momentarily perhaps forgive – the self he is bound to obliterate. Almost inevitably, therefore, his speech becomes more rhetorical, as he seeks from others the exculpation his own heart denies. Small self-extentuations – 'these un-lucky deeds' – give way to larger more pitiably self-pitying ones. For a last time, 'fancy' and 'conscience' (to use Johnson's phrases) come to 'act interchangeably' upon him, and they so often 'shift their places' that 'the illusions of one are not distinguished from the dictates of the other'. The speech reveals as sharply as any so far how compulsively Othello's fancy takes wing against reality whenever he is faced with the pressure and dread of his guilt. Thus, the humbly polite request – 'I pray you in your letters . . ./ Speak of me as I am: nothing extenuate,/ Nor set down aught in malice' – rapidly transforms itself into fully fledged, overt command. Othello attempts to *dictate* the story about himself that 'must' be published abroad: 'Then you must speak/ Of one that loved not wisely, but too well.' The size of that understatement – 'not wisely' – is matched only by the size of his need to speak it and believe it. Fancy is driven to supply the self-image, 'one that loved . . . too well', by a conscience dictating the as yet unutterable truth, 'too much, too desperately, and too little'. As Coleridge so well put it, 'Othello wishes to excuse himself on the score of ignorance, and yet not to excuse himself – to excuse himself by accusing.'[1] The great struggle of feeling in him is audible in the resonance of this public rhetoric stretched tight over the aching, unmed'cinable 'hollow hell' within. He creates, for the last time, a 'shadow' of himself – a vividly projected semblance of what he wishes he had been, is, and will be thought to have been. Each aspect of the projected image of himself leads instantly on to another; were his mind to dwell for a second more on its own productions it would founder in the recognition of everything he struggles to ignore.

This last tale of himself is superficially fluent and composed, with little pauses that allow only for a rhetorical catch of breath before gliding on to impede and outwit self-scrutiny. The sensuous language, the self-consoling

---

[1] S. T. Coleridge, *Shakespeare Criticism*, 2 vols., 2nd edn, ed. T. M. Raysor (London and New York, 1960 [1930]), vol. 1, p. 49.

glow of the understatements and fluent hyperboles, all momentarily lead the mind – his, the other characters', even ours perhaps – away from the deathly truths that prompt them. For the last time, reality seems cushioned by voluptuous assonance, seduced, softened and re-composed in statically picturesque images, tamed by the art of a lingering cadence:

> Then must you speak
> Of one that loved not wisely, but too well;
> Of one, not easily jealous but, being wrought,
> Perplexed in the extreme; of one whose hand
> Like the base Indian threw a pearl away
> Richer than all his tribe; of one whose sùbdued eyes,
> Albeit unusèd to the melting mood,
> Drop tears as fast as the Arabian trees
> Their med'cinable gum. (v, ii, 339–47)

For a second there is a pause – 'Set you down this.' But 'guiltiness will speak'. Almost imperceptibly at first, the elocution that has so far flowed with 'med'cinable' yet fatal sweetness at last channels itself into its natural course. From 'melting' sonority, the language tightens and chills suddenly, in the rigour of bleak, hard-cutting consonants. The rhythm of the voice drives forward with a now insatiable self-loathing finally to reach its prey in 'thus':

> Set you down this:
> And say, besides, that in Aleppo once
> Where a malignant and a turbaned Turk
> Beat a Venetian and traduced the state,
> I took by th'throat the circumcisèd dog
> And smote him thus.
> [*He stabs himself*] (v, ii, 347–52)

By this point, we cannot think that this is a sudden act of remorse. Ever since iii, iii, when he bound himself 'for ever' to the Spartan dog, Iago, Othello has been bound, by everything that distinguishes him from Iago and binds

him to Desdemona 'for ever', ultimately to recognize himself as 'malignant', a 'traducer', a 'circumcisèd dog'.
Throughout Acts IV and V he has struggled to kill in
himself the very capacity to feel; he has sought to 'whistle
off' Desdemona, to sever his very 'heart-strings' and turn
his heart into unliving, invulnerable stone. From the first
moment that some need, some lack of faith in himself,
turned to lack of faith in Desdemona's faith to him, and
dread created the object it needed – 'she's gone, I am
abused' – he has sought 'remedy' to kill his suffering; yet
we have never been able to doubt that the search has been
doomed to fail, and to bring him ultimately face to face
with the mortal guilt he has incurred in the course of it.
For us, his act of stabbing himself is the inevitable com-
pletion of the psychic self-murder he had attempted in
murdering Desdemona. Killing her could not stifle or
still the insufferable motions of his own heart. Except by
literally stabbing his heart, there is literally 'no way but
this' to endure the pressure of his feelings, to break free
of what has bound him to Iago, and to acknowledge his
inseverable bond with Desdemona which – in his demented
attempts to sever it – has driven him to murder and brought
him to the point of suicide.

At the end, with the extraordinary tact and integrity that
are the signs of his greatest art, Shakespeare realizes and
leaves open several ways for us to comprehend Othello's
act of suicide. We can see it as an outward action that
demonstrates 'in complement extern' the 'native act and
figure' of Othello's heart – his heart kills itself. We can see
his act, that is, as representing a self-indictment so total
that it actually *is* the act of self-annihilation. Alternatively,
yet no less dreadfully, it can be seen as his last desperate
effort *not* to have to face a guilt so total that his mind would
shatter in the recognition of it. Indeed, the play has pressed
us to enter into Othello's inner experience so far that we
can see his final action as both these at once. But we can

see too that, beyond these, his ultimate act is also paradoxically a recognition of his own ineradicable humanity, an acknowledgment that he can never finally gainsay the 'dictates' of his heart. His self-murder implies his final acknowledgment of what he has sometimes fleetingly recognized as the absolute ground of his emotional and moral life, but which another current of his being has always striven to master and deny: his absolute need of Desdemona's unalterable love – the need, always impossible of fulfilment in the flux of human life, to rest forever secure in her total love of him and her entire acceptance of his love. It is as if, at last, in this single act, he at once *acknowledges, accepts* and *cancels* that need and that impossibility forever. As her love for him gave him the power to hurt her past all surgery, so his love for her – with all her consequent power to reject and deny it – has all along empowered her to make him feel his capacity to *be* hurt past all surgery: and that necessary condition of loving is simultaneously confirmed and annulled by his suicide. This is why, in anticipation of the act, his very last words, which arise from and attest his dependence, are for the first time free of fear and all self-protective rhetoric. At last he can speak to her as 'thee', in a voice that is utterly simple, direct, and naked in its love:

> I kissed thee, ere I killed thee: no way but this,
> Killing myself, to die upon a kiss.

*

Just because they circumscribe, no articulated words could adequately sum up everything the end of the play brings us to think and feel. For all its inevitable bathos, Gratiano's ejaculation when Othello stabs himself is strictly true:

> All that's spoke is marred . . .

But the closing lines of the play, after Othello's death, bring us partially to realize something further as well:

297

LODOVICO   O, Spartan dog,
                  More fell than anguish, hunger, or the sea
                  Look on the tragic loading of this bed:
                  This is thy work. The object poisons sight:
                  Let it be hid.   (v, ii, 357–61)

Because we share a common bond of humanity with men like Cassio and Lodovico we too find it impossible to contemplate steadily 'the tragic loading' of the play's end. Our natural impulse, too, is to shield ourselves from its full recognition, to hide it from our sight. No doubt this would be so even if we knew only what the characters know about the disaster; but of course the play has brought us to know and realize far more than any of them can. And in the face of what we find hardest to contemplate steadily and whole, we too – more than any of the people left alive in the play – inevitably seek precisely the sort of 'relief' from our feelings that Othello had so disastrously sought for his: we instinctively try to divert our attention from 'what's past help', by imagining punitive reprisals. Trying to compensate where no real compensation is possible, we embrace the comforting idea of blaming Iago, 'enforcing torture' on him, needing to let our feelings erupt in 'the censure of this hellish villain'.

The urge to take control of the situation, to punish, to justify oneself and to mete out 'justice' on others, is partly what caused the tragedy of course; equally, the fear of negation, real loss and utter chaos was what aggravated that need in both Iago and Othello – the need not to have to suffer and be patient, not to have to 'be circumstanced', the need to find some or any 'cure' for what otherwise seemed insupportable. In Othello himself, ever since Act III, these needs have been all-consuming, insatiable. He has lurched from all to nothing, from a sense of Desdemona as an angel to the conviction that she must be a devil. The poles of his mind, like Hamlet's, were always heaven and hell; and amidst the violent storm of his feelings his capacity even to 'distinguish' them was 'quench'd', in the very moment when his only chance of 'bearing it out' lay in recognizing and accepting the possibility of some 'midway 'twixt these extremes'.

Because we have been shown and brought to feel the force of the whole story, the whole process by which Othello founders on the 'guttered rocks and congregated sands' of his own latent fears, moral panic and self-mistrust, we cannot at the end of the play find it sufficient to our fullest response to say what Lodovico (who knows only half the story) says to Iago: 'this is thy work'. For one thing, we have been shown that, as always in real tragedies (in literature as in life), the sources of this tragedy also lay in Othello and Desdemona's extraordinary positive capacities, their capacities to love absolutely and so risk total, irreparable loss, as much as they lay in their ordinary human shortcomings and susceptibilities. For another thing, we have seen that, despite our wish to think otherwise, it was not Iago who brought Othello to commit murder and suicide: it was Othello's own need for moral and emotional finality, moral and emotional certainty. So little could he stand any doubt, any moral query, that he presumed every 'if' meant 'must' and snatched at it before it could be given any 'overt test' at all. The working of that insecurity in him aborted every attempt to deny or leave in abeyance for a single moment his need to know for sure where he stood and who he was in relation to the woman who was his very source of life. For us, it is impossible not to realize what the play has shown in such dreadful detail: the pain and misery that can attend on trying to keep one's heart open to love and so open to being negated – on trying, that is, to live securely in a world of irreducibly 'skeined stained veined variety', as Hopkins puts it in 'Spelt from Sibyl's Leaves':

Lét life, wáned, ah lét life wind
Off hér once skéined stained véined varíety / upon, áll on twó
  spools; párt, pen, páck
Now her áll in twó flocks, twó folds – black, white; / right, wrong;
  reckon but, reck but, mind
But thése two; wáre of a wórld where bút these / twó tell, each
  off the óther; of a rack
Where, selfwrung, selfstrung, sheathe-and shelterless, / thóughts
  agaínst thoughts ín groans grínd.

And yet, in thus making us 'ware of a world where but
these two tell, each off the other', the play has made us
equally 'ware' of how mad it is to suppose life can ever be
rid of instability, perplexity and doubt. Because we have
seen the whole story from outside as well as from within,
we understand how and why Othello's frantic lust for
assurance has proved not less but infinitely more devastating
than his self-wrung struggles to live in suspense, to try to
distinguish what really is from what he darkly fears. Thus,
at the heart of the play, and centred in its full realization
of both Desdemona's and Othello's anguish, is Shakespeare's insight into the dire necessity for, and the often
impossible difficulty of sustaining, a life open to doubt and
uncertainty and therefore always at risk.

As usual, what applies to the play's characters applies
equally to us. Much of the power of *Othello* as a tragedy,
I believe, is to make us acutely aware of our *own* needs for
emotional and moral certainty, simplicity and finality –
our own impulse to think on two spools: black/white,
right/wrong – and to categorize people as fair or foul in
accordance with our own hot feelings about them. In
revealing the web of self-strung delusions in which its
characters trap themselves, the play forbids us (unless we
delude ourselves) to judge its characters absolutely in
terms of moral 'debit and credit', as angels or devils,
virtuous victims or hellish villains. But another part of its
power is to make us none the less urgently – in spite of

and because of all that it has shown us – continue to seek some way of sheltering ourselves from the full reality of its ending. As with the characters, so with us: to recognize that (as Iago put it) 'there's no remedy' is not to overcome our need for one. Even, indeed especially, at the end of the play, our rational awareness of the situation and our feelings about it pull in different directions. Inevitably, *we* seek to cheer ourselves up, 'endeavour to escape reality': by thinking, for example, that Othello's suicide somehow morally balances out the murder of Desdemona; or by trying to persuade ourselves that perhaps they are somehow better off dead than alive in a world that contained a Iago; or supposing that 'really' the catastrophe was entirely Iago's work; or by reminding ourselves a little too quickly that what we have witnessed is after all 'only a play'. Of course it is only a play – we are never in any doubt of it. Indeed, the comfort of being always in some sense aware that it is a fiction, together with the strange exhilaration which comes from contemplating the energy of Shakespeare's fully mature art, is exactly what enables us to stand what we see. But while we can bear the dramatic illusion, the full brunt of the tragedy, our urgent 'primary motive', willy-nilly, is to reach for some moral simplicity to lessen it. And it seems to me that our very need to try to lessen it is perhaps the clearest 'proof' of Shakespeare's insight here into the problems of reconciling honest judgment with honest feeling. In thinking about Shakespeare's art in *Othello* it is vital not to get trapped into too-ready feelings or too-ready judgments about its 'greatness' or its 'limitations'. Much more to the point is Lodovico's sober advice – 'As you shall prove us, praise us': the need and the difficulty of doing that are the subject and the substance of the tragedy. Like all the very greatest tragic works, *Othello* makes us realize with especial force that the fate of loving is precisely the conjunction of that difficulty and that need.

Printed in the United Kingdom
by Lightning Source UK Ltd.
134525UK00001B/325-327/A